From Individual to Community

Thank you for choosing a SAGE product! If you have any comment, observation or feedback, I would like to personally hear from you. Please write to me at contactceo@sagepub.in

—Vivek Mehra, Managing Director and CEO,
SAGE Publications India Pvt Ltd, New Delhi

Bulk Sales

SAGE India offers special discounts for purchase of books in bulk. We also make available special imprints and excerpts from our books on demand.

For orders and enquiries, write to us at

Marketing Department
SAGE Publications India Pvt Ltd
B1/I-1, Mohan Cooperative Industrial Area
Mathura Road, Post Bag 7
New Delhi 110044, India
E-mail us at marketing@sagepub.in

Get to know more about SAGE, be invited to SAGE events, get on our mailing list. Write today to marketing@sagepub.in

This book is also available as an e-book.

————૪૦ ૯૩————

it has also engendered some social and cultural dilemmas. Since the trickle-down effect of growth has been weak, the rate of reduction in poverty has been slow. Slower is the decline in the incidence of malnutrition, leaving close to half of the population, especially children and women, suffering from various forms of malnutrition including micronutrient deficiency. Though adult literacy rate has somewhat improved, about half of the children aged 15–19 years are out of school. Education is certainly a great equalizer of opportunities. Yet, privatization and commercialization tendencies severely limit the accessibility, equity and quality of education. Apart from social and economic inequalities, gender inequality also presents a serious problem in terms of gender-biased ownership and access of private and common properties. Although the reservation of open spaces in urban areas contributes to environmental conservation, the benefits of this activity go mainly to the high-income groups at the cost of poor people.

Development, ethics and human rights are intricately linked with each other. But, the strength of such linkage is influenced strongly by ideological considerations that influence the actual path of development. The magnitude of development benefits is determined by the way development interventions are planned, designed and implemented, especially by a careful exploitation of the local context and emerging situation. In a democratic system, politics play a major role in development. There are norms but such norms are often violated by various groups to gain economic and political advantage. The issue of social justice has always dominated development debates because of the increasing aspiration for social and economic equality.

While the coverage of the issues is selective rather than exhaustive, this volume does capture some of the most important issues dominating the cultural, social, economic and political landscape of India over the last decade. The issues are treated in a rigorous manner but in a language that can reach the public and policy-makers alike. Despite its focus on India, the volume does have relevance for other developing and emerging countries in Asia and Africa, which share a similar history and are facing similar problems and challenges. Given the span of issues covered and the richness of their treatment by eminent scholars, the volume represents a fitting tribute to the living memory of Professor Malcolm Adiseshiah, the founder of Madras Institute of Development Studies (MIDS) and a distinguished educationist, scholar, administrator and philanthropist, whose birth

Foreword

Development is a multidimensional phenomenon covering cultural, social, economic, political and institutional aspects. Development unleashes a variety of changes in all these spheres and its impacts are felt at all levels, spanning from a single individual to the community as a whole. The field of development studies, which has emerged as a distinct area of intellectual inquiry, investigates this social transformation both from disciplinary and transdisciplinary perspectives using different paradigms governed by their ideological foundations. What is the nature of the social transformation? How is it linked to the structure of the capitalist world? How are the recent economic reforms driven by globalization impacting poverty, horizontal and vertical inequality, gender disparity and environment? How does one evaluate social transformation in its totality? This volume tries to provide answers to these and related questions in the particular context of India. The individual chapters in this volume are written by some of the most eminent scholars in their respective fields of specialization.

India has achieved tremendous progress, especially since the early 1990s. With the policy of economic liberalization and subsequent globalization of the Indian economy, the economic growth rate has more than doubled. Many of the Indian industries have become very competitive at home and abroad. The service sector, particularly subsectors such as communications, IT-enabled services, etc., developed competitive edge and sustained high growth. The Indian market, along with that of China, is considered as one of the major engines of growth for the world economy. However, a worrisome development in the post-reform period is the sluggish growth of agriculture, and moreover, the rate of growth of food grains, which has fallen sharply and may have long-term implications on food security.

While globalization of the Indian economy has opened economic opportunities that were earlier limited to the elite and middle classes,

List of Tables and Figures

Tables

Figures

Contents

Professor Malcom Adiseshiah
(18 April 1910–21 November 1994)

Jointly published in 2012 by

 SAGE Publications India Pvt Ltd   and   **Madras Institute of**
B1/I-1 Mohan Cooperative Industrial Area   **Development Studies**
Mathura Road, New Delhi 110044, India   79, Second Main Road,
www.sagepub.in   Gandhinagar, Adyar
      Chennai 600 020
SAGE Publications Inc
2455 Teller Road
Thousand Oaks, California 91320, USA

SAGE Publications Ltd
1 Oliver's Yard
55 City Road
London EC1Y 1SP, United Kingdom

SAGE Publications Asia-Pacific Pte Ltd
33 Pekin Street
#02-01 Far East Square
Singapore 048763

Published by Vivek Mehra for SAGE Publications India Pvt Ltd, Phototypeset in 10/12 Calisto MT by Diligent Typesetter, Delhi and printed at Yash Printographics, Noida.

Library of Congress Cataloging-in-Publication Data Available

ISBN: 978-81-321-0731-6 (HB)

The SAGE Team: Sharel Simon, Pranab Jyoti Sarma, and Amrita Saha

From Individual to Community

Issues in Development Studies

Essays in Memory of Malcolm Adiseshiah

Edited by
R. Maria Saleth

m.i.d.s
Madras
Institute of
Development
Studies

SAGE   www.sagepublications.com
Los Angeles • London • New Delhi • Singapore • Washington DC

centenary was celebrated on 18 April 2010. I am sure this volume adds to the growing literature on development studies in India and elsewhere.

Professor R. Radhakrishna
Chairman, National Statistical Commission
Ministry of Statistics and Programme Implementation
Government of India, New Delhi
Chairperson, Madras Institute of Development Studies, Chennai

Preface

The Madras Institute of Development Studies (MIDS), Chennai, organizes two major events every year. One is the Founder's Day Lecture organized in April and the other is the Malcolm Adiseshiah Memorial Lecture organized in November. Both these events aim to commemorate the contributions of Professor Malcolm Adiseshiah, the founder of the Institute, former Deputy Director General of UNESCO, former Rajya Sabha Member and recipient of Padma Vibhushan Award. Both these events are supported with the generous grant from the Malcolm and Elizabeth Adiseshiah Trust. On both these occasions, an eminent Indian scholar is invited to present a paper on the subject of their choice. This volume brings together a select set of these papers. Even though the selected papers were presented by different scholars with varying disciplinary backgrounds, taken as a whole, they have a common theme of addressing various facets of development in India.

The aims of this volume are twofold. First, since the papers contained in this volume were originally prepared to venerate the memory of Professor Adiseshiah, it is only natural to bring them together in a volume that is brought out as part of his centenary celebration. Second, the papers, in their own right, are excellent pieces of intellectual work with considerable theoretical and policy significance. Given their academic quality and research value, they need to be taken to as wide an audience as possible. This volume will help in such dissemination. Although the subjects of some of the papers are technical, they are treated in a manner and written in a language that can well be appreciated both by general public as well as by policymakers. This fact ensures that the present volume will have a good reception from all kinds of readers with different backgrounds.

A number of people deserve credit for their varying contributions in producing this volume. My sincere thanks go first to all the contributors of the papers for writing such timeless papers. I am also grateful to Professor R. Radhakrishna, Chairperson, and Professor C.T. Kurien and Dr H.B.N. Shetty, both Trustees of the Madras Institute of Development Studies, for their encouragement. I also appreciate the valuable contributions of my predecessors: Professor S. Neelakantan, V.K. Natraj, Professor Padmini Swaminathan and Professor S. Janakarajan. Editorial help of Dr V. Jacob John, computer assistance of R. Dharumaperumal, documentation assistance of A. Arivazhagan and secretarial support of R. Vijayakumari and L. Celine are also appreciated. More importantly, the funding support from the Malcolm and Elizabeth Adiseshiah Trust is gratefully acknowledged. Finally, I would also like to thank the SAGE team for their excellent support and professionalism in producing this volume in such a nice form and in quick time.

R. Maria Saleth

1

Issues in Development Studies: An Overview

R. Maria Saleth and L. Venkatachalam

Introduction

Development is a long and multidimensional process encompassing changes in cultural, social, economic, political and institutional aspects. Obviously, discipline-specific approaches have inherent limitations in effectively tackling the nature and consequences of these multiple and interrelated aspects of development process. It is these limitations that have led to the emergence of 'development studies' as a separate field of intellectual inquiry. Since research in development studies relies on interdisciplinary approaches and pluralistic methodologies, it benefits from the cross-fertilization of theories and ideas from different disciplines. It is precisely this fact that makes the research in development studies relatively more realistic and comprehensive in terms of its ability to capture the full import of the process of development in a given context of time and space. While development studies are important for both research and policy, their importance is declining in recent years in India. This is partly due to the re-emergence of disciplinary domination in research funding and partly due to the declining public investment on social science research as a whole.

Within social sciences, the research in disciplines such as economics and political science dominate over the research in disciplines such as sociology and anthropology. Overall, public investment on social science research forms only a minute proportion of the public investment on science subjects, displaying definite bias against social science research. Despite this unfavourable climate, development studies in India, as a branch of social science research, is still able to keep its vigour and growth. The growing literature on the development studies provides ample evidence for this fact. The present volume aims to contribute to this growing literature. It has 11 chapters, each dealing with different dimensions of development in India. These chapters are contributed by some of the eminent Indian scholars. The objective of the present chapter is to set the stage and context for the volume and also to provide an overview of the papers included in this volume.

Achievements and Successes

India has undergone metamorphic changes since its Independence. These changes are obviously wide-ranging, covering the cultural, social, economic and political spheres. The economic change was much more pronounced and sharp, especially since the 1990s with the economic liberalization and subsequent globalization of Indian economy. The economic growth rate, which used to cover around 4 per cent in the early stages of development, has risen to about 8 to 10 per cent in recent years. The per capita income has also risen concurrently and the corresponding changes in the overall living standard of the masses have also been impressive. With the expansion of education and health facilities, the literacy rate and life expectancy level have also increased. Thanks to a major programme of infrastructural development implemented, especially in recent years, the road and railway networks and air and sea transport sectors have expanded rapidly. From the perspective of external sector, Indian commerce and trade have seen major transformation with a reduction in traditional export of primary goods and an enhancement in the export of industrial, commercial and software products. India was able to build huge foreign exchange reserves and Indian investment abroad is also growing.

There has also been an internal economic transformation of historical significance. Agriculture, which used to be the predominant source of growth in the initial years, is now contributing only to less than 20 per cent of the national income. Thanks to a massive level of investment in agricultural and irrigation development programmes and the spread of Green Revolution technologies, India was able to achieve food self-sufficiency since the early 1970s. Despite the problems of targeting and distribution, the public distribution system has made food security almost a reality in most part of the country at present. With the changed investment priorities, economic transition and international economic climate, the industry, trade and commerce and service sectors have now emerged as the major drivers of economic growth. The performance of the information and communication sectors has been especially phenomenal even notwithstanding the temporary setbacks witnessed in the aftermath of the recent global financial crisis and economic recession.

The developments in the social arena have also been remarkable. The once predominant system of caste has now lost its hold both in urban and rural areas. The curse of caste-based discrimination and untouchability has disappeared in most parts of the country. Dalits and other socially discriminated groups are now able to share and enjoy the benefits of education and employment almost in equal terms with other social groups. These were possible, thanks essentially to the concerted policy of reservation and affirmative action by the state. In this respect, a number of legal changes were made to protect the rights and benefits of the Dalits and other socially discriminated groups. The resultant upward mobility of these groups that occurred over time in the economic and social spheres has also led to similar ascendancy in the political sphere. They become well organized to articulate their interest in the political space that itself is expanding due to a number of major developments.

With the ongoing socio-economic transformation, the political power structure has changed with the entry of new interest groups and led to a corresponding alternation in the relative bargaining strength of existing interest groups. For instance, the power of the agricultural lobby has relatively declined, whereas that of the industrial and trade groups has increased. Similarly, with the deepening of democracy, the relative political clout of the traditionally rich groups has declined while that of the economically and socially marginal groups has increased. Notably, the development of multiparty system has led to the maturing of the political democracy. Since the coalition politics that has emerged since the 1990s makes even smaller parties to have a major say, it has made the political system much more open and participatory. The federal structure has been strengthened with a decline in the political predominance of the central government and corresponding ascendancy in the political power of the state governments. The judicial system is not only independent and free from political interference but also assuming the role of resolving political deadlocks, especially in the implementation and enforcement of environmental policies.

Issues and Challenges

As Indians, we can certainly be proud of the many achievements and successes that the country could make over the years since Independence. But, we cannot deny that there are also many challenges and unanswered questions still looming large in all spheres of development. While globalization has entailed many economic benefits, especially in the industrial and service sectors, it is not an unmixed blessing. This is in view of many social and cultural implications of globalization. Similarly, the structural transformation brought about by the process of development has sharply reduced the share of agriculture in national income. But, it has not reduced the role of agriculture in supporting a large segment of population through employment and livelihood. As a result, the income originating from agriculture is less and declining, whereas the population depending on agriculture and allied activities is more and increasing, which is especially so with the growth of population.

This is due to the nature of the development of the industrial and tertiary sectors, where the rapid growth observed has not resulted in a commensurate expansion of employment. In this sense, the economic transformation that has occurred in India so far is only partial and, therefore, remains incomplete. However, one cannot deny the fact that despite the incomplete nature of economic transformation, there have been profound changes in the village economy, thanks to the emergence of non-farm employment and the willingness of a segment of rural population to move to not only urban areas but even abroad in search of employment and income opportunities. The caste system, which was supported by an unequal land ownership and closed village economy, has also lost its grip over the village social system. With the availability of education, health and infrastructural facilities, the rural–urban divide is also getting gradually weakened over time.

Although there has been an increasing tendency for equality in the social arena, there are serious inequalities observed in the gender context. These inequalities, which are an outcome of the age-old customs and inappropriate norms, manifest more in terms of property rights. Unless the gender-based inequality in property ownership and control is addressed, the social development in its full form can never be achieved. But, social inequality is getting reproduced through other developments. One example is the environmental issues, especially in urban context, which are often used to strengthen the rights of economically rich groups while replacing the rights of the poor groups. Parks, common properties and other open spaces are reserved in the name of environmental protection or conservation that benefits the economically well-to-do groups at the cost of poor groups. Similarly, in the name of environment, slums are cleared and people are resettled out of cities, affecting the life and livelihood of the poor groups. Similar inter-group conflicts are also observed in rural areas in the allocation of land, water and other natural resources. The question that requires answer is: for whom and at what costs is the environment protected and resources conserved?

When considering social and economic inequality at the macro level, no one can ignore the equalizing role of education. Education is an important means to enhance the social and economic status of the poor sections of the society. But, this role depends on the accessibility and quality of education. While state policies related to reservation and scholarships improve accessibility, a number of changes happening within the education sector appear to work in the opposite direction. For instance, education is itself becoming costly due to a decline in state funding and the consequent increase in household expenditure. Increasing privatization and commercialization of educational sector leads to a kind of dualism, where rich groups monopolize quality education while poor groups are left with poor schools. These changes raise a horde of questions related to the equality, quality and quantity dimensions of education.

Ideology plays a major role as it determines the nature and direction of development. The development process in India has been influenced by several ideologies or visions of development. These aspects raise several important questions. In what way does ideology influence development? What are the dominant ideologies of visions of development that have affected the development process in India? What role do ethics play in development? Is development a human right or a political largesse? Besides these questions, there are also issues related to the design and implementation of development programmes. These issues are important as they determine the magnitude of impact and direction of the flow of programme benefits across socio-economic groups. The most important among these issues pertain to the role played by uncertainty in development planning and programme implementation. Contrary to intuition and expectation, uncertainty can have many positive roles in development planning. What are these positive roles? How can they be used to enhance development impacts and benefits?

There are serious issues and challenges on the political dimension of development as well. In a democratic system, different social groups have different strategies for politically articulating their interests. What roles do violent demonstrations play in the process of political bargaining? How does the relative political power of groups deviating from the existing norms lead to political equilibrium? To what extent do the Western political theories account for the norm-deviation behaviour in political bargaining? These are the larger political issues that have a major bearing on the overall development. There are also questions related to the specific political aspects such as those related to the politics of social justice. While reservation and other affirmative actions contribute to social justice and equality, these actions also, at the same time, tend to reinforce the influence of some of the very factors that are to be rooted away such as the caste system. This fact raises the issue of how to promote social justice and equality without the reliance on caste as an identification device for affirmative action. Why does democratic system coexist with high level of socio-economic inequality? What are the instruments for promoting social justice and inequality? How effective are they? What roles do economic growth and prosperity play in addressing socio-economic inequality? These questions also need answers.

An Overview

This section not only provides an overview of the chapters but also shows how some of the issues and challenges noted above are addressed by individual chapters. To begin with, Professor Ananthamurthy, in his chapter dealing with the issue of globalization and its portents for Indian culture, considers the cultural and social implications of globalization. He identifies important cultural aspects, which become vulnerable by the current pattern of globalization. Globalization, according to Professor Murthy, creates a conflict between the global culture that a person with no real conception of the world acquires and his or her native culture. The conflict ultimately compels him or her to return to his or her native culture in order to regain what he or she has lost in the desire to expand beyond his or her limit. The global culture tends to destroy the creativity and imagination of the person by making him or her in the process a 'mere bag of words'.

According to Professor Murthy, the ongoing process of globalization does not recognize time and space. He argues that there exists a blend of centralization and decentralization in the way in which the language and culture were created and interpreted. In a pre-liberalization era, one could find 'oneness' among the languages and cultures without in any manner spoiling the plurality among them. There was recognition of a single concept which could be described simultaneously in different ways. The two aspects of 'unity' and 'diversity' cannot be separately treated and emphasized due to the fact that overemphasizing any one of them would lead to different and often negative kind of reaction from the other one. Thus, there was, in fact, no trade-off between the two and there has been a vast scope for utilizing both of them in a balanced and symbiotic way. At present, the politics practised in India makes the identities of people as 'discrete' and 'contradictory', which once upon a time was 'continuous' and 'non-contradictory'. To Professor Murthy, this form of discontinuity and contradiction has become an integral component of globalization.

As to the technology that forms the pillar of globalization, Professor Murthy argues that the technology destroys the 'aura' in the art and culture. For instance, while technology makes copying or reproduction of arts on a large scale possible, it cannot in any case ensure the aura possessed by the originals. In certain cases such as the Ayyappa Cult, the technology brings not only vigour but also vulgarity, taking away the 'inner core' as well as the 'reality' of things such as those inherent in modern 'bhakti' movements, social functions, etc. According to him, the sad part is that the opponents of globalization themselves also utilize the very instruments embedded in the modern technological arena.

Having critically evaluated the globalization and its impact on language and culture, Professor Murthy provides an alternative suggestion to deal with globalization. That is either to follow the Leavisian path by discriminating and resisting against globalization or just to remain passive by allowing the globalization to take over us. Globalization benefits only very limited sections of the society and not all. He concludes that under the ongoing process of globalization, we will be 'culturally' nowhere. The inevitable conclusion is that despite its material and technical benefits, globalization has a deleterious role as far as the social and cultural areas are concerned.

Next to globalization, another but related issue that affected vast sections of Indian population relates to the policy of economic liberalization, which was pursued with vigour since the early 1990s. In his chapter on the growth of wasteland, Professor Amit Bhaduri deals with the social and economic impacts of this policy in a figurative manner. He is mainly concerned with the 'waste lands' created by the kind of economic growth under the liberalization programme. Income inequality is one such wasteland in the Indian context. According to Professor Bhaduri, the 'trickle-down effect', which is supposed to distribute the economic benefits to the poor, has not worked well at the ground level. The high growth-based industrialization is currently pursued in India under the principle of 'there is no alternative' (TINA) syndrome. The author argues that justifying liberalization in India on the ground that such policies are pursued in China and Vietnam is not a valid argument. This is because of the reason that unlike India where a flawed multiparty democracy is being followed, China and Vietnam with a regimented single party system have been implementing extensive pro-poor policies. These safety net policies implemented so effectively are able to insulate the poor and vulnerable sections from the ill effects of the ongoing industrialization process in China and Vietnam.

Although the national income of India has grown, on an average, at 7 to 8 per cent during the last two decades, the growth of employment is much lower and slower. Notably, the increased productivity during this period has come essentially from an increased use of capital and technology, reduced level of labour force and longer hours of work. This is particularly so in the industrial and service sectors. International competition has resulted in a 'zero-sum game' in the sense that one country's gain from trade and commerce comes only from another country's loss of economic welfare. Increased investment by foreign companies and growth of financial markets contribute to the inequality in income due to the accumulation of enormous wealth among corporate owners. The increasing wealth among the rich leads to a demand pattern that leads to the production of a particular set of goods and services, which the poor could neither use nor afford to buy. This pattern obviously leads to lopsided composition of goods, making, thereby, a 'waste land' of the countryside where majority of the poor lives.

The resource crunch and debt-ridden farmers in the countryside are not capable of producing the kind of agricultural goods demanded by the rich, ultimately forcing them to give way for corporate sector to enter into the agricultural operations. In a liberalized and market-based economy, the natural resources such as water and energy are allocated for the urban areas and big corporate firms, depriving these resources to the rural poor. This fact actually represents an act of internal colonization of the resources of the poor, leading to serious social and political resistance from the affected groups. Professor Bhaduri argues that the suggestions from the pro-market intellectuals regarding the alternative arrangements for the poor come from an economic and policy vacuum. He has criticized the liberalization policies for their negative effects in terms unemployment and economic inequality and warned that no society, not even ours with a malfunctioning democratic system, can withstand these negative effects beyond a point. Thus, the high economic growth that is being nurtured by the increasing inequality cannot be sustained. Professor Bhaduri advocates an alternative path of development that involves poor people to participate effectively in the economic process and that converts the wastelands created by liberalization into productive economic assets yielding long-term dividends.

In his chapter on the evolving relationship between rural culture and agriculture, Professor Dipankar Gupta deals with the causes and consequences of the profound changes that are taking place within Indian villages in recent years. According to him, these changes are wide-ranging, covering the economic, social, political and cultural dimensions of rural India. Unfortunately, these changes are not recognized well by the city dwellers and urban intellectuals, who continue to believe that Indian villages remain as those depicted in some of the old films, where rural life is glorified and every villager is believed to prefer to live in rural setting. As a result, the conventional theoretical and analytical framework continues to be relied on for analyzing the rural issues. But, social surveys and field visits clearly show that things in the villages at present are not what they used to be. Interestingly, it is not urbanization that has brought changes in villages from outside but the main impetus for change has come from within the rural areas themselves. The sources for change range from the Green Revolution and education expansion to population pressure and migration. Although agricultural activities are shrinking, non-farm employment is increasing in villages. Regrettably, the real changes that are taking place in rural areas are not being captured by the current system of information generation.

The influences of traditional institutions such as caste hierarchy, though not completely eliminated altogether, have really become very weak. The caste hierarchy emerged mainly because of the existence of unequal distribution of wealth and power in a closed village economy and social system. Thanks to the economic transformation, the village itself is shrinking as a sociological reality, though it still exists as a space. The lower caste groups, without the support of the upper caste ones, could create their own identity equivalent to that of the upper caste ones in cases such as worshipping god, establishing beauty salons, etc. Some of the lower caste people are no longer interested in working as agricultural labourers. Rather, they prefer to do non-farm jobs outside the villages. The village caste system has collapsed and caste identities are seen in an exaggerated form. The assertion of caste identities is becoming more obvious in villages and this paves the way for the caste politics to emerge not only in the rural context but also in the national context.

In terms of political mobilization of the rural groups, the farmers' movements are no longer addressing the core issues of the farm labourers. These movements are obviously fighting for the interest of the owner cultivators. The core demands of these movements have also changed over time. For instance, there are farmer leaders, who even welcome open markets for agricultural produces, which is a major deviation from the conventional perception of protectionism. Though owner cultivators are protected with subsidies, their future is grim due to the fact that agriculture is increasingly becoming a relatively unattractive profession. This is indicated by the declining profitability of agriculture and increasing suicides among farmers.

In general, the rural non-farm employment has been increasing in many states over a period of time. The landowning community is also actively involved in non-farm employment. But, in the case of the lower caste people, the participation in non-farm activities not only changes their economic status but also brings changes in their attitude and prejudices in relation to caste. The off-farm employment outside the villages has also been increasing providing more income options for the villagers. Professor Gupta concludes that it is within the context of these economic, social and political changes, the culture in the village needs to be understood. This culture is not a stable one as being assumed. From the rich to the poor, the common trend is to leave the village and if that entails going abroad, then so be it.

In her chapter on gender inequality, Professor Bina Agarwal tries to bring to light certain neglected dimensions and hidden facts on the subject. She highlights how both women and men experience inequality in terms of their property rights under different contexts. According to her, gender inequality has some distinct patterns and features. First, gender inequality is observed not only outside the home but also within the household itself. This contradicts with the economic theory that subscribes to 'unitary household model' suggesting equitable distribution of goods and tasks across gender, which is mediated by the 'altruistic motive' of the head of the household. It is this contradiction that led to an alternative theory based on 'collective model' that suggests that intra-household allocation of goods and tasks is done through the relative bargaining power of the members within the household. Second, gender inequality is influenced not only by unequal economic endowments across men and women but also by the prevailing social norms and perceptions. And, third, gender inequality not only pre-exists but also the new one can arise from and get reinforced by the already existing institutions.

Gender inequality in terms of property rights has certain important features. First, inequality in the command over property is a major source of economic inequality between men and women. Second, mere ownership of property alone is not sufficient but the control over it is more important. Third, when property advantage is emanating from public property as well, men's control over the public property results in a lack of control of it by women. Fourth, men can also control those instruments which generate advantages and benefits from the property. And, finally, command over property can also influence institutions shaping the ideas about gender such as media and communication.

The social and economic implications of widening gender inequality are many and wide-ranging. First of all, men's control over the larger portion of land does not ensure welfare to the women. In fact, this control makes women more vulnerable to poverty, desertion, divorce and widowhood. On the other hand, women's access and control over the land will make them empowered, both economically and socially, and would improve the welfare of the entire family. Women's control over land and other assets facilitates access to credit, provides opportunity of diversified livelihood and improves intergenerational benefits. Access to and control over land by women improves the efficiency of resource use as demonstrated by empirical studies from Kenya, where improved weeding technology has increased the productivity in farmlands owned by women greater than that observed in farmlands owned by men.

What women actually contribute and what is being socially perceived are two entirely different things. For instance, women are considered unskilled and very often, their contributions are significant and invisible in nature. It is also the case that perceptions make the women's public presence invisible. Though social norms reduce transaction costs and increase economic efficiency, these norms do not work well for women and their contribution. This is because these norms restrict the mobility and public interaction of women. It is also the case that these norms also usually affect the material outcomes for women. Taking Join Forest Management approach as a case, Professor Agarwal illustrates how women's 'participatory exclusions' lead to negative consequences. For example, the restriction to enter the forests increases the burden on the women, especially the poor women, in terms of increased burden of collection of fuel wood and fodder.

How can gender inequalities be reduced? Professor Agarwal argues that economic analysis using 'bargaining framework' where the women's role in changing the rules, regulations and perceptions studied with a sharper focus should be able to address the issue in a much better way. Within such a bargaining framework, not only the role of qualitative information about perception needs to be incorporated but also the effects of non-market and non-household arenas such as the state and community have to be added. Making women realize their worth and creating external interventions, especially through non-governmental organizations are expected to change the existing rules and, thereby, enhance the socio-economic status and promote the real empowerment of women.

Professor Amita Baviskar's chapter focuses on the environmental politics in urban India, a subject that has long been neglected both in the academic discourse and policy debates. She builds her arguments on environmental politics by highlighting an untoward incident that occurred in Delhi. A migrant worker in Delhi was beaten up to death when he entered a park, which has been used by the rich in the neighbourhood, for the purpose of defecation. When poorer people joined together and protested against this killing, police opened fire on them, killing four more people. This sort of state violence against poor people, who contest for limited open space in urban areas, has become a recent phenomenon, though this kind of violence has been noticed in forests and rural areas for quite some time in the past. But, the fact remains that the environmental concern in urban areas pertains essentially to the rich people as it is being used to displace the poor people and make them more vulnerable to poverty. In this sense, most of the urban developmental activities such as air and water pollution control and slum clearance benefit the rich but make the poor people more vulnerable to poverty and insecurity.

Urban–rural conflicts over land, water and other natural resources involve class struggle and state violence. Even though environment is a public good, it is being privatized by the powerful. Prior to 1970, there was only agrarian question and no environmental question was raised in social sciences. In academics, B.B. Vohra and Ramachandra Guha were some of the pioneers who raised the awareness over environmental issues in India. Many social movements such as 'Chipko' that emerged during this period have also generated considerable debate about the environmental question and its implications for the poor and vulnerable groups. These movements have also been successful in influencing various scholars such as Ramachandra Guha to write about peasant resistance and saving forestlands. In the early 1990s, equity issues and issues related to the cost-benefit analysis of big dams cropped up. Big dams were constructed in the name of generating benefits to the 'nation' but the real question was whether the poor displaced by the dams are part of the conception of 'nation' or not.

The developments noted above paved way for the emergence of 'cultural politics' on environment and development. The emergence of cultural politics was actually the outcome of a learned critique of the 'political ecology' approach. What is cultural politics? Cultural politics has the following attributes. Departing from the conventional treatment based on compartmentalized approach, cultural politics treats the subject of environment and development based on a 'holistic approach'. Cultural politics approach treats environment not merely as a factor of production but also as a life supporting system in a larger sense. It recognizes the social and ecological limits to growth and reintroduces a focused view on how power operates in the inter-action between environment and development. The cultural politics framework focuses on how to improve the welfare of the people who act in multiple ways under multiple institutional settings, rather than on how to safeguard the resources as such. Cultural politics has the potential to play a vital role in articulating the environmental issues in a more effective and realistic manner.

Education is one avenue that is available for the poor to change the economic and social status of their sons and daughters. In this sense, education can be a great equalizer over time provided it is equitable and widely accessible to all sections of the society. The state has a major role to play in ensuring that educational facilities are expanded to meet the requirements and educational opportunities are available to all groups. In this effort, public expenditure on education and state educational policies assume critical importance. In his chapter on ed-ucational financing, Professor Tilak deals with three interrelated is-sues involved in the financing of education in India. These issues are: an increasing reluctance of the state to enhance education financing, the increasing compulsion on the families to pay for education and the emerging role of market in the educational sector. He argues that these three issues underline the three domains in which investment decisions on education are being made, namely, the public domain, individual domain and the market domain. He analyzes the decision processes and their implications in each one of these domains sepa-rately.

In the case of the public domain, the investment decision on educa-tion is made on three grounds: education as a public good, education as a social merit good and education as human right and as an input to human development. Although investment on education increased by 900 per cent in absolute terms during the five decades ending with the year 2000, the increase is only a mere 6 per cent in real terms dur-ing this period. It is also the case that public expenditure on educa-tion in India is relatively small as compared to other countries. Also, the proportion of educational expenditure in total plan expenditure has been gradually declining over the plan periods. Overall, in real terms, the expenditure on education has not increased significantly.

The subsidy to higher education is continuously declining and higher education is increasingly being forced to become more and more self-financed over time. Why is this so? First, it was believed that public expenditure on education did not have significant impact on social welfare. Second, it was believed that as a developing nation, India could not afford to spend more on education. But, as Professor Tilak argues, these beliefs are not true and, therefore, unwarranted. In fact, the government expenditure has been the second most important factor for the development of education and some of the economically poorer states in India spend relatively more on education. Because of government's unwillingness to increase its investment on education, the onus of payment for education shifts towards the families. As a result, household expenditure on education is increasing rapidly over a period of time. But, according to Professor Tilak, the increase in household expenditure on education is not due to households' willingness to voluntarily pay more for the education but due to the compulsion on them as imposed by the government's inefficiency in providing education. The shift in the investment on education from the government to the household has serious implications for the equity and accessibility of educational opportunities. With the increasing cost of education, poor families could not afford to pay for education. In most cases, quality education is being monopolized by the rich households and the poor households are crowded out of good schools. Although reservation has some positive effects, it could not completely neutralize the inequality resulting from inaccessibility.

Professor Tilak is also concerned with another major development in the education sector. This pertains to the increasing privatization of education and some of its negative consequences. Private sector participation in education, as observed in the recent years, is strongly influenced by profit motive. Several initiatives taken by the government suggest that the higher education is being rapidly privatized with the emergence of many private universities and institutes. This process of privatization is adversely affecting the quantity, quality and equity of research and supply of qualified teachers in the higher education sector. The mushrooming of fake national and foreign universities in the education sector feeds into the existing problem. Professor Tilak concludes that in future, the state should play a major role not only in providing good quality education by financing out of tax and non-tax revenues but also in regulating the private universities and institutions in an effective manner.

Professor Upendra Baxi, in his chapter on development and human right, critically evaluates the notion of development and argues that development occurs in a variety of ways and diverse forms. In this sense, development is a multidimensional concept capturing a ubiquitous process of social, economic, political and institutional change. Development, when conceived as 'developmentalism' remains also as a dominant ideology or as 'several histories of mentality', influencing strongly the political and policymaking communities. Professor Baxi also elaborates the subject on a large canvas encompassing different itineraries of the Indian development visions and experience. He also notes the decisive moments of ruptures and fissures that occurred within the Indian development discourse over the years.

Having established the broad conceptual basis of development, Professor Baxi raises 12 important questions relating to the notion of development. These questions relate to (*a*) the constructive arena of development, (*b*) the agency or representative that makes the decision, (*c*) the relative autonomy or dependency in terms of decision-making, (*d*) the distribution of goods and material resources, (*e*) the role of time dimension, (*f*) the influence of spatial concerns, (*g*) the directionality of development, (*h*) the violence of developmental judgments or decisions, (*i*) the way in which militarization of governance practices taking place, (*j*) the orders of reciprocal and mutuality of respect between government and social change agents, (*k*) the issues of learning in the process of development and (*l*) about the reversibility dimension of development.

Professor Baxi, then, examines what he calls as the 'Mohandasian Legacy' that underlines development ethic. The Mohandasian conception of development is intertwined tightly with the issue of justice. The Mahatma's preoccupation with installing a blueprint for just governance and just development stand in stark contrast to the Nehruvian and post-Nehruvian conception of development. He describes the Nehruvian model of development as 'mediation' since it 'creatively adapts the Mohandasian legacy in terms of presenting an inaugural post-colonial version of the idea of progress both within and beyond the framing discourse of the European Enlightenment'. In answering whether the talk of development is a human right or political largesse, Professor Baxi concludes that it hardly matters to the impoverished people targeted by the process of development since it failed despondently to take into account the people's existential issues of negotiating for subhuman survival.

Dr Shah provides an entirely new and fascinating perspective on the concepts 'certainty' and 'uncertainty' and their implications for the transformational initiatives undertaken both at the micro and macro levels. Drawing from the economic, social and anthropological literature and utilizing practical instances from the field and public policy arena, Dr Shah argues that certainty implies the notion of a 'single truth' or the 'correct path' and requires a top-down approach and a unilateral vision of change. On the other hand, uncertainty liberates us from the tyranny of certainty and enables us to benefit from multiple perspectives, multidimensional approach and multi-stakeholder dialogue. Uncertainty helps us to recognize that the dynamics of change process is governed by the multidirectional and multidisciplinary matrix of relationships.

Dr Shah deals particularly with three kinds of uncertainties related respectively to time, context and nature. He also elucidates what they mean for the design, implementation and evaluation of the transformational initiatives. According to him, the principles that need to guide and characterize transformational initiatives under uncertainty have implications for action in four key areas.

First, the approach to transformational initiatives needs to recognize uncertainty as the best corrective to fundamentalism as fostered by the illusion of certainty and the arrogance of complete knowledge. The approach under uncertainty has, therefore, to be open-minded, flexible, dialogue-oriented and inclusive of history, stakeholders and disciplines.

Second, the transformational initiatives are to be weaved with the flows and dynamics of the natural process, especially with a location-specific approach. The unity and integrity of natural cycles requires the abandonment of the silo-based approach and the creation of resilient systems resistant to external perturbations.

Third, as to the handling of conflicts and contentions inherent in any transformational initiative, Dr Shah suggests that the uncertainty related to conflicts involves three issues, that is, power, justice and love. Citing Martin Luther King, he argues that power and love need not be polar opposites, especially when love is interpreted in the sense of the Greek word 'agape', which means an overflowing love, which seeks nothing in return. Although this form of love is a weapon against injustice, it does not aim to defeat or humiliate anyone but to transform only the opponent's viewpoints.

A conflict is not so much of a victory as a resolution. From this perspective, Dr Shah aims to underline the link between individuals' inner transformation and the larger social change process. For such an inner transformation to get initiated, social mobilization of the weak and voiceless and the inclusive approach in sharing project costs and benefits are necessary. Finally, the transformational initiatives under uncertainty have important implications for institutional linkages and forging partnership among different agencies and organizations, which are lean and open-minded. Since transformational initiatives will succeed only when there is an active participation of all concerned, there is an urgent need to create the legal and organizational space and technical capacity necessary to promote such participation as well as to have a new and more inclusive definition of 'reform'.

Dr Shah concludes that with the increasing recognition of the limits of the three main bastions of certainty, that is, the totalitarian state, the invisible hand of the market and science and technology, there is now a real possibility for taking the full advantage of the power of uncertainty for achieving the goals of transformational initiatives. What we need are the patience, imagination, resourcefulness and creativity of the people and organizations involved in the design, implementation and evaluation of transformational initiatives.

In his chapter on Western political theory and Indian political practice, Professor Partha Chatterjee wonders how political outcomes such as colonial exploitation, racial discrimination and class conflicts that dominated the real history of the modern world 'have managed not to displace in even the slightest way the stable location of modern political theory within the abstract discursive space of normative reasoning'. According to him, the institutions prevailing in different countries at different time periods do influence the evolution of the normative political theory. He argues that the postcolonial politics provides a moral critique of the normative standards upheld by Western political theory and improvises practices that are parallel to the approved forms. From this perspective, the real theoretical challenge, according to him is twofold. The first is to break the abstract homogeneity of the mythical time-space maintained by the Western normative theory. And, the second is to expand and redefine the normative standards of modern political theory in the light of the considerable accumulation of the new political practices as observed, for instance, in countries such as India.

Professor Chatterjee argues that the phenomenon of violators of law becoming legitimate representatives of people is not necessarily a symptom of popular foolhardiness or perversion of electoral democracy. It is rather a sign of the inability of the existing theories to account for power relations in society. According to him, in every society, a 'normal' level of violence is established, which represents the empirical equilibrium existing in the prevailing power relations among political groups. When a situation has to be demonstrated as outrageous or intolerable, a spectacular show of violence, involving the destruction of public property, is made to elicit the desired political responses to the situation from the government and the public. In this case, the observed level of violence goes beyond the normal level of violence. To understand the realities of politics in the management of violence and, in general, the realities of postcolonial societies, the normative political theories developed in the West need to be expanded and also redefined. What is needed is a 'norm-exception' or a 'norm-deviation' model of the formation of political systems.

Using the 'norm-exception' or a 'norm-deviation' model of political system, Professor Chatterjee explains the establishment of squatter colonies in urban slums in India. While establishing such colonies, the established or existing code of laws remains as the 'norm'. But, due to the political realities, 'exceptions' to the 'norms' were created to accommodate the needs of the squatters, who had a real political significance beyond civil society, which usually adhered to the 'norms'. This kind of analysis would have to be extended to create postcolonial political theory, which broke the abstract homogeneity of the Western normative theory, by emphasizing the 'real history of its formation through violent conflict and hegemonic power'. The other challenge was to redefine the normative standards of modern politics by absorbing into the theory what were considered 'exceptions', but were actually the core of a richer, more diverse and inclusive set of norms.

The politics of social justice is the focus of the chapter by Professor Pratab Bhanu Mehta. The politics of social justice is a major challenge of our times. For the first time in our history, real social and economic change seems like a possibility, and the sheer unleashing of aspiration and energy across different sections of Indian society is staggering. But, there are some concerns about the form the politics of justice will take, even in this newly buoyant and optimistic era. First, we have a limited set of instruments to do justice to the aspiration of social equality. Second, caste still remains an entrenched category around which the politics of social justice is constructed. The present challenge of the politics of social justice must be seen against the backdrop of a general, perhaps more global and historical, pessimism about the relationship between democracy and equality. The most obvious instrument is redistribution through taxation. But, there is no serious politics structured around using this instrument for several reasons. What are these reasons? What are the consequences of the institutionalization of caste as the basis of equality? Why are identity politics and other forms of politics centred on welfare and justice often posed as alternatives? Professor Mehta tries to provide answers to these and related questions.

Political democracies generally coexist with high levels of economic and social inequalities. This fact naturally leads to the question, namely, why democracies are unable to mitigate inequality? Though other scholars used different reasons to answer this question, Professor Mehta brings in 'small liberty effects' explaining how small differences in the basic freedom at the micro level leads to the accumulation of greater inequalities at the aggregate societal level. Redistributive instruments such as taxes can play an effective role in reducing inequality but they are, according to Professor Mehta, associated with some practical problems. For him, even politics itself is a weak instrument for asset quality. The land reform measures to bring down inequality in the present context are less relevant because of the current agrarian crisis that the farmers in India are experiencing now.

The State may also bring down inequality by way of providing health and education to the poor but this is also constrained by factors such as appropriate targeting and accurate delivery. The criteria being used to identify the poor also ran into various practical and logistical problems, especially at the implementation stage. However, Professor Mehta feels that measures like issuing Unique Identification (UID) number may help in identifying the poor in future. Even though the constitution promised political equality, the actual social life is characterized by social and economic inequality. The political equality acquired some normative depth wherein the equality extended to Dalits has now been extended to other backward castes as well. According to Professor Mehta, the institutionalization of caste has the following consequences: (*a*) it has legitimized the class difference; (*b*) there exists no serious discourse on the relationship between justice and discrimination; (*c*) equality can be claimed only on the basis of immutable identity and (*d*) identity politics and other forms of politics centred around welfare and justice are often posed as alternatives.

Concluding Remarks

The volume represents a wide canvass of issues that has emerged in the social, cultural, economic, political and institutional dimensions of the development process as observed in India. Admittedly, the coverage of issues here is more eclectic and selective rather than extensive and exhaustive. But, they are certainly the ones that have dominated the development debate in India during the past two decades. The treatment is both disciplinary and trans-disciplinary in nature. The methodological frameworks are based on descriptive, analytical and quantitative approaches. While the chapters individually address some dimensions of development, the volume, taken as a whole, provides an overall picture of an assessment of the kind of development process that is ongoing in India. The volume tries to provide answers to some issues, but it also raises several new questions. The answers can become the basis for change in development policy. The questions, on the other hand, can give direction for future research in the area of development studies. In this sense, the volume contributes to both research and policy. This indeed is the rationale and justification for its prominent publication.

2

Globalization: Its Portents for Indian Culture

U.R. Ananthamurthy

Frog in the Well

Let me start with an unusual metaphor, that of the *koopamandooka* or the frog in the well which thinks of the well as the universe. We use this metaphor to decry a very limited person who has no real conception of the world. But a great Kannada poet, Gopalakrishna Adiga, a modern poet of renown, has written a poem called 'Koopamandooka'. The hero in the poem flies all over the globe; he is a dreamer and an idealist who tries to embrace the whole universe and ends up as a mere bag of words—forever repeating all the great clichés about humanity and losing his creativity. In the end he decides to be a frog in the well and stay within its confines, literally in the mud of the well. Why? For it is believed that when the skin of a frog dries up it has to go back to the mud to recapture its golden sheen. Probably, for all the attractions that globalization offers, there is a compelling need to return as a frog in the well in the sense that you then try to recover what you have lost in the desire to expand beyond your limits.

Why do I say this? I have a reason. In the South and North Canara districts of Karnataka, there emerged two styles of Yakshagana, hardly a few miles from each other—*Badgu* and *Tenku Tittu*. That was when India was not globalized. If you go to Rajasthan, within an area of 10 miles you will find a variety of musical drums and different ways of playing them. Then again, take languages. India has so many of them. When I was President of the Sahitya Akademi there was pressure on me to recognize the tribal languages since injustice had been done to them. I responded saying that I would not recognize any language; we are not here to recognize languages but literatures. If there is a great work in any tribal language it should receive the same honour as one in a recognized Indian language. I hope this practice which started then continues. As a writer I realized that a tribal language may have a Homer in it. In the past it was a tribal language which had a Homer. Most languages then were tribal; perhaps some were only dialects. When a dialect has an army and a national poet it becomes a language. Most developments in the old world of arts were of this kind.

The first great writer in Kannada, a thousand years ago, was a man (in fact a king) called Nripatunga (or Srivijaya) who wrote a book called *Kavirajamarga*. There he says: 'In this land of Karnataka there are many varieties of languages like the thousand hooded Adisesha but we have to find in one of them the language of the whole land.' He tries, merely, to reduce the great plurality and find one language which could be used all over. In other words, a thousand years ago, the search was for oneness and at the same time for the recognition of plurality. Nripatunga was aware that when he set out to make one language 'the language of the land' other languages would be under its umbrella. He hegemonizes one language over the others but does not destroy them. Sometimes countries which believe in hegemonizing do not take to destruction, they allow others to remain at a lower level and thus they do have the opportunity of gaining in stature later on. Nripatunga made one form of Kannada superior to all others but this was the Kannada used in a particular geographical space. Even at that time there was a search for something which was common to and could be shared with a larger group of people, but along with this there was concern that we should not lose the pluralities that are nurtured by small areas.

Unity and Diversity

Globalization does not respect time and space. The multitude of varieties that India produced were at a time when we had no World Bank money, no Obama overseeing our development and foreign affairs as he does now. We had variety even as we searched for oneness. The two great quests of the human mind, paradoxical as it may seem, are for centralization and decentralization, which represent respectively oneness and plurality/diversity. In India, you have *Advaita* (non-duality), which tries to fuse all theories into one great principle. At the same time, you have numerous gods who satisfy local needs. There is a *Kshetradevata*, a *Grihadevata* and also an *Ishtadevata* for the individual. But, there is also a Brahman who is common to all. I think both these movements, to centralize and to decentralize, are two essential needs of the human soul. One of my close friends K.V. Subbanna, writer, critic and Magasasay Award winner, has founded a globalized cultural centre, Neenasam, in a village in Karnataka. And this centre attracts people from all over India.

Subbanna says that India has two languages, Ramayana and Mahabharata. Europeans come to know Homer when they read him for the first time. But no Indian reads the Ramayana and Mahabharata for the first time. They just 'know' these epics. A.K. Ramanujan, scholar, poet and translator, used to tell me a story which I often narrate as it conveys to me a powerful message. Ramanujan had collected more than a thousand versions of the Ramayana in Kannada. In one oral version Rama and Sita are illiterate. They converse about going to the forest. Rama tells Sita: 'You can't come, you are a princess, your feet are tender, you are not used to hardship, so don't come.' Sita says: 'No, I have to come, I am your *ardhaangi*.' Rama persists and Sita counters by saying: '[I]n every Ramayana Sita goes to the forest, how can you deny it to me.' This illiterate Sita knows Valmiki Ramayana without being conscious of it. There is certain richness in this blend of centralization and decentralization, of having one concept and simultaneously several ways of describing it.

That is why, when the phrase 'unity in diversity' is used in India, it has become a cliché—my response is if you overstress unity and claim there is only one India, then we all become conscious of diversity— each of us will claim to be Tamils, Kannadigas, Assamese, Bengalis and so forth. If, on the contrary you insist on diversity and say 'we are Kannadigas and have nothing to do with others, that will provoke a quite different reaction. We shall say 'no, there is something common to all the great sages, who created our Upanishads, Ramayana and Mahabharata; we are a united country'. This is the reason why neither unity nor diversity can be exclusively emphasized. That is why I hope the Bharatiya Janata Party (BJP) will fail in this country in their attempt to find a common principle among all of us.

The Indian Mind

There is certain suppleness in the Indian mind, in Indian culture, and it has been there for thousands of years. It is because of this that a small Gujarati like Gandhi could become an all-India figure. He spoke Gujarati, wrote in Gujarati, he had all the characteristics of a Vaishya. One could recognize him in terms of his caste, language, place of origin and yet see him as a national and global figure. I wrote a poem and addressed it to Mr L.K. Advani when he was setting out on his Rath Yatra. I said that if someone asked me who I was I would say Indian if I were in London. I would want to make myself distinct from a Pakistani since we look alike.

In Delhi I would say that I was from Karnataka, in Bangalore I would say I am from Shimoga and in the latter I would mention Melige. But in Melige I need say nothing. Everyone knows my caste, subcaste and even my *gotra* (the word *gotra* denotes the progeny [of a sage] beginning with the son's son). All these identities are continuous, not contradictory. However, Indian politics wishes to make them discrete and conflictual. When that is done we lose something valuable. How can one be Kannadiga and also an Indian, how can you be a Tamilian and also patriotic? These contradictions emerge from modern politics suggesting that there is a higher reality than being an Indian or a speaker of a particular language or a member of a specific caste. And this is integral to globalization as well.

Technology and Aura

Another major influence to reckon with is technology. When technology permeates into the world of culture people develop new varieties of musical instruments and new forms of music and dance. According to the great German thinker and philosopher Walter Benjamin (in his essay: 'Art in the age of mechanical reproduction') in the age of mechanical reproduction a certain 'aura' in the work of art is lost. There is only one Mona Lisa, in one place, securely guarded. It has an aura. When you can mechanically reproduce it, I can have a Mona Lisa poster in my bathroom. When you remove it from a particular time and space where it has aura it becomes commonplace. Thinkers like the literary critic F.R. Leavis felt that aura should be protected. He and his ilk warned against the loss of aura. I too shared this view once. I am still quarrelling with it but I understand the historical relevance of this theory.

Walter Benjamin wrote his essay during the Second World War. He died in 1940. He had seen Hitler's rise to power. He was witness to what aura could do. Aura is undemocratic and can be dangerous, whereas mechanical reproduction makes it available for mass consumption.

What precisely does technology do to our lives? Consider the Ayyappa pilgrimage as an example. Pilgrims carry a bundle on their heads with rice and coconut, which are a sacred necessity for the pious journey. But they also carry a two-in-one music system. Modern technology has already entered the realm of pilgrimage. In the past the Ayyappa cult was founded on Bhakti. In all Bhakti cults there is a congregation in which all are equal. In the Ayyappa cult everyone is a swami. The moment you wear the prescribed robe you are casteless. I know Dalits who have done this pilgrimage. For 40 days they abjure meat, drink and smoking. They are not individuals anymore; all are equal when on the pilgrimage. Now, though, technology has provided the pilgrims with powerful microphones and so they can guarantee the rest of us sleepless nights. But more important, the earlier Bhakti movements created poetry of the first order, poets of the quality of Tukaram and Kabir in the north and Basava and Purandaradasa in Kannada, but not now. Ayyappa cult has vigour and vulgarity, as well.

Purandaradasa lived during the time of the Vijayanagar Empire. He provides a sharp contrast to Hegel. Hegel posits the view that the mind had its childhood in India, developed in Europe, grew further in Germany and would reach its pinnacle in his King's time. Purandara, quite different, says in a poem: 'Uttama Prabhutva Lolalotte'. Literally it translates into: 'great/good statehood (governance) is a meaningless expectation.' Lolalotte is a term children use to signify something that is empty or bereft of meaning. Purandara is saying that even 'Uttama Prabhutva' is meaningless; it has no significance. Purandara is the product of a Bhakti movement. Poetry or thought of this genre we do not meet in the Ayyappa cult.

What has caused this? Modern technology, modernized ways of building a movement such as advertising and 'publicising' it? Does some inner core disappear from the Bhakti movements of today when they come under the spell of modern technology? In Bangalore I see movements for spiritual regeneration, supported by NRIs, advertised on big hoardings featuring leaders with longer beards than perhaps the sages of the past. But they seem empty. It is technology at work, there is nothing 'real' in them. I miss the aura I found in a Ramana sitting on a rock.

The omnipresence of technology brings to mind the recollection of a friend—a good man in every sense, a true family man who looked after his ageing parents. He had 'correct' political ideas but would not like his daughter to marry outside the caste. When his mother died he was not at home and got back only in time for the funeral. His wife had very capably taken care of everything including getting hold of a video camera. The camera had captured everything, even the local minister paying homage and naturally it had focused a little longer on the minister and other VIPs, their heads bowed. All that we attach to death and sorrow was present—the priest, white cloth, flowers, weeping—all of these captured on video (and of course properly edited).

In the process, the camera had fundamentally altered the communication of bereavement. When my friend played this recording for me, I had a problem. You do not know whether to respond to the bereavement or to the quality of the video? This happens when you are confronted with an album of photos of death. As you turn the pages do you speak about the sadness death induces or do you comment on the photographs? It occurs to me that you may even have to go through the critical wedding rite twice, that is, if the video has failed to capture the tying of the *mangalasutra* (sacred thread of love and goodwill worn by women as a symbol of their marriage). Again, somewhere the aura of the priest has been supplanted by technology and the possibility of mechanical reproduction.

Why is a funeral videographed? In one instance, a few sons could not attend the funeral. They were working in the Gulf but they had to have the satisfaction of catching the picture of the funeral. Here we have the nexus between the family, technology and globalization. Without the latter two, the family would not have been able to send its siblings to the Gulf and for that very same reason we cannot fault them for wanting a video of the funeral. If they were part of an agricultural community, there would have been no photographs at all. When a girl leaves home after marriage, all she leaves behind is the red mark of her hand on the wall. In fact, this mark makes a deeper impression than a photograph of which copies can be made. There is only one 'mark'. It has an aura.

For an ancient civilization like India, going through the impact of globalization is a torment. But we should realize that this cannot be reversed. The reactions to this impact are, sadly, not what we would find in Kabir or Purandaradasa. The responses we encounter are 'fundamentalist' in nature. The opposition to 'false' globalization utilizes the same instruments afforded by modern technology. The agony is not expressed in deeply felt spiritual terms but in mechanical, reproducible syntax.

I feel that the Indian mind can respond to globalization in one of two ways. One is to follow the Leavisian path—the essence here is to discriminate and resist, to hold on to what you consider valuable, ensure that at least in a minority this is inculcated, do not allow the essence to be lost through globalizing influences. The other alternative is to remain passive, let it take us over.

We are critical of India getting Westernized and of the prospect of Sonia Gandhi, a foreigner, becoming our prime minister. But let us not forget, we are getting Westernized all the time. In our metropolitan cities almost every young man behaves as if he were born in New York. Many youngsters work in places where they are required to change names, voice and adopt a non-Indian intonation. They are happy because they are fairly profitably employed and can sport a cell phone. They believe, I am certain, that through globalization we shall all overcome our caste distinctions and get 'modernised'. I wonder though if this can ever be a realistic expectation.

The United States is not letting Palestine modernize. The American objective is to confine Palestine to the status of a 'factory' which will produce its enemies, and ensure their perpetuation such that all hatred gets boiled over. Globalization will see to it that we lose what our tradition has bequeathed us to be replaced by something new which we cannot comprehend fully. We shall all be speaking English, preferably with an American accent since the British (and therefore the British accent) are now deemed second-class citizens.

Globalization for Whom?

For whom is the world getting globalized? I attended a Kannada conference in the United States. I said that our *yajnopaveetam* (the triple stranded sacrificial strand of thread that is worn by those initiated into the Gayatri recital) is like a software; it wears hot on our bodies. I made this remark since many in the audience were software professionals and largely drawn from the upper castes. But even though there is a shortage of barbers in America why don't our barbers go there? There is a big demand for women to take care of children, yet our unemployed young women do not migrate. I understand that California has become so expensive that teachers cannot afford to live there; schools consequently suffer from teacher shortages. Why should not our teachers go there? Birds globalized the universe long before we did; they go in search of food and a suitable climate, flying thousands of miles. If only that kind of bird-like existence is made possible would globalization become meaningful.

As a writer I know that our languages will get globalized for the fortunate few but the process will also bring in results which are not of our making. Our small, region-specific identities and cultural specificities get lost. Similarly, mechanical reproduction entails costs and generates evil, just as the aura did and still does. Take this instance: temple entry was banned to untouchables because of aura. I bathe every day and that confers aura on me, you cannot touch me and so aura became evil. India's creativity, whether of Tagore, Premchand or Bharati, fought against this kind of aura which tradition created. They tried to remove aura from these spheres but those who fight against it often end up creating aura about something else. Globalization is one phenomenon which will be the undoing of aura because under its sway virtually everything will be marketed as mechanical reproductions. That is why Tirupati Thimmappa looks much more beautiful in New York. They have made a better image and the priest speaks English (and better Sanskrit than his counterparts here) and has moved away from the sacred seven hills to some small hill in New York.

In one sense I think this is bad. But I ask myself in the same breath, 'Why shouldn't it be so?' In essence, I am trying to communicate to you this perpetual dual state in which we find ourselves. I think clarity must come to us only through suffering—suffering of loss and the desire to replace it with something else. In India there is much less intellectual suffering than in the past. Intellectual suffering means grappling with choices. Do we wish to keep to our own language, our own traditions? There was a time when Pampa wrote in Kannada, a thousand years ago, and he wanted to excel Kalidasa. There was no question of a small province as against a big India. India meant the whole of India—Delhi was not the only centre, Kanyakumari and Kashi were centres too. India was multi-centred. We were, therefore, not *koopamandooka*s in the sense of not knowing the world. We were where we were but imaginatively where we wanted to be.

Under the spell of globalization we shall be nowhere. We shall have lost our culture—Tamil, Telugu, Kannada—but will not acquire any other, not even American culture in the true sense of the term. That state of mind is dangerous—it represents the tiredness of the human soul. That is the final message of Adiga's poem: 'I am tired, I would like to be a frog in the well', says the poet so that the sheen is regained. Perhaps we will all feel this way after globalization goes a little too far.

3

Growth of a Wasteland

Amit Bhaduri

Introduction

Economic growth tends to be sustained over a period of time by mutually reinforcing tendencies. This process has appeared in different guises in various fields of enquiry to describe essentially similar phenomena. Biologists have long known it as symbiosis or mutualism between two species; they appear as autocatalysis in chemical reactions, and engineers dealing with electrical circuits call similar mechanisms systems of positive mutual feedback. Economists Myrdal and Kaldor tried to capture this phenomenon occurring during the process of economic growth as the mechanism of 'cumulative causation' and 'dynamic increasing returns', respectively. While most processes of economic growth sustained over a period of time might be characterized by this somewhat abstract notion of mutually reinforcing tendencies, each historical process is also different insofar as it generates its own specific tendencies. It is the specificity of these reinforcing tendencies that determine to a large extent the developmental politics underlying this growth process.

The growing despair and anger in large part of Indian countryside about India's recent and unprecedented high growth has to be placed in this context. It is not simply that growth coexists with the persistence of widespread poverty and inequality. That has always been the case, and continues to be so after 60 years of political independence and democratic governance. The current pattern of high growth is different, because it requires rising inequality as its driving force. Growth feeds on increasing inequality, and increasing inequality promotes growth in a mutually reinforcing cycle of positive feedbacks. It is a World Bank–IMF promoted platitude, shared by most economists and all mainstream political parties from the traditional Right to the traditional Left, that this growth and the accompanying pattern of industrialization would gradually alleviate poverty, as the benefits of growth begins to 'trickle down' to the poor.

The actual truth is less comfortable. This high growth based on a certain pattern of industrialization can continue only so long as inequality and relative poverty in our society is allowed to increase, while growing inequality is justified in the name of liberalization, globalization, the link between capital, foreign investment and industrialization, in short 'there is no alternative' (TINA) syndrome. It is also absurd to provide ideological justification along the line that the 'socialism' in Vietnam and China follows this route. These countries do not have a functioning democracy. Their extensive pro-poor policies inherited from their revolutions still survive to some extent despite market-oriented reforms. The Indian context is very different. India has a flawed but functioning multiparty democracy. Its most glaring failure has been our inability to remove extensive subhuman poverty to which we continue to subject anywhere between one-third and one-fourth of our citizens. One cannot hope to understand the historical process of growth under Indian democracy, if one ignores this specific historical context.

Inequality as Growth Source

The mechanism by which growing inequality drives this growth, while growth reinforces further inequality is caused apparently by two different factors. First, while India is experiencing a growth rate of some 7–8 per cent in recent years, the growth in regular employment has hardly exceeded 1 per cent. According to official statistics, between 1991 and 2004 employment fell in the organized public sector, and the private sector did not compensate for it. This means most of the growth, some 5–6 per cent of the GDP, is the result not of employment expansion, but of higher output per worker in contrast to earlier times when less than 4 per cent growth on an average was associated with 2 per cent growth in employment. This high growth in labour productivity comes in turn from two major sources.

In the corporate sector and in some organized industries, it comes mostly from mechanization, longer hours of work and downsizing of the labour force. Tata Steel, for example, increased its output five-fold in the last decade, but cut down labour force by nearly half, implying an almost ten-fold increase in productivity. Without a corresponding increase in wages and salaries, by cutting down labour cost per unit of output this becomes an enormous source of profit, and also a source of international price competitiveness in a globalizing world. One could multiply such examples, but this is broadly the name of the game everywhere in the private corporate sector. Nevertheless, this is not the entire story, perhaps not even the most important part of the story, because the corporate sector belonging to the organized industries account for at most about one-tenth of the labour force. Simply by the arithmetic of weighted average, a 5–6 per cent growth in labour productivity for the whole economy is possible only if the unorganized sector accounting for the remaining 90 per cent of the labour force also experiences considerable growth in labour productivity.

As many field surveys show, this comes mostly from lengthening the hours of work in the unorganized sector which has no labour laws worth the name, and no social security to protect workers. Subcontracting to the unorganized sector along with casualization of labour become convenient devices to force longer hours of work without higher pay as a source of growth in labour productivity as well as corporate profit. In this context, self-employment of workers becomes another name for ruthless self-exploitation in a desperate attempt to survive by doing long hours of work with very little hourly earning. It is this category of self-employed workers (about 260 million workers) which has expanded fastest during the high growth regime proving an invisible source of labour productivity growth.

The increase in labour efficiency driving growth is partly the result of economic openness in a globalizing world in two respects. The first relevant aspect is trade openness. Given the overall size and rate of expansion of the global market, which is beyond the control of an individual country like India, the thrust of trade-related economic policy becomes capturing a larger share of the global market for exports. In this respect, India, like many other countries, behaves like a giant corporation and tries to achieve a greater share of a given world market through higher competitiveness by cutting unit cost of production. This means imposing greater wage restraint on the one hand, and attempts at raising labour productivity through measures like longer hours, mechanization and downsizing of the labour force, on the other—policies known as needed for greater labour market flexibility.

It has turned international trade into an extremely competitive zero-sum game, where one country winning through greater export surplus entails some other countries losing through larger export deficit. It should not be forgotten that attempts at enhancing international competitiveness also put greater pressure on a country to invite direct foreign investments, raising concern at times over dependency to foreigners. For instance, China has been a winner in this zero-sum game, nearly 77 per cent of Chinese communication industry is controlled by foreign investors, with foreign capital controlling the top five firms in each and every industry where the Chinese government allows foreign investment. It forced the government to introduce in September 2006 regulations requiring companies to seek official approvals for all mergers and acquisitions involving more than 2,000 employees or 25 per cent of market share.

While trade in goods and services is the more visible aspect of openness, the openness to international finance and capital flows might well be of greater consequence. Much of India's comfortable foreign reserves position (crossing US$230 billion in 2008), despite the fact that we continue to import more than we export (unlike China) is the result of portfolio investments and short-term capital inflows from foreign financial institutions. To keep the show going in this way constrains government's policy, for it requires the government policies to be compatible with the interests of the financial markets. Successive Indian governments have willingly accepted this; for example, the *Financial Responsibility and Budget Management Act* (2003) restricting deficit spending serves this purpose, and so does the complementary idea that the government should raise resources through privatization but not through raising fiscal deficit or not imposing a significant turnover tax on transactions of securities. The hidden agenda behind these measures have been to please the large players in the financial markets who mostly take their lead from the IMF and the World Bank. The burden of such policies is borne largely by the poor of this country. It has had a crippling effect on policies for expanding public sector expenditure on health, education, public distribution as well as on employment generation.

The 'discipline' imposed by the financial markets serves the rich but harms the poor. This is the other reason for growing inequality, which expresses itself in the ideological rolling back of public expenditure in social services like health, education and public distribution. The result is a picture of striking contrasts that is India today. On the front page of its 8 October 2007 edition, the *Times of India* reported that the collective wealth of India's top 10 billionaires had increased by over US$65 billion or 27 per cent in the third quarter of the year 2007. The number of Indian billionaires rose from 9 in 2004 to 36 in 2006 with a combined wealth of US$191, which works out to about one-fifth of India's current GDP. Estimates based on corporate profits suggest that, since 2000–01 to date, on an average each one additional per cent growth of GDP has led to some 2.5 per cent growth in corporate profits. India's high growth is sheer music to the ears of the corporates. However, for ordinary Indians it is a land devoid of hope.

Nearly half of Indian children under 6 years of age suffer from underweight and malnutrition, nearly 80 per cent from anaemia, while some 40 per cent of Indian adults suffer from chronic energy deficit. Destitution, chronic hunger and poverty are systematically more acute in rural India, and among more vulnerable groups like females, Dalits and *Adivasi*s, and also concentrated in poorer states since recent market-oriented policies have widened regional disparities. After several years of high growth, India now has the distinction of being only second to the United States in terms of the combined total wealth of its corporate billionaires coexisting with the largest number of homeless, ill-fed and illiterates. It is this mechanism of the high growth process that we need to analyze. This is a process of high growth which traps roughly one in three citizens of India in extreme poverty with no possibility of escape. The high growth scene of India appears to them like a wasteland leading to the Hell once described by the great Italian poet Dante. On the gate of his imagined Hell is written, 'This is the land you enter after abandoning all hopes.'

Efficiency with Unemployment

Extremely slow growth in employment and feeble public action exacerbates inequality, as a disproportionately large share of the increasing output and income from growth goes to the rich, not more than say the top 20 per cent of the income groups. With their income rapidly growing, this group of privileged Indians demands a set of goods which lie mostly outside the reach of the rest in the society. The market expands rapidly, but only for a selected set of high-income goods; typically, they also have high service content. For instance, we are told that more than three in four Indians do not have a daily income of US$2. They can hardly be a part of this growing market. Since the market votes with purchasing power, its logic is to produce those goods for which there is enough demand backed by money so that high prices can be charged and handsome profit can be made. As the income of the privileged grows rapidly in the process of this growth, the goods they demand expand even faster through the operation of the 'income elasticities of demand' which roughly measures the per cent growth in the demand for a particular commodity due to 1 per cent growth in income.

Typically, goods consumed by the rich have income elasticities greater than unity. Consequently, the demand for the goods consumed by the rich expands even faster than the growth in their income. As a result, a lopsided composition of goods emerges in our otherwise poor country. Examples abound. We have state-of-the-art corporate-run expensive hospitals and nursing homes for the rich, but not enough money to control malaria and tuberculosis which require inexpensive treatment. So they continue to kill the largest numbers. Lack of sanitation and clean drinking water transmit easily preventable deadly diseases, especially to small children, while bottled water of various brands multiply for those who can afford. Private schools for rich kids often have fees that are higher than the annual income of an average Indian, while the poor have to be satisfied with schools without teachers, and enough classrooms because the government feels itself constrained to spend.

Resource-intensive Production

The resulting composition of output produced by the market in the liberalized economic regime of high growth is highly energy, water and other non-reproducible resources intensive. We only have to think of the energy and material content of air-conditioned malls, luxury hotels and apartments, air travels and private cars as means of transport. These become the symbols of 'world class' cities in a poor country, while by diverting resources they make a wasteland of our country-side where most people live. This is the black hole of urbanization with a giant appetite to gobble resources to help the rich by robbing the poor. Many are forced to migrate to cities. And it becomes another case of mutually reinforcing cumulative causation, that is, more depressed countryside and more impoverished agriculture leading to more migration and more migration leading to bigger cities. The poor are forced to migrate to escape the wasteland of an increasingly impoverished agriculture, only to be pushed out of the city as unwelcome, illegal shanty dwellers and street hawkers, because a world-class city cannot tolerate them.

The composition of output demanded by the rich is hardly producible by village artisans or the small producers. Naturally, they find no place as either producers or consumers; instead, it has to be handed over to large corporations who enter in a big way into the scene. The cycle of high growth with rising inequality is now completed. The corporations are needed to produce goods for the rich, and in the process they make their high profits and provide well-paid employment for the rich in a poor country. The obliging economist or politician, usually an intellectual slave to the platitudes that go under the name of development discourse sees nothing wrong in this process. Their sermon goes that investments must flow to the most productive and profitable sectors for the efficient allocation of resources in a market economy. It is conveniently forgotten that the price mechanism guides, but the prices are a consequence of the distribution of income in the society. Which sectors are most profitable and productive are determined largely by the pattern of income distribution ruling in a market system. An increasingly unequal distribution of income might indicate a particular set of goods and lines of production as most profitable (like air-conditioned malls, luxury apartments, private cars as modes of travel, etc.). However, they would cease to be so with a more equal distribution of income in a poor country. The name of the game is to be a knowing or unknowing slave to economic platitudes, and talk of 'inclusive growth', while ignoring the link between greater inequality and higher growth. And yet, this is the link that binds the corporations with the government, and becomes the defining characteristic of India's recent high growth regime.

A common pattern of resource use dictated by a liberalized market and a corporate led state begins to emerge. This is most visible in the large developmental projects each of which displaces thousands of labourers. Hydroelectric power from the big dams is transmitted mostly to corporate industries, and a few posh urban localities, while the nearby villages are left in darkness. Peasants even close to the cities do not get electricity or water to irrigate their land as urban India increasingly gobbles up these resources. Take the case of water use. According to the Comptroller and Auditor General report released to the public on 30 March 2007, Gujarat has increased the allocation of Narmada waters to industry five-fold last year, eating into the share of drought-affected villages. Despite many promises made to villagers by different governments, water allocation stagnated at 0.86 million acres feet (MAF), and now even this is being cut. Water companies and soft drink giants like Coca-Cola sink deeper to take out pure ground water as free raw material for their products. Because peasants cannot match their technology or capital cost, the land in surrounding areas is left starved of water.

Iron ore is mined out from distant tribal lands where people would hardly ever use iron beams or any other metal for their mud houses or roads. Common lands which traditionally provided some supplementary income to the poor are taken over systematically by the local rich as well as the corporations with active connivance of the government. While natural resources like land and water are being handed over under various guises mostly to a few corporations turning the Indian countryside to a wasteland for the poor, the rich and the powerful celebrate it as the progress of the whole country. And yet, it is nothing less than the internal colonization of many of our poorest citizens. The manifest crisis engulfing Indian agriculture is a pointer to this process, with more than a hundred thousand suicides by farmers over the last decade according to official statistics. We are indeed colonizing successfully our own agriculture, where most of our fellow citizens live.

Internal Colonization

The large corporations and the rich citizens of India who mostly benefit from this process of destructive creation of corporate wealth find that their interests increasingly coincide. A new coalition cutting across traditional Right and Left political division is being formed in the process. The name of the game is 'progress through industrialisation'. In effect, this leads to ganging up against the poor by the rich and upper classes who believe it their birthright to have all the industrial luxuries in the name of economic progress. The meagre livelihood of the poor have to be destroyed, the small and marginal peasants' lands have to be snatched and consent has to be forcibly manufactured, if and where necessary at gunpoint, from the *adivasis*, so that their thousand-year-old habitats can be handed over to large private corporations in the name of public interest by a democratic government. Such practices are extensive particularly in the resource-rich states of Orissa, Jharkhand, Chhattisgarh and Madhya Pradesh, but even the Marxist government in West Bengal is not lagging far behind.

The *adivasis* or tribals who constitute only 8 per cent of India's total population accounted for an overwhelming 55 per cent of the people displaced in the name of economic progress in recent years. In this central part of India, where these states have parts of their land mass, in some 160 districts covering nearly one-fourth of the land area of the country, extremist left wing movements have gathered momentum. It would have been surprising if it did not. When people are preached continuously about the eventual benefits of industrialization, but are left with nothing but destruction of their livelihood, resistance cannot be unexpected. The governments, at the federal as well as at the state level, irrespective of their political colour consider it the 'greatest security threat' to the country. However, they do not quite explain what the dispossessed rural poor should do when all the security of their livelihoods are snatched in the name of high growth.

The middle-class opinion makers, learned economists, democratic politicians, legal experts and the media persons unite occasionally to restrict their liberal talk carefully to 'fair compensation' for the dispossessed. They are at a loss about how to create alternative dignified livelihood due to such large-scale displacement and destruction. Even discussion about compensation is one-sided, and focuses usually on ownership and, at best, usage rights to land property. However, the multitude of the poor who eke out a living without any title to landed property like agricultural labourers, fishermen or cart-drivers in rural areas, or illegal squatters and small hawkers in cities seldom figure in this discussion about compensation. And yet, they outnumber by far, perhaps in the ratio of 4 to 1, those who have some title to property.

In the meantime, the state acquires with single-minded devotion land, water and resources for the private corporations for mining, industrialization or Special Economic Zones in the name of public interest. It destroys in the process livelihoods of numerous poor people with or without titles to property; presumably these poor people do not count in defining 'public interest'. None stops to ask why the poor, who are least able, should bear the burden of 'economic progress', which constitutes a rapidly growing basket of goods and services as gross domestic product without any relevance to their lives. But rich India of a mostly urban, smooth-talking upper middle class pleased with their lifestyles as never before needs these goods and services, and helps corporate billionaires to shine by multiplying their number and wealth at a furious rate.

Dispossession of the Poor

The process of internal colonization of the poor, of the dalits and the *adivasi*s and of other marginalized and forcibly dispossessed groups has set in motion a relatively little noticed social process, not altogether unknown as the relation between an imperialist 'master race' and the colonized natives. As the privileged thin layers of the society distance themselves from the poor, the speed at which the secession takes place is celebrated as a measure of the rapid growth of the country. Thus, India is poised to become a global power in the twenty-first century, with the largest number of homeless, undernourished and illiterates. Over them rules an unbridled market whose rules are fixed by the corporations aided by state power.

The ideology of progress through dispossession of the poor, preached relentlessly by the united power of the rich, the middle class and the corporations colonize directly the poor, and has begun to colonize indirectly even our minds. The result is a sort of uniform industrialization of the mind which sees no alternative. And yet, no matter how powerful this public relations campaign is, the combined power of the corporations, the media and the politicians is still defenceless in a way against the life experiences of the poor. If this process of growth continues for long, it would produce its own demons. No society, not even our malfunctioning democratic system, can withstand beyond a point the increasing inequality that nurtures this high growth. The dissent of the poor must either be suppressed with increasing state violence against the poor flouting every norm of democracy, and violence will be met with violence to engulf the whole society. Or, an alternative path to development that deepens our democracy with popular participation has to be found. Neither the rulers nor the ruled can escape for long this challenge thrown up by high growth.

References

Alternative Survey Group. 2007. *Alternative Economic Survey, India 2006–2007.* New Delhi: Dannish Books.

Dev, S. Mahendra. 2008. *Inclusive Growth in India.* New Delhi: Oxford University Press.

Government of India. 2007. *Economic Survey, 2006–2007.* New Delhi: Ministry of Finance.

———. 2007. *Green Left Weekly* issue no. 710, May.

Radhakrishna, R., ed. 2008. *India Development Report.* New Delhi: Oxford University Press.

Rakshit, Mihir. 2007. 'Service-led Growth', *Money and Finance*, February.

Rangarajan, C., Padma Kaul, and Seema. 2007. 'Revisiting Employment and Growth', *Money and Finance*, September.

4

Whither the Indian Village?
Culture and Agriculture in 'Rural' India
Dipankar Gupta

Country–Town Nexus

There is a certain resistance in accepting the fact that the Indian village is undergoing major changes, not just economically, but culturally as well. The reluctance in coming to terms with this reality arises largely from the widely prevalent belief among intellectuals that the Indian village is timeless and unchanging and that the Indian villager likes nothing more than living in a rural setting. These notions need to be revised, not just for the sake of factual accuracy, but also because of the imperatives of the planning and developmental process. If the village is really the mainstay of India's economy, then that would require a certain set of policy prescriptions that would centralize agriculture. But if, on the other hand, the agrarian character of the village is fast changing then that should certainly inspire a significant shift in perspective, especially when thinking in developmental terms.

It is not as if these changes have not been noticed by others. In fact, this presentation will refer to such studies and, hopefully, build on them. There are two points that need to be noted in this connection. The first is that while there is the acknowledgement that rural India is changing in factual terms, yet at the conceptual level the village and the villagers remain resolutely in the past.[1] This is probably because

---

[1] Rural life was portrayed in a variety of ways in the past. For example, *Do Bigha Zameen*, a 1950s classic gave a moving account of a poor peasant eking out a living in the harsh environs of a metropolis as a rickshaw puller so that his family could survive

of the hangover of earlier scholarship, as well as popular conceptions regarding India, that depict Indian society to be essentially rural. So the theoretical cum analytical frameworks remain largely unchanged, while at the level of facts there is a clear recognition that things are not what they used to be.

The second feature that needs to be recognized in terms of contemporary rural dynamics is that it is not urbanization that is always the critical factor that is impacting the village from the outside. The village landholding structure is such that there are few jobs available in the fields that can engage the rural population on a sustained, albeit suboptimal, basis. It is true that the availability of urban jobs has made a difference; it is also true that there are more electrified villages in India, many more motorized vehicles and better roads connecting

back in the village. The film begins with a song in praise of the rain gods, but when the monsoon fails, the protagonist of the film has no other option but to seek work in the cities in order to pay back the loans he had taken. Shyam Benegal, ideologically committed to a radical revision of a placid village commune, directed films that bring to the fore the colours of rural violence. It is usually the landlords or their henchmen who are the perpetrators of such violence. If in movies such as *Mirch Masala* or *Nishant*, Benegal gives a vivid picture of exploitation in rural India, other films such as Manoj Kumar's *Upkaar* glorifies the village, the agriculturalists and the rural way of life in general. The village is presented largely as a homogeneous community where the moral economy thrives. The agriculturalist is the salt of the earth in more ways than one, and mother India yields food in the villages for her millions. The hit song, 'Is Desh ki Dharti', exemplifies this sentiment.

The city is where the undesirables live with their crass and immoral ways. The city is the home of the black marketer, the cheat, the swindler. Villagers do not drink, smoke or play the fool in nightclubs like city people do. *Khottey Sikke* and *Adalat* are two other films which put forward a similar message. *Lagaan*, the mega hit, also showed the village as a community where everybody pulled as one against the extortionate demands of the British administrators in colonial times. In this case, even the native upper crust was presented with sympathy.

The opposition between town and country, or between India and Bharat (Manoj Kumar was called Bharat in one of his movies), is a fairly recurrent theme when Indian cinema deals with the village. In Bimal Roy's other great classic *Devdas*, the hero Devdas lives in idyllic enchantment with his lover in the villages. When Devdas is forbidden from marrying the woman he loves he takes off for the city of Calcutta and it is there that he gives himself up to alcohol with dogged determination. In Mehbooob Khans' *Mother India*, the heroine looks for her husband who has run off to the city and consequently can hardly keep track of his disintegrated character (see Dwyer and Patel 2002: 63–64). Today, the bucolic characters of the Indian village rarely attract viewers any more. It is hard to recall a film made in the late 1990s that extols the Indian village, or glorifies it at the expense of the city. In fact, these counter positions no longer seem to resonate.

country to town than was the case a few decades ago. Yet, it is not as if the village is transforming internally on account of urban inputs, but rather because it is expelling people outside because of the sheer inertia of the agrarian economy that hardly allows for any optimism. In this sense then it is not that the village is changing in one direction towards urbanization, but rather the impetus for change is taking place in the village itself. The town is not coming to the country, as much as the country is reaching out to the town, leaving behind a host of untidy rural debris.

It is better then to look at the relationship between country and town not only in terms of how the urban world is changing rural life, but also enquiring into the modalities by which villagers are leaving their agrarian pasts for an uncertain non-agrarian present. It would not be quite right to liken their contemporary situation as 'urban', but it is not agrarian either though they continue to live, in the main, in what are still called 'villages'. To live in the village and be alienated from agriculture surely demands a new analytical optic, but for that it needs to be admitted that rural India cannot be comprehended under earlier rubrics. The uprooting of village life from within and the linkages with towns and cities bring to light a country–town nexus within which those who are deracinated at home are structurally compelled to function.

Village under Duress

The Indian village is not what it used to be, and even further from what it has been for long imagined to be. There are unambiguous statistics that point to the falling rates of growth in agriculture, and to the increasing exodus from country to town. On top of it, we have the phenomenon of non-farm employment whose scale has increased tremendously over the years. It is estimated today that about 24 per cent of villagers are engaged in non-agricultural occupations. This is not a small number, and in all likelihood, it is probably a conservative estimate.

While these gross statistics do suggest a whittling down of the importance of agriculture as the mainstay of Indian society, there is in addition a general undermining of values and practices that have their origins in the villages and are imbued with the so-called rural ethos. There was a time, not too long ago, when a Jat farmer in Uttar

Pradesh or Punjab would proudly proclaim that farming was the noblest of all occupations. Today this swagger is missing amongst them. They want an urban foothold, and would even condescend to take up occupations in towns and cities that they would deign to perform in their own villages.

The profundity of changes in rural India is not fully captured by census figures, or by statistical surveys. Useful though they are, it is necessary to comprehend the depth of disenchantment that prevails in the villages through in-depth field investigations. This disenchantment is on a variety of fronts. Indian agriculture has always lurched from crisis to crisis. If the monsoons are good then there are floods, if they are bad there are droughts, if the production of mangoes is excellent then there is a glut and prices fall, if the onion crops fail then that too brings tears. The artisanal nature of agriculture has always kept farmers on tenterhooks, not knowing quite how to manage their economy, except to play it by year.

Even in Green Revolution areas, where there has been a spectacular increase in mechanization and chemical inputs, the dependence on the vagaries of the weather and on the insufficiency, and irregularity, of electrical supply and other infrastructural inputs can throw the best agricultural calculations out of gear. It is not surprising then that whenever the occasion arises villagers are more than willing to up and leave for a future outside the mud walls of their homes and in fields as distant from agriculture as industrial labour. The village is shrinking as a sociological reality, though it still exists as space. Nowhere else does one find the level of hopeless disenchantment as one does in the rural regions of India. In urban slums, there is squalor, there is filth and crime, but there is hope and the excitement that tomorrow might be quite different from today.

Rarely would a villager today want to be a farmer if given an opportunity elsewhere. Indeed, there are few rural institutions that have not been mauled severely from within. The joint family is disappearing, the rural caste hierarchy is losing its tenacity and the much romanticized harmony of village life is now exposed for the sham it perhaps always was. If anything, it is perhaps Dr B.R. Ambedkar's analysis of the Indian village that strikes the truest of all. It was Ambedkar who said that the village was a cesspool of degradation, corruption and worse. That village India was able to carry on in spite of all this in the past was because there was little option for most people, rich or poor outside the confines of the rural space.

If rural India has lost its centrality in the minds of most villagers in contemporary India today it is not, as we mentioned earlier, only because an urban world has opened up their horizons, but also because the village economy itself has lost its sustaining power. Consequently, the countryside has witnessed a kind of cultural implosion that has shaken many of the verities of the past. With the abolition of landlordism and the introduction of adult franchise (the two must necessarily go hand in hand), old social relations that dominated the countryside are today in a highly emaciated form, when not actually dead. Roughly 85 per cent of landholdings are below 5 acres and about 63 per cent are below even 3 acres. What land reforms and land redistribution could not do, demography and subdivision of holdings have done to land ownership. Where are the big landlords? There are some, but they are few and far between. But does this make the village an egalitarian utopia? Far from it!

Medium-sized owner-cultivators contend against landless labourers, both economically and socially. While the rigidities of the caste systems no longer operate in their pristine form, caste prejudices and identities die hard. The stigma of tradition sits incubus like on social relations even if the prescriptions of tradition cannot be followed with equal facility these days. Other than the lack of economic opportunities, it is the nature of social relations in rural India that drive many poorer castes and classes out of the village. Clearly, the poorer one is, the greater the temptation to up and leave the village before the sun finally sets on one.

Where landholdings are so fragmented there is little scope for agricultural regeneration. Planners would be happy if agricultural production could be sustained year after year, and elated if there is a modest increase of even 1 per cent. Last year, there was in fact a negative growth rate. In small plots, there is always a preponderance of family labour and the Chayanovian logic of balancing drudgery and needs usually operates in such cases. But for that to happen without emotional philippics, the needs horizon must curve within the village perimeter. Only then is the family farm a precious gift to be harvested in perpetuity. But now needs have escalated and the family farm is no longer what it was earlier cut out to be. It cannot support the ambition to be where the bright lights are. Nor can family farms provide employment to the landless youth in the villages. Therefore, no matter which way one looks at it, as owner-cultivators or as landless labourers, the village is no longer a site where futures can be planned.

Preconceptions and Conceptions of Village India

That India's villages were changing was noticed in the late 1950s. Several studies, the most renowned being McKim Marriot's edited volume, *Village India* (1955), indicated that India's villages were not little republics. A select group of distinguished anthropologists commented on the fact that the great culture of Hinduism interacts with the little cultures of the villages and in that process both are transformed. Scarlett Epstein's work, which was a longitudinal time study of two villages, also demonstrated the growing relationship between town and country. Even so, till the late 1960s and early 1970s the importance of farming was overwhelmingly visible, as also the incidence of hired labour even though mechanization had made some inroads into agriculture (Epstein 1973: 86, 99, 192). There is not much evidence by way of non-farm occupations except for the number of cafes that have sprung up in the villages she studied (ibid.: 117). She also found that the poor in these villages have suffered a definite fall in their standards of living (ibid.: 165), though the rich peasants have certainly grown richer with the opening up of the jaggery market (ibid.: 171). But otherwise the villages were not terribly influenced by the world outside: their shops buy from without but sell wholly within, and even their university graduates were not expected to 'exert much influence over village affairs' (ibid.: 240). In spite of changes noticed by Epstein, it appears that the villages she examined over 40 years ago still looked up to agriculture as the mainstay of their economic life. This is notwithstanding the fact that a large number of poorer farmers had become distinctly worse off in the 15-year interim between her first study and the second one.

The village has often been essentialized as an idyllic locale where community ties bind the population together. These villages were little republics, timeless and unchanging—obdurate too, in their stasis, but engagingly so. In such conceptions, the Indian village knows no evil, and is counterposed to the harsh and immoral life of the cities. This is where the native 'authentically' lives. Charles Metcalfe and James Mill were among the early popularizers of this view. Even

Marx, who tirelessly championed dialectical movement, fell prey to this 'village republic' conception of rural India. Dynasties may come and go, great wars may be fought by ambitious monarchs and potentates, but the steady hum of village life is scarcely ever disturbed (see Cohn 1987: 213). According to Ronald Inden, colonial administrators saw the village as the atom of Indian civilization, no less (Inden 1991: 131). Much of this can be found in Gandhi's exhortation to revive the Indian village to its earlier authentic existence. He, of course, recognized many of the shortcomings of rural life, but nursed the political goal of returning the village to its pristine ways.

Gandhi was not, however, unchallenged in the years leading up to the national movement. Peasant leaders like Swami Sahajanand Saraswati brought forth the harshness of village life where the landlords plundered poor peasants and lived off the fat of the land (see Rasul 1974). The much written about jajmani system was clearly a much romanticized phenomenon (see Wiser 1969; Beidelman 1959). Even if the perfectly orchestrated organic division of labour based on caste did not quite exist, nevertheless, M.N. Srinivas argued, 'the power wielded by the dominant caste was real' (Srinivas 1987: 59). Members of the dominant caste were the chief patrons of the village (see Beteille 1980: 110–15), though, they had to encounter factional rivalries within (see Dumont 1970: 163–64). What remained largely undisputed was that everyday life, politics, economics and rituals included, pivoted around the dispensations of the dominant caste. Social anthropology was clearly cured of any romantic naiveté primarily because leaders in the field insisted on the field view and not the book view. The fact that the village community, howsoever defined, did not mean egalitarianism comes through quite clearly in the works of several scholars, foremost among whom is perhaps M.N. Srinivas. Even so, the concept of the dominant caste does not illumine village India today like it used to a few decades ago. Bose (1991), Bandopadhyay and von Eschen (1991), Harriss (1982), Sahay (2001), Chakravarti (2001) and a host of other authors discussed tensions between agrarian classes, bringing out the severe asymmetry of rural social relations. So for some time now, village India has ceased to be a quiet, idyllic rural haven in academic writings.

Traditionally, caste and village called out to each other in synergy. If the village was said to be tranquil it was argued that caste ideology was responsible for it. This is how the much vaunted jajmani system was understood. Each caste had its specific locus and all castes agreed in the hierarchy of purity where the Brahman sat on top. What most scholars failed to notice was that the hierarchy on the ground was not an outcome of ideological acquiescence but an outcome of an unequal distribution of wealth and power in a closed agrarian economy. In fact, every caste values itself and its ritual practices very highly, and no caste actually believes that it is essentially impure. Origin myths of castes clearly demonstrate this. In every instance, these origin tales recall a mythic past when a supposedly 'low caste' actually held a very high status in the distant past. Loss of status took place in such cases because of chicanery, deceit, reversals in war and sometimes also because the gods were idiosyncratic. But on no account did the members of the so-called lower caste participate willingly in their own subjugation. Nor is it that ideas of grandeur crop up once a caste has economic and political power. In fact, these ideas are always there, except that they cannot be extraverted when conditions are not propitious as in a closed village economy under the sway of a dominant caste. As this aspect of unconditional dominance is rapidly becoming a thing of the past in Indian villages, the assertion of caste identities is becoming much more strident and out in the open. This is also why caste politics has so much purchase in contemporary India (see Gupta [2000] for details).

Caste Identity and Caste System

The gradual diminution of status of the dominant castes and of the earlier village oligarchs who controlled the agrarian economy of the village have brought about a number of changes at the cultural level too. One instance is the stridency with which backward castes and scheduled castes express their political views and preferences. In Uttar Pradesh (UP), the impact of the Bahujan Samaj Party has been written about quite extensively and does not need repetition here (see Jaffrelot 2003). The reason for the rise of scheduled caste political assertion in recent times is primarily that the propertied classes in rural India can no longer exercise economic domination over the landless peasants. As they cannot employ the landless any more because of the shrinking size of their own landholdings, the power of landowners as patrons and as political leaders has also diminished over time.

Apart from the political side of scheduled caste mobilization in recent years what needs also to be mentioned is the symbolic defiance of the hitherto subaltern castes towards those who, till less than a generation ago, were their unchallenged social superiors. In Punjab, the once low caste Chamars now identify themselves as Adi-Dharmis (Jodhka 2002: 1816). Without formally giving up Sikhism they have established their own Gurudwaras and do not go to those that are controlled by Jat Sikhs. In order to mark their distance further from Jats, the Adi-Dharmis display a portrait or statue of Guru Ravi Das in their Gurudwaras. Most Adi-Dharmis have given up wearing the Sikh turban and are clean-shaven though their parents adorned the Sikh visage till not so long ago. In Talhan Village in Jalandhar District the Ramgarhias (carpenters by caste occupation) have also been drawn into the Adi-Dharmi fold. The Jat Sikhs do not approve of the ascendance of the Adi-Dharmis but there is little they can do about it. In fact, in Talhan every third Adi-Dharmi household has a family member living abroad. I found three beauty salons in the Adi-Dharmi hamlet of Talhan village. All these are signs of prosperity and a clear indication that the Adi-Dharmis can do without Jat patronage. Even in districts where the Adi-Dharmis are not as assertive as in Jalandhar, such as in Taran Taran, they, nevertheless, refuse to do menial work, nor will they work in fields owned by Jats as agricultural labourers. The Mazhabi Sikhs, who were traditionally scavengers, have now begun to be employed as agricultural labourers, when the occasion presents itself, but the Adi-Dharmis refuse to be engaged in that kind of work anymore as they consider it humiliating to bow before Jat landowners. The Mazhabi Sikhs still do not have the economic capabilities to oppose Jats frontally. Though many of them have their own Gurudwaras, as they feel slighted in those run by Jats, yet they have not made a defiant, symbolic break with Jat culture and orthodoxy as the Adi-Dharmis have.

This story is a familiar one and is played out in different parts of India by different castes. In UP, the Jatavs refuse to be agricultural labourers and so the Valmikis have taken their place. Even so, the Valmikis are not as supine either any longer. During my visit to Behrichi Village in Saharnapur District of UP, I found that a large number of Valmikis had left the village in search of jobs outside to the utter disapproval of the landowning Tyagis of that region. The Tyagis, like the Jat Sikhs of Punjab, cannot complain enough against what they consider the upstart effrontery of those whom they consider to be of low caste. The Tygais never let scheduled castes enter their Shiv Temple, and this is an age-old phenomenon. In recent years, however, the scheduled castes have built their own temple dedicated to Ravidas and play recorded hymns (*bhajans*) which are often lifted from popular Hindi films. In Maharashtra, the literate and culturally advanced Mahars have for a long time now given up their traditional occupation and have moved over to cities and towns where they are employed in a variety of services. This process has a much longer history in Tamil Nadu, with the Chakaliyar (Arunthodiar), the Pariyar (Adi-Dravida) and the Pallar (Devendrakula Vellala) showing scant respect today to local dominant castes. In recent years, the Arunthodiars have raised their levels of defiance by setting up Ambedkar statues which the landed Gouders find objectionable. The Arunthodiars (or Chakaliyars) are also very mobile and clearly prefer non-farming jobs to working on Gouder fields.

Caste identity has resurfaced at every level now. It is no longer the case that the property-less castes in the village could only speak of their origin tales in hushed tones. Now every caste proudly digs into deep pockets of heritage in order to claim an elevated status, frontally denying the station that tradition had accorded to them. Thus while the caste system has collapsed, caste identities are to be seen everywhere in a highly exaggerated form. This has given rise to the optical illusion that the caste system is enjoying a fresh lease of life. In fact, because caste as a system is dying in rural India that caste identities can now afford to come up. In the reign of the closed village economy ruled by the oligarchs of the dominant caste there was little scope for poorer castes to express their sense of self-worth through origin myths without being subjected to persecution from the superior communities. Now that the pressure of the upper class, landed castes has been lifted in the economic domain, the ex-untouchable castes have the space and the opportunity to proudly extravert their origin myths and their sense of identity without fearing reprisals. There are still some pockets where landed castes can be quite domineering, but the writing is already on the wall and the trend is irrevocably set against them.

Farmers' Movement

Rural agitations today are no longer between the agricultural labourer and landlord as used to be the case as late as the 1970s. During this period, there were a large number of organizations with political allegiance to left-wing national parties that were active in rural India campaigning for the landless labourer and poor sharecropper. Such mobilizations are things of the past and except for certain pockets in Bihar and Andhra Pradesh, they do not exist anywhere else. Even in these areas, such as Bihar, it is not clear to what extent the Naxalite brigades are actually Maoist in their orientation and to what extent they are now extortionate groups feeding off a poorly organized state machinery. The simple reason why such organizations have lost their initial focus is because agricultural labour is no longer a critical issue that involves masses of rural Indians. As most holdings are run on family labour, the need for wage labour is intermittent during peak seasons. This has reduced the scope for left-wing organizations to be active on their own terms.

By the 1980s it was clear that landless labourers had no viable future in the economy of the village. The increasing incidence of family farms made hired labour less critical for agricultural production than before. Where there was substantial agricultural prosperity in the years following the Green Revolution, such as Punjab and Haryana, labour could be hired from among migrants who came from East India in search of employment. Agricultural prosperity among capitalist farmers almost always meant a scarcity of local labour. This is primarily because even in large farms the amount of labour required per acre decreased substantially owing to mechanization. Increased prosperity of the region also meant greater opportunities outside the farm, which is where the local labour set off for in search of employment. This left the field open for migrants from East India who were happy to get some employment even though they were far from home.

In this context it must also be kept in mind that in many parts of India, particularly in Punjab and West UP, those who worked earlier as agrestic labour are no longer willing to work in the same capacity. As we mentioned earlier, Harijans and Adi-Dharmis of UP and Punjab respectively have more or less set their minds against labouring on others' fields. Cumulatively, this led to the diminution of the agricultural labourer's presence in rural India. By the time the 1980s came around, agricultural labourer movements that involved huge rural unions and supra-local organizers became more or less a thing of the past. Now was the turn of Mahendra Singh Tikait and Nanjudaswamy to lead agitations espousing the interests of owner-cultivators. In these mobilizations it was clearly stated that anyone who did not own land was not really a farmer. There was no room now for agricultural labourers in these movements which the Bharatiya Kisan Union (BKU) of UP and Haryana articulated most cogently. Even as the owner-cultivators were getting restive, a new configuration was taking place in rural politics. In the past when agricultural labourers mattered most in rural uprisings the target was always the local landlord, *jotedar* or *thanedar*. With the shift to owner-cultivator brand of agitation the enemy was no longer local, but supra-local, even the government of India. Not surprisingly, BKU and Kshetkari Sangathan were constantly moving into cities to impress upon the public, and upon recalcitrant politicians, the authenticity of their demands. Thus, while they were still agriculturalists, in the main, already the link between town and country was being strongly established (see Gupta 1997). Concurrently, there was the demand among the same category of owner-cultivators for reservations in urban jobs and in educational institutions. The Mandal Recommendations of 1990 were timed just right to coincide with the urban aspirations of cultivating castes such as Yadavas, Gujars and Jats. An urban job was clearly a prize catch for communities that for generations prided themselves in being farmers first and last. There is a play on a famous couplet in West UP that captures this sentiment rather nicely. The famous Urdu poet, Ghagh, had once eulogized rural life when he wrote: 'Uttam kheti, madhyam baan; nishidh chakri, bhikh nidam.' Translated it means that agriculture is the best, followed by business, salaried jobs and beggary. Today, the villagers have recast the ditty along the following lines: 'Uttam chakri, madhyma baan; nikrisht krishi, bhik mahan.' In this case a politician who begs for vote is on top, followed by a salaried job and at the bottom of the heap is the agriculturist.

The Marginalized World of the Owner-Cultivator

Though it is difficult to say where the process of cultural alienation from the village began, it can nevertheless be maintained that the relative stagnation of the rural economy has contributed significantly to it. This can be gauged not just from the growth rates between industry and agriculture, but also in terms of the quite remarkable shift that is taking place in the number of agricultural workers of all descriptions.

The belief that India is overwhelmingly an agricultural society obviously is in need of further finessing. The sectoral distribution of Rural Net Domestic Product for agriculture is down to 54.41 per cent from 72.37 per cent in 1970–71 (Chadha 2003: 58). As G. Parthasarathy et al. argue, workforce changes in India did not match the production structure of its economy (Parthasarathy et al. 1998: 140). The National Sample Survey points out that the number of rural people working in urban India has doubled between 1987–88 and 1993–94. Also the annual GDP growth in agriculture in value added terms has declined from 3.5 per cent in the 1980s to 2.8 per cent in the 1990s. Thereafter, the figure dipped even more dismally to 1.3 per cent in 1999–2000 and unbelievably to a negative growth rate of −2 per cent in 2000–01 (Mujumdar 2002: 3983). Further, trends show that urban households earn more than their counterparts in villages and that the disparity is growing. In a 1975–76 survey urban households earned on an average 1.82 times more than rural households, but today the figure stands closer to 2.1 per cent (Pradhan et al. 2000: 2531). Though there is a noticeable increase in inequality in urban India, poverty levels are on the whole much lower than in the countryside (Vaidyanathan 2001: 1814).

Just because a majority of Indians live in villages, it would be rather hasty to conclude from this that India's national culture is determined by the village. Most of the political debates in the country do not have a rural character at all. This is rather surprising given the fact that a large number of politicians in the parliament and legislatures have rural origins. Occasionally a Mahender Singh Tikait or a Nanjudaswamy will stir things up in the villages, but in the main, political ideologies that inform most of the national parties do not have a strong rural component. The usual concessions are made in terms of subsidies or minimum price for agricultural produce, but the kernel of political ideologies do not reflect any major preoccupation with the village. Even Laloo Yadav and Maulayam Singh Yadav demonstrate little by way of rural concerns. Playing the arithmetic of caste does not necessarily mean committing oneself to the chemistry of the village.

Yet, because it is also a question of arithmetic, politicians often vie against each other in coming through as champions of the beleaguered owner-cultivators. There is very little concern shown today with respect to agricultural labourers in political discourses nationwide. But even here there is a strong element of political gamesmanship at work.

In the name of protecting the poor farmer, political parties have in general opposed the institution of tax on agricultural incomes. Yet, as many owner-cultivators have told me repeatedly, this tax concession makes no difference to them as their incomes would be below the taxable amount anyway. These farmers argue that the exemption on agricultural tax is to help the rich entrepreneurial farmers and those in cities who want to escape the burden of taxation by diversifying into agricultural production, or in animal husbandry, or poultry farming and so forth. At the same time, politicians are alive to the fact that the opening up of agricultural imports would ruin the owner-cultivators who are in substantial numbers. As this would lead to political and economic stability, they are obviously cautious about it. Even so, there are peasant activists like Sharad Joshi of Kshetkari Sangathan who welcomes an open market for he believes that the peasants in Maharashtra would do very well if they could take their produce abroad. Mr Joshi's calculations need to be looked into closely, for he is obviously not keeping his books very carefully. To imagine that the Indian farmer could compete against the West where agriculture is an industry is quite difficult to conceive. Indeed this is precisely the reason why India constantly opposes moves in international forums to let the market dynamics control Indian agriculture.

While the owner-cultivators are protected politically, their futures are left unplanned. In 2000, the National Agricultural Policy formally recognized that agriculture has become 'a relatively unrewarding profession', and that efforts to revive it have to be multi-pronged in character. Horticulture, floriculture, the cultivation of aromatic and medicinal plants, over and above animal husbandry and fisheries are some of the alternatives they have presented to straighten agriculture. While these recommendations sound good on paper, there are vast infrastructural deficits that have to be overcome. To begin with, the conditions of owner-cultivators do not in general favour heavy investments in chancy cash crops. The suicide rate of farmers in Andhra Pradesh and Punjab is most alarming. In search for a better economic future, they had taken loans to upgrade their agricultural production which they could not repay. According to reports, the overwhelming number of suicides among farmers is on account of their inability to pay back loans. Further, this happens with those agriculturists who are ambitious and want to move on, but are suddenly pulled up because the empirical structures are far too unyielding which makes their attempts to take off lack throttle and thrust. Further, the village lacks other kinds of basic facilities like transportation systems, cold storages, modern silos and a sound marketing framework.

Without this kind of infrastructural backup, the hope that the production of non-food crops will revive the village is not very realistic. Regardless of how feasible this strategy will eventually be, there is no gainsaying the fact that agricultural production of food is far from being either romanticized or valorized for its own sake any longer. Though the majority of Indians live in villages, the village leaves little impress upon the national culture today.

Rural Non-Farm Employment

Perhaps the most telling aspect of the transformations that are being wrought on rural culture can be gauged from the extent of rural non-farm employment. Till 1983, there were 12 states where the Rural Non-Farm Employment (RNFE) was below 20 per cent. These states included Punjab, Maharashtra and Gujarat. This left only five states where the RNFE was more than 20 per cent. In 1999–2000, roughly 20 years later the situation has changed dramatically. Now 12 states have RNFE figures above 20 per cent and only 5 are below 20 per cent. In the 50th round of the NSS held in 1993–94, the data suggest that about 32.9 per cent of rural households were outside agriculture. By the 57th round in 2001–02 the percentage has gone up to 35.2 per cent. In fact in Kerela, Haryana and Punjab over 50 per cent of rural households are non-agricultural in the 57th round of the NSS. Further, in Jammu and Kashmir, West Bengal, Himachal Pradesh and Bihar (yes, Bihar), about 40 per cent of households are non-agricultural. These figures are indeed staggering!

It is, however, difficult to see any pattern beyond this except to say that RNFE is widely prevalent across the country and is not exactly in proportion to rural prosperity, or the lack of it. This is because Maharashtra and Gujarat have RNFE below 20 per cent in the 1999–2000 survey. These states rank below even Orissa, Rajasthan and UP. But in Punjab the RNFE climbed from a modest 17.4 per cent in 1983 to 27.1 per cent in 1999–2000. In Haryana, likewise, the figure went up from 22.3 per cent in 1983 to over 30 per cent in 1999–2000. Himachal Pradesh showed a dramatic increase for the figure doubled in these years from 12.4 per cent to 25.2 per cent (Chadha 2003: 55).

We cán approach the same scenario from another angle of vision. If one takes into account the number of male workers engaged in agriculture one again finds a significant drop in numbers from 77.5 per cent in 1983 to 71.4 per cent in 1999–2000. In other words, about 30 per cent of male workers in rural India are not working in the primary sector any more (ibid.: 12; Simmons and Supri 1995: 136). Chadha estimates that the services sector attracts a majority of those who are engaged in RNFE. According to him, in 12 of the 17 states in the country, the service sector plays a much 'weightier' role than manufacturing when it comes to RNFE (Chadha 2003). At any rate the rural non-farm sector contributes as much 45.59 per cent of Rural Net Domestic Product (Simmons and Supri 1995: 58).

But what accounts for the growing incidence of RNFE? True, as we mentioned earlier, the scope for agricultural employment has fallen rapidly, but alongside that there has been a refocusing of aspirations as well. It is argued that the growth in agricultural production creates many types of post-harvesting activities that relate to trade where a high degree of non-farm employment takes place. Though this argument can be sustained up to a point by demonstrating the extent of RNFE in Punjab and Haryana, it is difficult to explain how the figure is so low in this regard in Maharashtra and rather high in Assam (ibid.: 55).

It has also been argued that RNFE is an instance of 'distress employment'. Unlike many other historical instances when the fall in rural employment is accompanied by high rate of agricultural growth, RNFE has continuously increased in India in spite of stagnant rates of agricultural growth. Thus, the rural unemployed go out searching for jobs and are willing to do whatever comes their way (see Parthasarathy et al. 1998: 141). Simmons and Supri show from their research an inverse relationship between land ownership and RNFE (Simmons and Supri 1995: 145). Eighty-eight per cent of their sample who were engaged in RNFE had less than 10 acres of land and hence the deduction that there is a distress aspect in RNFE (ibid.: 149). There is little doubt that the poorer one is the greater the pressure to seek off-farm employment. Yet, it must also be mentioned that owning around 10 acres of land in India does not really signify a poor farmer who is in distress.

Our field studies indicate that in Punjab and West UP villages, all castes are active in rural non-farm employment. Adi-Dharmis and

Jats in Jalandhar own stores, run STD booths, sell grocery, sweets and snacks and stitch footballs for multinational companies. Surprisingly, in Village Khara in Taran Taran District, we also found Jats who work as tailors (see also Abbi and Singh 1997). But it also needs to be mentioned that in UP villages the non-landowning caste is more active in RNFE than the landowning communities. In Behirchi in Saharnapur District and Baijalpur in Ballia District, both in UP, the Tyagis and Thakurs, respectively, are not as active in non-farm occupations as the other poorer castes are. In fact, in Baijalpur in Ballia, very few Thakurs were involved in non-farm occupations, other than joining the army or buying truck and taxis for commercial purposes.

Thus, while there are indications that villages in East India are less dynamic than those in northwest India in shedding some of their values and prejudices, what is common in all instances is the general disenchantment with village life. The ambition to leave the village for a better life outside it, or to stay in the village but not to work on land, is too pronounced to be overlooked. It is also true that while RNFE attracts people from diverse castes, their location in the structure of employment outside the farm depends a lot on where they come from, and to the kinds of household they belong. What is also common is that the SCs are not without ambition, and in terms of RNFE they show a much greater degree of aggressiveness. In every village the SCs resent the treatment of the hitherto dominant castes, and have in many instances given up performing those menial tasks that they traditionally performed and which they believed, rightly so, to be humiliating in character.

Quite clearly, at an all-India level there is no pattern as such, though traditional and landowning castes in regions such as UP are less prone to step out of agriculture than their counterparts in places like Punjab. But these are caste-specific predispositions, and they cannot be generalized across the country. Nevertheless, what our findings show is that the recourse to non-farm employment varies, not just with respect to one's economic position, but also with caste-related attitudes and prejudices.

In an interesting case study by Ruthven and Kumar (2002) it is the availability of off-farm employment that drives the local villagers to seek jobs outside the village. This exodus of locals from the village obviously draws in a sizable number of migrants who are willing to work for less. And yet, because wages outside agriculture are better, it is those who live in the vicinity who can take advantage of it first. Yet, the study conducted by Parthasarathy et al. suggests that the degree of urbanization in a district has little impact on RNFE (Parthasarathy et al. 1998: 149). Certainly, if agricultural income had been plentiful, perhaps such labouring jobs in urban areas would be less attractive, but the jury is still out on whether or not it is distress employment, or pure urbanization, that drives up the figures of RNFE (see Basu and Kashyap 2002: A-180-1).

The availability of jobs outside agriculture is certainly an important factor for RNFE, almost axiomatically so. What one would really like to know is the nature of these jobs and their provenance. Pravin Visaria details the contribution of public utilities investments that have spurred RNVE (Visaria 1995: 404). Indeed, Ruthven and Kumar's study of a UP village provides empirical micro-level data that substantiates this position (Ruthven and Kumar 2002). Men are the main takers of jobs that arise from investments in public utilities and construction. In addition, as Visaria pointed out, villages which have gas, electricity and water are places where there is a greater incidence of RNFE (Visaria 1995: 404). Statistically, where land productivity is high, RNFE is also high (Basu and Kashyap 1992: A-181), but this cannot be posited as a general condition either. In some cases it is distress RNFE, in other cases, the incidence of RNFE is driven up by better wages (ibid.: A-187). When this happens it helps to increase the bargaining power of farm labourers. What, however, remains incontrovertible is that there is a growing increase in the number of those who work in non-agricultural operations in the village.

Finally, it is not as if all the non-farm employment is in the villages. Indeed, the number of people working in off-farm jobs outside the village must not be ignored. This is a factor that the census enumerators have not quite grasped and hence the census figures are probably not very reliable. In an earlier work I had pointed out, with data from Western UP, that a large number of landless villagers work in towns and cities in the day, but return at night, or even during the weekend (see Gupta 1997). It is, therefore, safe to conclude that RNFE can well be a local phenomenon that is often encouraged by supra-local factors. Further, RNFE is also an indicator of other changes that are occurring in the culture of the village, some of which we have already mentioned.

Is the Indian Village Vanishing?

In terms of the many diacritics of village life, a lot seems to be changing in rural culture. Old taboos against holding certain kinds of jobs
are disappearing; the caste system does not operate, though there is
a strong assertion of caste pride and caste identity. Untouchability
is not practised widely, though there are pockets of upper caste in-
transigence. On the economic front, even prosperous landowners
seek a future outside the village or in non-farm enterprises. We did
not find too many instances of satisfied farmers. Most of them have
grievances against the government for not providing them with better
amenities.

The most striking feature of all, of course, is the growing incidence
of rural non-farm employment across the board. The importance of
this cannot be exaggerated. It is not possible to convincingly demonstrate that there are linkages between agriculture and RNFE, other
than saying that better-off farmers are investing their money and
their ambitions outside agriculture. The poor in rural India do not
see a future in the village either but for them the recourse is primarily
in terms of manual labour and long-distance migration.

Predictably, wealthy landed people often have considerable political leverage in villages and form a vested interest group. While many
of them draw their wealth and esteem from the village, they either
live in cities, or they recreate an affluent urban ambiance in their
rural setting. In stark contrast to the poorer villagers with urban aspirations, when the rural rich engage with the outside world they do
so from a position of relative strength. Yet, they too see their future
outside the village, or in interacting with the town in enterprises that
require rural and urban inputs. It is against this background that the
culture surrounding agriculture must be understood. This culture is
not a stable one. History has not left behind a consistent legacy, nor
does rural culture have a temporal overhang that is safely cantilev-
ered on present commitments. Agriculture is an economic residue
that generously accommodates non-achievers resigned to a life of sad
satisfaction. The villager is as bloodless as the rural economy is life-
less. From rich to poor, the trend is to leave the village, and, if that
entails going abroad, then so be it.

All this may sound a trifle alarming, but this is what India's villages are telling us whether or not we are inclined to listen to these
rustic murmurs.

References

Abbi, B.L. and Kesar Singh. 1997. *Post Green Revolution Rural Punjab: A Profile of Economic and Socio-cultural Change.* Chandigarh: Centre for Research in Rural and Industrial Development.

Bandopadhyay, Suraj and Donald Von Eschen. 1991. 'Agricultural Failure: Caste, Class and Power in Rural West Bengal', in *Social Stratification,* ed. Dipankar Gupta. Delhi: Oxford University Press.

Basu, D.N. and S.P. Kashyap. 1992. 'Rural Non-agricultural Employment in India: Role of Development Process and Rural–Urban Employment Linkages', *Economic and Political Weekly* 27 (Review of Agriculture): A-178–A-189.

Beidelman, T.O. 1959. *A Comparative Study of the Jajmani System.* New York: Locust Valley.

Beteille, Andre. 1980. 'The Indian Village: Past and Present', in *Peasants in History: Essays in Honour of Daniel Thorner,* eds. E.J. Hobsbawm, Witold Kula and Ashok Mitra. Calcutta: Oxford Univeristy Press.

Bose, Pradip K. 1991. 'Mobility and Conflict: Social Roots of Caste Violence in Bihar', in *Social Stratification,* ed. Dipankar Gupta. Delhi: Oxford University Press.

Chadha, G.K. 2003. 'Rural Non-Farm Sector in Indian Economy: Growth, Challenges and Future Direction' (Mimeo), paper presented in the joint JNU–IFPRI Workshop on 'The Dragon and the Elephant: A Comparative Study of Economic and Agricultural Reforms in China and India', 25–26 March, India Habitat Centre, New Delhi.

Chakravarti, Anand. 2001. *Social Power and Everyday Class Relations: Agrarian Transformation in North Bihar.* New Delhi: SAGE.

Cohn, Bernard. 1987. *An Anthropologist Among Historians.* Delhi: Oxford University Press.

Dumont, Louis. 1970. *Homo Hierarchicus: The Caste System and its Implications.* London: George, Weidenfeld and Nicolson.

Dwyer, Rachel and Divia Patel. 2002. *Cinema India: The Visual Culture of Hindi Film.* Delhi: Oxford University Press.

Epstein, Scarlett. 1973. *South India: Yesterday, Today and Tomorrow.* London: Macmillan.

Gupta, Dipankar. 1997. *Rivalry and Brotherhood: Politics in the life of Farmers of North India.* Delhi: Oxford University Press.

———. 2000. *Interrogating Caste: Understanding Hierarchy and Difference in Indian Society.* New Delhi: Penguin.

Harriss, John. 1982. *Capitalism and Peasant Farming: Agrarian Structure and Ideology in Northern Tamilnadu.* Delhi: Oxford University Press.

Inden, Ronald. 1991. *Imagining India.* Oxford: Basil Blackwell.

Jaffrelot, Christophe. 2003. *The Silent Revolution: The Rise of the Low Castes in North Indian Politics.* Delhi: Permanent Black.

Jodhka, Surinder. 2002. 'Caste and Untouchability in Rural Punjab', *Economic and Political Weekly* 37: 1813–23.

Marriot, McKim. 1955. *Village India: Studies in the Little Community*. Chicago: Chicago University Press.

Mujumdar, N.A. 2002. 'Rural Development: New Perspectives', *Economic and Political Weekly* 37: 3983–87.

Parthasarathy, G., Shameem and B. Sami Reddy. 1998. 'Determinants of Rural Non-agricultural Employment: The Indian Case', *Indian Journal of Agricultural Economics* 53: 139–54.

Pradhan, Basanta, P.K. Roy, M.R. Saluja and S. Venkatram. 2000. 'Rural–Urban Disparities: Income Distribution, Expenditure Pattern and Social Sector', *Economic and Political Weekly* 35: 2527–39.

Rasul, M.A. 1974. *A History of the All India Kisan Sabha*. Calcutta: National Book Agency.

Ruthven, Orlanda and Sushil Kumar. 2002. 'Moving Mud, Shifting Soil: Change and Development in Wage Labour Livelihoods in Uttar Pradesh, India' (Mimeo), Working Paper 176, Overseas Development Institute, London.

Sahay, Gaurang Ranjan. 2001. *Village Studies in India: A Case of Bihar*. Jaipur: Rawat/New Delhi.

Simmons, Colin and Salinder Supri. 1995. 'Participation in Rural Non-farm Activity in India: A Case Study of Cultivating Households in Jalandhar District, Punjab', *International Journal of Punjab Studies* 2: 133–53.

Srinivas, M.N. 1987. *The Dominant Caste and Other Essays*. Delhi: Oxford University Press.

Vaidyanathan, A. 2001. 'Poverty and Development Policy', *Economic and Political Weekly* 36: 1807–14.

Visaria, Pravin. 1995. 'Rural Non-farm Employment in India: Trends and Issues for Research', *Indian Journal of Agricultural Economics* 50: 398–409.

Wiser, W.H. 1969. *The Hindu Jajmani System: A Socio-economic System Interrelating Members of Hindu Community*. Lucknow: Lucknow Publishing House.

5

Gender Inequalities: Neglected Dimensions and Hidden Facets

Bina Agarwal

Gender Inequality

Rural women in northwest India, married to strangers miles away from their birth villages, use folk songs to decry their estrangement from the green pastures of their childhood homes—homes to which their brothers, who inherit the ancestral land, have automatic access. I quote excerpts from two folk songs:

> To my brother belong your green fields
> O father, while I am banished afar.

> Always you said
> Your brother and you are the same
> O father. But today you betray me ...
> My *doli* leaves your house, O father
> My *doli* leaves your house.
> These dowry jewels are not jewels
> but wounds around my neck, O father.
> My *doli* leaves ...[1]

Women in Sri Lanka, by contrast, traditionally inherited immovable property, and sometimes their husbands moved in with them. But according to folklore such a husband was advised to always keep

---

[1] These verses are taken from folk songs sung by women in northwest India when the bride leaves her parent's home on marriage. *Doli* means a palanquin. I am grateful to Veena Das for sharing the second song with me.

a walking stick, an umbrella and an oil lamp handy. Why? In case his wife evicted him when he was ill, and in the rain, in the middle of the night! And some wives indeed did so.

Both examples depict gender inequality. In the first the woman has no property and social norms require her to join her husband—a dislocation she sees as banishment. In the second, the man has no property and social norms allow him to join his wife, but in a home from which he can easily be evicted. In the first example, the woman is the less equal, in the second the man.

These examples illustrate several things. They highlight that gender inequality and indeed gender in general, is a relational category. And although most times we are grappling with women's disadvantaged position, in rare cases men too might occupy that position. In particular, these examples highlight the importance of women's property status and enabling social norms in determining gender relations.

Compared with other inequalities such as those of class or race, gender inequality also has some distinct features. One, it dwells not only outside the home but also centrally within it. Mainstream economic theory has long treated the household as a unitary entity in relation to both consumption and production. The unitary household model assumes that all household resources and incomes are pooled, and family members either share common interests and preferences, or an altruistic household head (who represents the household's tastes and preferences and seeks to maximize household utility) ensures equitable allocation of goods and tasks (see also, Agarwal 1997).

Most people know from personal experience that this is not how real families behave. But academically too, in recent years, virtually every assumption of the unitary household model has been challenged effectively through empirical evidence, including assumptions of shared preferences and interests, pooled incomes and altruism as the guiding principle of intra-household allocations. Gender, in particular, is noted to be an important signifier of differences in interests, preferences, endowments and allocations. And in alternative 'bargaining models' of the household, bargaining power rather than altruism is seen as guiding intra-household allocations.

Two, gender inequalities stem not only from differences in economic endowments between women and men but also from social norms and perceptions, that is, the inequalities are also ideologically embedded. While norms and perceptions impinge on other social inequalities like race and caste as well, gendered norms and perceptions cut across these categories and exist additionally.

Three, gender inequalities not only pre-exist, new ones can arise from the foundations of the old ones, and people with prior advantage can set in place rules that perpetuate that advantage, such as rules governing new institutions now being promoted to manage common pool resources. Although based on principles of cooperation, such institutions can effectively exclude significant sections, such as women, from their decision-making bodies and their benefits. In other words, gender inequality can be *in the process of constant recreation in new forms*.

Gender inequality is thus a vast subject with a vast literature on it. But some aspects are more neglected and hidden than others. And it is on these aspects that I will now focus, namely,

1. Inequality in command over property—a notably neglected dimension.
2. Inequalities in social perceptions and social norms, the workings of which are often hidden but which have visible economic outcomes.

   The former is a significant material form of inequality, the latter a significant ideological form.
3. New inequalities arising in emergent institutions through the interaction of the above two dimensions of pre-existing inequalities. This will also throw light on the process of inequality creation.

In addition, I will illustrate how gender inequalities are simultaneously constituted in several arenas: the family, the community, the market and the state. And the bargaining approach provides a promising analytical framework for understanding how both the material and the ideological aspects of gender inequality can be challenged within these arenas.

Gender Gap in Command over Property

The Nature of the Gap

Consider first the issue of property. Economists have long emphasized the importance of property rights for incentives and efficiency. But relatively few have looked at the gender gap in command over property. And although there has been some progress on this count in recent years, it still remains a largely neglected issue. Economic analysis and policies concerning women continue to be preoccupied with employment, and relatedly with education.

In the process, inequality in command over property has largely been neglected. Yet it is this aspect of inequality which remains one of the most important forms of persisting economic inequality between women and men—one which has a critical bearing not only on women's economic well-being but also on their social and political status.

The idea of 'command' over property is more complex than appears on the surface (for a detailed discussion, see Agarwal 1994). First, it takes us away from the narrow legalistic way in which many think of property rights. Command over property implies not merely rights in law, but effective rights in practice. Equality in legal rights to own property need not guarantee equality in actual ownership. This is especially true of inheritance where the gap between law and practice can be vast.

In India, for example, legally women enjoy significant inheritance rights, even if unequal to men's (Agarwal 1994). In practice, only a small percentage of women inherit. A sample survey of rural widows in 1991, by development sociologist Martha Chen, found that only 13 per cent of the surveyed women with landowning fathers inherited any land as daughters. And only 51 per cent of widows whose deceased husbands owned land inherited any. Thus 87 per cent of daughters and 49 per cent of widows with legal claims did not inherit (cited in Agarwal 1998).

Second, property advantage can arise not only from ownership but also from effective control over it. Ownership alone does not always guarantee control. In many countries, even when women inherit they do not fully control what they receive. Some obstacles are social. For example, some cultures restrict women's interactions in the public sphere and hence their ability to manage their property effectively. Other barriers can be legal. For instance, in Sri Lanka's Jaffna Province, a married Tamil woman, under local law, needs her husband's permission to lease out or sell her own property. Similar laws prevailed earlier in parts of Europe. The distinctions between law and practice, and between ownership and control are thus especially critical for women.

Third, property advantage can stem from not only private property but also public property. For instance, in most societies today, control over wealth-generating public property is largely in male hands, be they managers in large corporations, or heads of government bureaucracies. Even in the former socialist Union of Soviet Socialist Republics (USSR), although private property ownership was abolished, decision-making over public property remained mostly with men.

Four, men (as a gender, even if not all men as individuals) also largely control the instruments through which existing property advantages get perpetuated, such as institutions that enact and implement property laws (for example, parliaments and law courts) and the mechanisms of recruitment into bodies which control property.

Fifth, command over property can also significantly influence the institutions that shape ideas about gender, such as the media, and educational and religious bodies. Predominantly male control over these institutions can thus affect the persistence of negative ideological assumptions about women's needs, work roles, capabilities and so on.

Seen in this broad way, gender inequality in command over property is thus important globally, in both developing and developed countries. However, which form of property is important can differ by context, and in large parts of the developing world, arable land has a pre-eminent position, as outlined below.

The Importance of Land

In largely agrarian economies, arable land is the most valued form of property. It is wealth creating, livelihood sustaining and status enhancing. For most rural households it provides security against poverty. Traditionally, it has been the basis of political power and social status. For many, it is even linked with personal identity and rootedness. And it has a permanence that few other assets possess. That is why people often end up spending more on litigation over ancestral land than its economic value would justify. It is notable that even in parts of central Europe today, as urban labour markets stagnate, people are returning to land and rural livelihoods for survival, as recent work on Uzbekistan shows (see Kandiyoti 2003).

While the links between access to land, economic well-being and social status are well recognized at the household level, their importance specifically for women has largely been neglected in both research and policy. The United Nations has long claimed that women own only 1 per cent of the world's property, but they provide no data to back this claim. In fact, in most countries, large-scale surveys do not collect gender-disaggregated data for land or other assets. (Nepal is a recent exception where such data are now being collected in their census.) Hence in order to estimate women's access to land we still have to depend mostly on small-scale surveys or village-level studies. These sources show, as noted, that few women own arable land and even fewer effectively control some. Why is this the case?

First of all, there are the noted biases in inheritance. Second, even government transfers of public land instead of narrowing the gender gap in private property tend to widen it, by transferring titles almost solely to men. This is true not only in India but in many other countries. In the Latin American agrarian reforms of the 1960s to the 1980s, for instance, less than 15 per cent of the beneficiaries across eight countries were women. Recent shifts toward joint titling remain regionally uneven (Deere and de Leon 2001).

In China, again, although the law promises gender equality in use rights in the distribution of household responsibility land, in practice, a range of gender inequalities can emerge. For instance, since most women leave their village on marriage, and land readjustments are infrequent, many have to wait long periods for land to be allotted for them in their husband's village. They also face special problems on divorce or widowhood (see for example, Li 1999). These problems could get compounded following the 1998 Land Management Law (LML) which has restricted readjustments by extending the duration of the household responsibility contract from 15 to 30 years (Li 2003; Brown 2003). According to Li (2003: 4), figures derived from a survey undertaken by the All-China Women's Federation and the State Statistics Bureau of 2000 showed that 70 per cent of people without their own land were women, and among these women, 20 per cent had never held land, while the others had lost their land on marriage, divorce or reallocation. It is as yet unclear to what extent the 2003 Rural Land Contracting Law (RLCL) can redress these gender inequalities.[2] Studies also show that typically officials get the husband

---

[2] For instance, on the one hand the RLCL further limits the practice of land readjustments, especially on account of population change; on the other hand, under this law, a collective cannot reassign land that is allotted to a woman if she later marries out of the village, unless the collective in her marital village allots land to her. Similarly, a collective cannot reassign land allotted to a woman during her marriage, if she divorces, unless she receives a new allotment in the village where she lives after divorce (Brown 2003).

to sign the contract for the family's land use allotments (Li 1999), embodying the assumptions of the unitary household. The third source of land is potentially through the market. But in many countries rural land markets are limited, and, in any case, given women's fewer financial resources, their access to land either by purchase or lease is substantially more restricted than men's. Support from the state or from NGOs can enhance this access, say, through the provision of subsidized credit to groups of women,[3] but only to a limited extent.

Implications of Women's Unequal Access to Land

The social and economic implications of this gender inequality can be wide-ranging. Millions of women in Asia, Africa and Latin America depend critically on land for a livelihood. The process of agrarian change under which labour shifts from agriculture to non-agriculture has been slow and gender-biased. In many countries, more men than women have moved to non-farm jobs. Hence, a disproportionate number of those left dependent on land are women. In India today, relative to 53 per cent of male workers 75 per cent of female workers are in agriculture. And the *gender gap is growing* (Agarwal 2003).

As more men shift to non-farm work, de facto female-headed households will also grow: estimates for India and Bangladesh already range between 20 per cent and 35 per cent. Many of these women bear growing responsibilities for running the farm, but can be seriously constrained by inadequate land rights.

Indeed a lack of effective land rights affects both welfare and productive efficiency. This is discussed in depth in my land rights book and recent papers (for example, Agarwal 1994, 2003), so I will only touch on some aspects here.

Welfare

Consider first, the welfare effects. These can be both direct and indirect. There is ample evidence that a household's property status does not automatically define the well-being of all its members. First, there is persistent gender inequality in the distribution of gains from

---

[3] The excellent work of the Deccan Development Society, an NGO working in Medak District in Andhra Pradesh, is a case in point (for details, see Agarwal 2003).

household resources. In South Asia, this impinges even on allocations for food and health care. Land solely in men's hands, therefore,
does not guarantee female welfare.

Women without their own land also face high risks of poverty in
case of desertion, divorce or widowhood. In parts of South Asia
often widows deprived of their property shares by family members
are found doing wage labour on the farms of well-off brothers or
brothers-in-law. In Bangladesh, widows living as dependents of male
relatives are found to face much greater mortality risks than those
heading their own households, and presumably owning some independent assets.

In China, similarly, in practice (even if not in law) divorced women
tend to lose their land allotments in their husbands' villages and may
not easily get land allotted for them in their parental village when
they return there, leaving them effectively landless and poverty prone.
This is especially likely following the above-mentioned 1998 Land
Management Law which restricts the frequency and scope of land
readjustments. This is likely to have negative implications for women
marrying into another village or returning to their birth villages on
divorce or widowhood (Brown 2003; Li 2003).

Hence, in most countries, to the extent that women, even of propertied households, own no property themselves, their class position
remains vicarious: a well-placed marriage can raise it, divorce or widowhood can lower it. Direct land access would provide a more certain means of welfare improvement and poverty reduction.

Second, land access would increase women's entitlement to family
welfare. For elderly women, owning land can improve support from
kin. As many elderly people say in India: 'without property children
do not look after their parents well' (Caldwell et al. 1988: 191).

Third, land access has interlinked livelihood effects. For instance,
it can improve credit and employment access. In South Asia, those
with land are more likely to obtain credit and put it to viable use. In
rural labour markets, those with land are found more likely to get
employment and higher wages. Also, even a small plot is found to be
a critical element in a *diversified livelihood system*. It can be used not
just for crops, but also to grow trees for fruit or fuelwood, or fodder
for animals, or to set up a vegetable garden or a microenterprise. The
landed are found to get much better returns than the landless, even in
rural non-farm activity.

Fourth, assets in women's hands can have intergenerational benefits. For a start, women are found to spend a much larger part of their

earnings on family needs than men (Dwyer and Bruce 1989). Several studies also show a positive link between children's welfare and the mother's assets. In Brazil, the effect on child survival probabilities was found to be almost 20 times greater when asset income accrued to the mother than when it accrued to the father (Thomas 1990). In rural India, children were found more likely to attend school and get medical care if the mother had assets (Duraiswamy and Duraiswamy 1991, 1992). On children's education, similar results obtain for Bangladesh, Indonesia and Ethiopia (Quisumbing and Maluccio 2003). It is no coincidence that in South Asia the best social indicators on health, education and fertility are found in Kerala in India and Sri Lanka in general—regions where women historically enjoyed notable rights in land and other property.

Efficiency

Welfare apart, in several contexts there can be efficiency gains from gender equal land access for several reasons. First, there is the issue of incentives. These are found to matter not only at the household level but also at the intra-household level. In Kenya, for instance, the introduction of new weeding technology was found to raise crop yields on women's plots by 56 per cent—plots from which women controlled the output, but it raised yields only by 15 per cent on the men's plots where too women weeded but men got the proceeds (Elson 1995). Second, there can be gender differences in preferences and efficiency of land use. In Burkina Faso, due to their choice of cropping patterns, women achieved much higher values of output per hectare on their own plots than did their husbands on theirs (Udry et al. 1999). Similar research is needed in other regions.

Empowerment

Last but not least, land is found to empower women socially. It adds to their voice, their sense of identity and their self-confidence. This is perhaps most graphically revealed in the voices of women themselves. In the 1970s Bodhgaya movement in Bihar, when landless women in two villages received land for the first time, after an extended land struggle in which they and their households had participated, they movingly recounted how having land of their own had given them the strength to speak and walk (Alaka and Chetna 1987). Women in China responded in similar ways when the Agrarian Reform Law of 1947 gave them separate land deeds for the first time, as described by William Hinton (1972) in his book *Fanshen* (see also Croll 1978).

Also, in our study based on a sample of some 500 households in Kerala, a colleague and I found a dramatically lower incidence of marital violence where the woman owned land or a house than where she owned neither (Agarwal and Panda 2003).

Indeed, in mainly agrarian economies there are many pointers that enhancing women's land access would help improve not just equity but also family welfare, production efficiency and women's bargaining power and sense of empowerment.

Having said this, however, I need to emphasize four points. One, there is scope for more empirical analysis in different regions of the world on the welfare and efficiency links of women's property status. For instance, are the links between women's land access and incentives noted in Kenya also found in Asia or Latin America, where the pattern of family-based farming is different? Are the links between the mother's assets and child survival found in Brazil as important in Africa or Asia? Does women's ownership of property serve as a deterrent to domestic violence in other regions as well? Two, although for illustration I have focused on land, my general purpose is to highlight the importance of property as such. In other contexts, a house may be as critical for women's economic and social security. Three, ownership confers only one form of right, but use rights or rights of control are also important. Indeed in public property, what matters is not ownership but managerial control—the ability to make rules, be it for government-run enterprises or for the management of local common pool resources, such as forests.

Four, it appears imperative that countries formulating new property laws do not repeat old biases. In post-apartheid South Africa, in Central Asia, in Central and Eastern Europe as well as in China, scholars are already expressing concern about the creation of new gender inequalities in land and other assets (see for example, Walker 2003; Kandiyoti 2003; Verdery 1996; Li 2003). To move toward such equality often requires taking into account the social context within which the laws will be implemented, since many laws which might in principle be gender-neutral can become unequal due to pre-existing social biases.

Social Perceptions

The second form of gender inequality I will explore today is ideological, as embedded in social perceptions and social norms. Although difficult to quantify and often hidden, these inequalities can affect economic outcomes for women in virtually every sphere, be it property rights, employment or intra-household allocations. And they remain understudied and under-theorized.

First consider perceptions. There can be, and often is, a divergence between what a person actually contributes, needs or is able to do, and perceptions about her contributions, needs or abilities. In particular, a person's contributions and needs may be undervalued because of her gender or race, or both. This affects outcomes in the market, the family, the community and the state (for elaboration, see Agarwal 1997).

In the labour market, for instance, gender, like race, often defines perceptions about abilities. The work women do is often labelled as 'unskilled' and that which men do as 'skilled', even if the tasks require equal skill. Or women are perceived as having lesser ability or commitment; or as being supplementary earners and men as being the breadwinners. Such assumptions often underlie discriminatory hiring and pay practices. Women on account of their gender may thus be paid less than men with the same abilities, for the same tasks.

Perceptions also guide intra-family allocations. For example, who gets what is often justified by referring to a person's contributions or needs. But a person's contributions may be undervalued because of gender, or because the work is less 'visible'. Home-based or unwaged work done mostly by women is often less valued than work which is more 'visible' in physical or monetary terms.

Female members would thus receive less than males because their contributions to the household are perceived as being less—what Amartya Sen terms 'perceived contribution response' (Sen 1990). Equally, women and girls may receive less because they are seen as needing less—what I term 'perceived need response' (Agarwal 1997). Systematic undervaluation of women's contributions or needs in systems where these are important distributive principles can thus reinforce gender-related deprivation. And such undervaluation is not confined to developing countries. Research on American households indicates that women doing paid work have more bargaining power than housewives, because housework is culturally devalued (England and Kilbourne 1990). Indeed, the Western feminist debate on 'wages for housework' arose from the recognition that unwaged work was 'invisible' and thus perceived as having little value.

Perceptions similarly influence community responses, and can hinder women's participation in collective activity. For instance, in my current research on forest management in the villages of India and Nepal, men typically exclude women from decision-making because they perceive them as making little contribution. Some characteristic responses are: 'Women can't make any helpful suggestions.' Or, 'women are illiterate. If they come to meetings, we men might as well stay at home....' I found that often the men who said this were themselves illiterate. Hence, their response clearly had more to do with their *perceptions* about gender differences in abilities rather than with *actual* differences in abilities.

The government's public policy is similarly affected by perceptions. For instance, that governments transfer land almost solely to men, even when women are significant farmers, has much to do with perceptions about, rather than the universal fact of male responsibility and female dependency. Similarly, perceptions can make women's public presence invisible. For instance, in matrilineal Meghalaya, when I asked officials why even in this society where traditionally women had property claims, they did not allot land to women, I was told: 'Women can't come to our office to fill out papers.' Yet outside their windows numerous women traders were selling their wares!

Indeed, perceptions underlie many assumptions in economic analysis and policy. They both constitute gender inequality in ideational terms and can lead to gender unequal material outcomes.

Social Norms

Like perceptions, gendered social norms embody an important form of ideological inequality. Conventionally few economists explicitly recognized the importance of social norms. Recent literature on social capital emphasizes the positive side of social norms. Social norms are seen to reduce transaction costs and enhance economic efficiency.

But are all social norms good? Not at all. Many social norms can also have a 'dark' side, especially for women. Such norms enter almost every sphere of activity both within and outside the home. Within the home, norms define the gender division of labour and goods. For instance, everywhere norms define housework and childcare as mainly women's work, and in many rural areas this is also the case for firewood collection and cattle care. Hence, firewood or fodder shortages adversely affect women more than men. Domestic responsibilities also undermine women's ability to participate in pubic decision-making, which may involve lengthy meetings at inconvenient times. Hence, a common response by rural women is that they don't have time to sit around for several hours in a meeting in the middle of the day.

Again, in north India, norms determine that males should eat before females and/or get more and better quality food. This makes for gender differences in nourishment and growth (Agarwal 1994). This is also the case in parts of China. For instance, Elizabeth Croll in her recent book, *Endangered Daughters*, quotes a young girl as saying: 'My mom, no matter what happened, always considered my elder brother first and ignored me. At the table, she kept putting food into my brother's bowl and not mine, as if I were not her own child' (Croll 2000: 145).

Social norms can similarly discourage women from asserting their rights, including in property. For instance, in northwest India social norms often dictate that a 'good' sister should forfeit her claim in parental property in favour of her brother.

Outside the household again, social norms restrict women's earning options by discouraging (or even preventing) them from working outside the home, limiting the range of tasks they may perform, placing double burdens of work on them, institutionalizing lower wages for them and so on. For instance, in many societies, norms restrict women's mobility and public interaction. In northern South Asia women of 'good character' are expected to avoid village spaces where men congregate. Hence while male farmers can sit in teashops and strike deals with other men for hiring labour or selling their crop, women farmers cannot do the same (Agarwal 1994). Similarly, a fear of reputation loss or reprimand from families makes women uncomfortable going to public meetings, unless men invite them. As a group of women in north India told Britt (1993: 148): 'The meetings are considered for men only. Women are never called' (see also Agarwal 2001).

Social norms also govern female behaviour. This can range from high female seclusion to more subtle gendering, such as the expectation in many societies that women will be soft-spoken and less visible. Women fish traders in parts of south India, if found haggling loudly, risk being dubbed as 'masculine' and losing social status. Women in public meetings often sit on one side or at the back of the meeting space where they are less visible and audible, making them less effective in public forums. Again, in most societies, norms dictate that women rather than men relocate on marriage or job shifts. In both India and China it is the woman who is usually expected to leave her natal home and go to the husband's village or home after marriage.

Basically gendered social perceptions and social norms embody inequalities which are hidden, sometimes difficult to name, often impossible to quantify. Yet they centrally affect material outcomes for women, impinging both on their employment status and their property status.

Emergent Inequalities: Community Forestry

Gender Inequalities in property endowments, norms and perceptions form the bedrock of pre-existing material and ideological disadvantage. And their persistence can create new inequalities. Consider examples from my current research on community forestry and collective action in India and Nepal, where I have done detailed fieldwork (see Agarwal 2000, 2001).

Forests and commons have always been important sources of basic needs such as fuelwood, fodder and other items for rural households. But because women often lack private property resources such as land and since social norms make firewood and fodder gathering mainly women's responsibility, their dependence on the commons is greater than that of men.

Traditionally, rights in local forests were based on village citizenship. Access to these communal resources thus mitigated, to some degree, inequalities in private property. However, to reduce deforestation, today governments in many countries (including developed ones such as the Scandinavian countries and Canada) are involving communities in local forest management. Certainly, across South Asia today, community forestry groups (CFGs) are mushrooming. Most are state-initiated under the Joint Forest Management (JFM) programme launched in 1990, in which government and villagers share the costs and benefits from protection. There are over 64,000 JFM groups in India alone, in addition to self-initiated groups.

The JFM groups have a two-tier management structure: a general body (GB) which can draw members from the whole village and an executive committee (EC) of 9–15 persons. Both bodies, interactively, define the rules for forest use, the punishments for abuse and the methods of protection and benefit distribution. Who has a voice in the GB and EC bears centrally on who gains or loses from these initiatives.

These groups were based on modern ideas of cooperation and participation and are meant to include all villagers, but effectively many have excluded significant sections such as women from their decision-making and main benefit sharing. For instance, in many Indian states the criteria for GB membership is one person per household. Although technically gender neutral, it is usually men alone who join, since they are seen as the household heads.

But even where women can become members, few attend meetings or speak up at them, due to restrictive social norms and perceptions. Some women's groups explained this to me as follows (see Agarwal 2001): 'Men don't listen. They feel they should be the spokespersons.''When we open our mouths, men shout us down.'

Or take a male response: 'I am a man, I attend the meeting. If I am prepared to make the female members of my family act according to what I say, why should they attend the meeting?'

These 'participatory exclusions' as I term them, that is, exclusions within seeming participative institutions, have other negative consequences. Without women's participation, the rules framed for forest use tend to take little account of their concerns. Typically, CFGs ban forest entry. This affects women more than men. Men mostly use the forest for small timber for agricultural implements or house building—both are sporadic needs, and purchase is also an option. Women need the forests almost daily for firewood and fodder, and for most women firewood purchase is not an option both because they have limited control over cash, and because firewood is not easily available for purchase in the rural areas. Hence women are the worst affected by the ban on entry.

In some regions women who before forest closure spent one to two hours for a headload of firewood ended up spending four to five hours after closure, and journeys of half a kilometre grew to eight to nine kilometres (Sarin 1995). And although over time the forests have regenerated, the strict bans on extractions often continue. Firewood extractions are sometimes as low as 10–15 per cent of sustainable limits (Agarwal 2002). Hence, even several years into protection, firewood shortages persist in most cases. Paradoxically, as some poor women in one Indian village told me: 'Earlier too there was a shortage but not as acute.'

Most women have switched in varying degrees to using crop waste and some even use weeds as cooking fuel. These firewood substitutes take more time to ignite and keep alight, thus increasing cooking time. They also seriously increase smoke-related health risks, both for women and for infants playing in smoky kitchens.

Benefits from the regenerated resource are, however, largely male controlled. To begin with, any cash generated typically goes into a community fund controlled by men and mostly used for purposes from which women do not usually benefit, such as for purchasing rugs, drums or community utensils which the men use or lease out, or for travel to other villages, etc. Where benefits are distributed in cash or kind, entitlements are linked to membership and often also to contribution to protection. Thus non-member households, that are mostly the poor, are excluded, with the exclusion especially affecting poor women. Also, implicitly embodying the assumptions of a unitary household, benefit shares are on a household basis, so even if both spouses are members they get only one share.

Inequities arise too from the distributive principles followed. Distribution can be market determined (willingness to pay) or by contribution or need. While seemingly neutral, these principles have notable gender (and class) bias since people differ in their ability to pay or to contribute, or in their needs. In practice, distribution is usually by contribution and sometimes by sale. Sales adversely affect women more than men, since women have fewer financial means. But even distribution by contribution can prove inequitable where social norms bar women from making specific types of important contributions, such as doing patrol duty.

Not surprisingly, women especially the poor, often resent the closures. Some common responses are: 'What forest? ... Since the men have started protecting it, they don't even allow us to look at it!' Or 'the community forest belongs to the men, we own nothing'. The new arrangements are thus creating a system of property rights in communal land which, like existing rights in privatized land, are strongly male centred and inequitable.

Here new gender inequality is being created through male control of public property and the rules that govern its use. All the rules are gender neutral on the surface. But they become unequal when filtered through the prism of pre-existing inequalities. Hence, membership by one person per household translates to one man per household. A lack of private property resources increases women's dependence on common pool resources. Both norms and perception restrict women's participation and voice in rule making and implementation. And much of this remains hidden, since most evaluations still deem the CFGs to be success stories of decentralized management and participative community involvement.

Reducing the Inequalities

How can the noted inequalities be reduced in both their material and ideological forms. A promising analytical framework for examining the prospects for change is that of bargaining. In terms of this framework, women's ability to change rules, norms, perceptions and property distribution in a gender-progressive direction would depend especially on their bargaining power with the state, the community and the family, as the case may be (for a detailed discussion, see Agarwal 1997).

Traditionally, economists have applied ideas about bargaining within the game-theoretic mode and with little attention to gender. Recent interest in intra-household gender dynamics has yielded some interesting formulations of bargaining models, but with little application to extra-household arenas or to qualitative factors. In my discussion, at least two types of shifts from this standard approach appear necessary: First, taking account of qualitative factors such as social norms and perceptions which have particular gender implications. Second, extending the framework to include non-household non-market arenas, such as the state and community. Both extensions need a less restrictive formulation than that of a formal game-theoretic model. Here it is useful to distinguish between a bargaining *approach* and formal models. A bargaining approach that is not constrained by the structure that formal modelling requires would allow us to more freely apply concepts such as bargaining power to new arenas; and also allow us a freer engagement with qualitative factors.

In the present discussion, applying the bargaining approach to interactions within three major arenas—the state, the community and the family—is especially relevant. It is relevant whether we are concerned with land rights, or changing social norms, or with community forestry. Consider community forestry by way of illustration.

Some CFG rules, such as eligibility to GB membership are made at the state level, others that relate to forest closure are made at the

community level. And social norms, perceptions, and property endowments are constituted in all three arenas. What would affect
women's ability to bargain effectively in these arenas? A key element would clearly be women's own attitude to seeking change, as
discussed below.

Women's Attitudes or Socio-economic Constraints?

One influential view has been that a notable barrier to improving
women's situation can be their lack of perception of self-interest.
Nobel Laureate Amartya Sen, for instance, has argued that one reason for persistent gender inequality in intra-family allocations in
traditional societies is women's lack of perception of self-interest,
or what he terms false perception and Marxists term false con-
sciousness. He notes: '... acute inequalities often survive precisely
by making allies out of the deprived. The underdog comes to accept
the legitimacy of the unequal order and becomes an implicit accom-
plice' (Sen 1990: 126).

But the question is, how can one tell? Observationally, it is difficult to infer from people's overt behaviour whether they are conform-
ing to an unequal order because they accept its legitimacy, or out
of fear, or because they lack other options. Empirical work which
probes women's covert responses, suggests that a lack of options is
especially relevant.

There are numerous examples of women's 'everyday resistance'
to intra-household inequalities. In Bangladesh, a number of studies
have found many instances of rural women secretly trying to earn
some cash by selling small amounts of rice without their husband's
knowledge (Abdullah and Zeidenstein 1982). In Nepal rural wom-
en have been found treating themselves to their favourite dishes by
cooking secret meals in the woods when fetching firewood, etc. Even
American housewives in the early twentieth century were found to
pad bills to get extra cash (Zelizer 1994). Everywhere women complain about their double work burden. Consider what some landless
Indian women had to say. I quote (cited in Sharma 1980: 207): 'We
women stay at home and do back-breaking work even if we are ill or
pregnant. There is no sick leave for us. But we do not have any money
of our own and when the men come home we have to cast our eyes
down and bow our heads.'

Here the overt appearance of compliance ('cast our eyes down') does not mean women lack a perception of their best interest. Rather, it reflects a survival strategy stemming from constraints on their ability to overtly pursue those interests ('we do not have any money of our own'). Compliance should not be read as implying complicity.

The policy emphasis here should thus be less on making women realize they deserve better, and more on providing options that would help them do better. Women's noted resistance to inequality is often individual and covert. And there are inherent limitations to the effectiveness of covert resistance. To be effective agents of change often requires that women overtly challenge the formal structures that disempower them.

This returns us centrally to the question: how do we enhance women's bargaining power in different arenas—the family, the community and the state?

Enhancing Women's Bargaining Power

As I have discussed at length, both in a theoretical paper and in other work, the determinants of women's bargaining power could vary by context and could include their command over economic resources, support from external agents such as the state and NGOs, and enabling social norms and social perceptions (Agarwal 1997, 2001). But at least two factors appear especially important for all three arenas and for different contexts: external agent support and women's group strength. For illustration, again consider community forestry.

Community forestry experience indicates that pressure from external agents such as NGOs, donors and key individuals can prove significant in changing the initial rules of entry at the state level. For example, several states in India have now made their membership rules more gender inclusive, say by instituting that one man and one woman should be members of the GB, rather than only one person per household. Here village women did not need to bargain explicitly for change. External agent support and the larger women's movement gave village women implicit bargaining power vis-à-vis the state (Agarwal 2001).

However, bargaining with the community, for ensuring that women have more voice in CFG forums, is more difficult. Here again, external agent support can help to some extent. For instance, some

NGOs have used their bargaining power on women's behalf to insist that meetings would be held only if men invited the women. Women on being so invited, often turn up in strength. Not all regions, however, have external agents committed to gender equity. A larger and sustained impact needs women's own input.

Ground experience suggests that for women to have more voice in mixed forums and for them to challenge restrictive social norms, they would need, for a start: (a) a critical mass of vocal women, and (b) a sense of group identity.

In many villages the women I interviewed stressed: 'without a good majority of women present it is impossible to express opinions'. The importance of a critical mass has also been noted in the Western context. A study of Scandinavian women politicians found that as women became a significant percentage (say 30 per cent or more) in Parliament or local councils, there was less stereotyping and open exclusion by men, a less aggressive tone in discussions, a greater accommodation of family obligations in scheduling meetings and more weight given to women's policy concerns (Dahlerup 1988).

However, in South Asia, an additional step appears necessary, namely building women's self-confidence in public interactions and increasing their sense of group identity. One way by which this is being attempted in India is by women's credit and self-help groups. Such groups are found to enhance women's self-confidence and collective identity. They also tend to improve male perceptions about women's capabilities and weaken restrictive social norms. The following responses from women I interviewed are fairly typical: 'Initially men objected to our going to meetings. But our women's group helped men understand better. When we women became united in the women's group, men saw we were doing good work. That also helped.'

These factors also help in bargaining within the family. Again I quote from my interviews with rural women in India:

> There were one or two men who objected to their wives attending our meetings .... But when our women's association came to their aid, the men let their wives go.

> My husband feels I contribute financially, take up employment, obtain credit for the home. This increases his respect for me.

In fact, these experiences are common to many women's groups across South Asia, namely that women's collective strength and visible contributions, along with external agent support, can change at least some norms and perceptions. Of course dilemmas persist. Many separate women's groups remain un-integrated into mixed groups, and unable to change the gender dynamics of the latter. Also certain norms, such as the gender division of domestic work, and gender inequalities in property, are more difficult to alter. To have an impact on them, a deeper structural change would be needed.

Concluding Remarks

Gender inequality takes both material and ideological forms. A critical neglected dimension of the material form is embedded in who commands public and private property, especially land. A critical hidden dimension of the ideological form are social norms and perceptions. The interactive effects of these gender disadvantages can lead to new inequality creation.

Of course, which type of property is central, or the specific nature of norms and perceptions, can vary by country and culture. But the fact of their importance everywhere is indisputable, as is the need to enhance women's bargaining power through collective action, for mitigating such inequalities. In academic terms, understanding how such collective action among women and among progressive groups can emerge and sustain is, I believe, a challenge both for gender economics and for the social sciences more generally. In political terms, there is a challenge here for forging new strategic alliances.

References

Abdullah, Tahrunnesa and Sondra Zeidenstein. 1982. *Village Women of Bangladesh: Prospects for Change.* Oxford: Pergamon Press.

Agarwal, Bina. 1994. *A Field of One's Own: Gender and Land Rights in South Asia.* Cambridge: Cambridge University Press.

———. 1997. '"Bargaining" and Gender Relations: Within and Beyond the Household', *Feminist Economics* 3(1): 1–50.

———. 1998. 'Widows Versus Daughters or Widows as Daughters? Property, Land and Economic Security in Rural India', *Modern Asian Studies* 32(1): 1–48.

———. 2000. 'Conceptualizing Environmental Collective Action: Why Gender Matters', *Cambridge Journal of Economics* 24(3): 283–310.

Agarwal, Bina. 2001. 'Participatory Exclusions, Community Forestry and Gender: An Analysis and Conceptual Framework', *World Development* 29(10): 1623–48.

———. 2002. 'Gender Inequality, Cooperation and Environmental Sustainability', Paper presented at a workshop on 'Inequality, Collective Action and Environmental Sustainability', Working Paper 02-10-058, Santa Fe Institute, New Mexico.

———. 2003. 'Gender and Land Rights Revisited: Exploring New Prospects via the State, the Family and the Market', *Journal of Agrarian Change* 3(1, 2): 184–224.

Agarwal, Bina, and Pradeep Panda. 2003. 'Home and the World: Revisiting Violence', *Indian Express*, 7 August, p. 9.

Alaka, and Chetna. 1987. 'When Women Get Land—A Report from Bodhgaya', *Manushi* 40: 25–26.

Britt, Charla. 1993. 'Out of the Wood? Local Institutions and Community Forest Management in Two Central Himalayan Villages' (Monograph), Cornell University, Ithaca.

Brown, Jennifer. 2003. 'Protecting Women's Land Rights through RLCL Implementing Regulations' (Mimeo), Rural Development Institute, Seattle, Washington DC.

Caldwell, John H., P.H. Reddy, and Pat Caldwell. 1988. *The Causes of Demographic Change: Experimental Research in South India*. Wisconsin: The University of Wisconsin Press.

Croll, Elizabeth. 1978. *Feminism and Socialism in China*. London: Routledge and Kegan Paul.

———. 2000. *Endangered Daughters: Discrimination and Development in Asia*. London and New York: Routledge.

Deere, Carmen Diana, and Magdalena de Leon. 2001. *Empowering Women: Land and Property Rights in Latin America*. Pittsburg: Pittsburg University Press.

Dahlerup, Drude. 1988. 'From a Small to a Large Majority: Women in Scandinavian Politics', *Scandinavian Political Studies* 11(4): 275–98.

Duraisamy, P. 1992. 'Gender, Intrafamily Allocations of Resources and Child Schooling South India', Economic Growth Center Discussion Paper No. 667, Yale University, New Haven, CT.

Duaraiswamy, P., and R. Malathy. 1991. 'Impact of Public Programs on Fertility and Gender Specific Investment in Human Capital of Children in Rural India: Cross Sectional and Time Series Analyses', in *Population Economics*, Vol. 7, ed. T. Schultz, pp. 157–87. Greenwich, CT: JAI Press.

Dwyer, Daisy, and Judith Bruce, eds. 1989. *A Home Divided: Women and Income Control in the Third World*. Stanford: Stanford University Press.

Elson, Diane. 1995. 'Gender Awareness in Modelling Structural Adjustment', *World Development* 23(11): 1851–68.

England, Paula, and Barbara Kilbourne. 1990. 'Markets, Marriages and other Mates: The Problem of Power', in *Beyond the Market: Rethinking Economy and Society*, eds. R. Friedman and A.F. Robertson. New York: Aldine de Gruyter.

Hinton, William. 1972. *Fanshen: A Documentary of Revolution in a Chinese Village*. Harmondsworth, Middlesex: Penguin Books Ltd.

Kandiyoti, Deniz. 2003. 'The Cry for Land: Agrarian Reform, Gender and Land rights in Uzbekistan', *Journal of Agrarian Change* 3(1, 2): 225–56.

Li, Zongmin. 1999. 'Changing Land and Housing use by Rural Women in Northern China', in *Women's rights to house and land: China, Laos, Vietnam*, eds. I. Tinker and G. Summerfield. Boulder and London: Lynne Rienner Publishers.

———. 2003. 'Women's Land Tenure Rights in Rural China: A Synthesis' (Mimeo), Ford Foundation, Beijing.

Quisumbing, Agnes R., and John A. Maluccio. 2003. 'Resources at Marriage and Intrahousehold Allocation: Evidence from Bangladesh, Ethiopia, Indonesia, and South Africa', *Oxford Bulletin of Economics and Statistics* 65(3): 283–328.

Sarin, M. 1995. 'Regenerating India's Forest: Reconciling Gender Equity and Joint Forest Management', *IDS Bulletin* 26(1): 83–91.

Sen, Amartya K. 1990. 'Gender and Cooperative Conflicts', in *Persistent Inequalities: Women and World Development*, ed. Irene Tinker, pp. 123–49. New York: Oxford University Press.

Sharma, Ursula. 1980. *Women, Work and Property in North-West India*. London and New York: Tavistock Publications.

Thomas, Duncan. 1990. 'Intra-household Resource Allocation: An Inferential Approach', *Journal of Human Resources* 25(4): 635–63.

Udry, Christopher, John Hoddinott, Harold Alderman, and Lawrence Haddad. 1995. 'Gender Differentials in Farm Productivity: Implications for Household Efficiency and Agricultural Policy', *Food Policy* 20(5): 407–23.

Verdery, Katherine. 1996. *What Was Socialism, and What Comes Next?* New Jersey: Princeton University Press.

Walker, Cherryl. 2003. 'Piety in the Sky? Gender Policy and Land Reform in South Africa', *Journal of Agrarian Change* 3(1): 113–48.

Zelizer, Viviana. 1994. 'The Creation of Domestic Currencies', *American Economic Review, Papers and Proceedings* 84(2): 238–42.

6

Cultural Politics of Environment and Development: The Indian Experience

Amita Baviskar

A City Story

Let me begin by recounting an incident that happened 10 years ago, an incident that has a central bearing on the subject of my lecture, the cultural politics of environment and development in India. On the morning of 30 January 1995, Delhi was waking up to another chilly winter day. Imagine the well-to-do colony of Ashok Vihar in north Delhi, posh houses shrouded in grey mist, early risers setting off on morning walks, some with their pet dogs—Pomeranians and Alsatians, straining at the leash. As one of these morning walkers entered the neighbourhood 'park', the only open area in the locality, he saw a young man, poorly clad, walking away with an empty bottle in hand. Outraged, he caught hold of the man and called out to his neighbours. Someone phoned the police. A group of enraged house-owners and two police constables descended on the youth and, within minutes, beat him to death.

The young man was 18-year-old Dilip, a visitor to Delhi, who had come to watch the Republic Day parade in the capital. He was staying with his uncle in a jhuggi (shanty house) along the railway tracks bordering Ashok Vihar. His uncle worked as a labourer in the Wazirpur industrial estate nearby. Like all other planned industrial areas in Delhi, Wazirpur too has no provision for workers' housing. The jhuggi cluster with more than 10,000 households shared 3 public toilets, each one with 8 latrines, effectively 1 toilet between more than 2,000 persons. For most residents, then, any large open space, under cover of dark, became a place to defecate. Their use of the 'park' brought the industrial workers and their families up against the more affluent residents of the area who paid to have a wall constructed between the dirty, unsightly jhuggis and their own homes. The wall was soon breached, to allow the traffic of domestic workers who lived in the jhuggis but worked to clean the homes and cars of the rich and to offer access to the delinquent defecators.

Dilip's death was thus the culmination of a long-standing battle over a contested space that, to one set of residents, embodied their sense of gracious urban living, a place of trees and grass devoted to leisure and recreation, and that to another set of residents, was the only available space that could be used as a toilet. If he had known this history of simmering conflict, Dilip would probably have been more wary and would have run away when challenged, and perhaps he would still be alive. The violence did not end there. When a group of people from the jhuggis gathered to protest against this killing, the police opened fire and killed four more people (PUDR 1995).[1]

This incident made a profound impression on me. During my research in central India, the site of struggles over displacement due to dams and forestry projects, as well as the more gradual but no less compelling processes of impoverishment due to insecure land tenure, I had witnessed only too often state violence that tried to crush the aspirations of poor people striving to craft basic subsistence and dignity (Baviskar 2001). Now I was watching a similar contestation over space unfold in my own backyard. I had previously analyzed struggles over the environment in rural India; now my attention was directed towards how, in an urban context, the varied meanings at stake in struggles over the environment were negotiated. This concern has been strengthened over the last five years by two sets of processes, each an extraordinarily powerful attempt to remake the urban landscape of Delhi. Through a series of judicial orders, the Supreme Court of India initiated the closure of all polluting and non-conforming industries in the city, throwing out of work an estimated 2 million people employed in and around 98,000 industrial units.

For the first time since Independence, perhaps for the first time since the British sacked Shahjehanabad in 1857, workers who had come to the city to earn a living are leaving Delhi, retracing their steps and returning home. At the same time, the Delhi High Court

---

[1] I have narrated this incident in Baviskar (2003a).

has ordered the removal and relocation of all jhuggi squatter settlements on public lands, an order that has already resulted in large-scale demolitions and that may ultimately affect the homes of more than three million people. Both these processes, which were set in motion through public interest litigation by environmentalists and consumer rights groups, indicate that upper-class concerns around health and safety, aesthetics and order and the desire to live in a 'world-class' city, have come to significantly shape the disposition of urban spaces. In a city of 12 million people, the enormity of these changes is mind-boggling. Already, before our eyes, we have seen the cityscape transformed, new malls and multiplexes, flyovers and wider roads, the Metro, and shops, shops everywhere. And yet, the darker side of this development, the demolitions and displacement, remains invisible to all except those who endure it. The resounding media silence about how workers are losing livelihoods and homes is perhaps not all that remarkable; as P. Sainath points out, there are more important things like fashion shows to report.

I dwell on these events because, to my mind, they pose a challenge both intellectual and political. On the one hand, there are striking resonances between these conflicts over urban resources—land, water, air and conflicts over rural resources—land, water, pastures and forests. Both pit different classes of people against each other; both involve powerful state institutions that are markedly biased and both sets of conflicts contain invocations of a transcendental public interest: a 'clean and green city' in one case, and 'national development', 'economic growth', and 'biodiversity conservation' in the other. On the other hand, the urban question raises some perplexing issues, which do not come up in the case of rural conflicts over environment and development, or at least not with the same intensity. One, if clean air and green areas are environmental goods, and indeed no one would dispute that they are, then the protagonists in this case are bourgeois environmentalists who use all the weapons at their command to make the city liveable. This is rather different from what has now come to be an accepted position in debates about rural resource management, that it is those who directly depend on these resources for their subsistence who are best placed to conserve them.

It seems as if the connection between ecology and equity, and the related issue of which cause and whose efforts to support, is harder to establish in the urban case. Also, there is the problem of 'environment' and 'natural resources'. What exactly is the environment?

In the rural case, it seems to be self-evident that we are referring to land, water, animals and plants and other elements of the biophysical world. In the urban case, we often fall back on an idea of nature derived from rurality—green areas, clean air and water. But the urban environment, that apparently unnatural, artefactual space of concrete and steel, cement and tar, is in its own way merely nature transformed. And when workers describe *their* environmental concerns, they rarely mention clean air or parks as a priority; most often, they speak of *space*, just the sheer ability to have a secure foothold in the city, a place to live. They, and this is especially true of women, also talk about toilets and taps. Shelter, sanitation and water, these are the environmental goods that are most meaningful for the urban poor. There is thus a lack of consensus on what defines an urban environmental issue, and who speaks for the urban environment. Into this discursive gap have disappeared the environmental concerns of an urban underclass that makes cities possible.

Why have we, as scholars and researchers on environment and development, neglected the urban question? Despite a strong secular trend towards urbanization, why have we concentrated single-mindedly on the rural? As the ecological footprint of urban India grows larger and deeper by the day, rural–urban resource flows acquire greater importance, as does the traffic of migration. Why have we ignored the fact that 'the relation of country and city is not only an objective problem and history, but has been and still is for many millions of people a direct and intense preoccupation and experience' (Williams 1973: 3)? In my own case, I suspect that it has something to do with growing up as an urban, upper-middle-class nature lover, and presuming that environmentalism means mainly caring about trees and birds. But in order to address these questions more substantively, I now present before you a short, spotty and highly idiosyncratic survey of what we *have* done in the last 30 or so years in terms of engaging with the cultural politics of environment and development.

By tracing the trajectory of Indian environmental questions in the social sciences, I intend to show that scholarship has been inspired and shaped by popular mobilizations on the ground. In turn, academic research has lent greater legitimacy to the positions espoused by progressive environmental movements. This has been both its strength and its limitation. Such a survey also enables me to pay homage to some of the stalwarts in this field whose work has inspired and influenced me over the years. While I did not have the privilege of personally knowing Dr Malcolm Adiseshiah, the institution that he founded and the scholarship that it fostered have been major resources for me. Professor Vaidyanathan's early writings on agriculture and irrigation had an environmental sensibility that was rare among economists (and still is). To him and to Professor Nirmal Sengupta, for his work on tribal identity and social movements (rather unusual subjects for an economist!), and both of them together for their critical perspectives on large dams, I owe a large intellectual debt. To the Madras Institute of Development Studies (MIDS) as a whole must go the credit of showing us the importance of paying attention to the *region* as a unit of analysis. In our preoccupation with the village and the nation, we ignore all too often the regional specificities of landscape, history and culture. In correcting this and other oversights, MIDS leads the way.

Social Movements and the Social Sciences

It would not be an exaggeration to say that, in the social sciences of the 1970s, there was no environmental question; there was only the agrarian question. Political economists concerned about poverty, inequality and social change concentrated on areas of irrigated agriculture and how social relations had been transformed by the Green Revolution. Sociologists studied caste and class in villages and, if the subtitle of many books of that time is an indication, usually found both 'continuity and change'. It took two landmark intellectual contributions in the early 1980s—one by a bureaucrat and the other by a journalist—to open up the field. In 1980, B.B. Vohra drew attention to the massive degradation of the rural environment due to intensive agriculture, ill-planned irrigation and deforestation (Vohra 1980).

In 1982, Anil Agarwal published *The State of India's Environment: A Citizen's Report*, a monumental work drawing on the work of researchers and activists all over the country (CSE: 1982). If Vohra's alarm call was directed towards the government, Agarwal's encyclopaedia alerted an urban, educated audience. Both were, to some extent, influenced by the emerging environmental movement in the West, but a more proximate cause, especially for Agarwal, was that remarkable movement happening in the Himalaya—Chipko. Of course, there is more than one story to tell about the rise of environmentalism in India—others will emphasize the key importance of the Kerala Sastra Sahitya Parishad and its campaign to save Silent Valley. Still others will recall the campaign against eucalyptus plantations in Karnataka and the Mitti Bachao Andolan in Madhya Pradesh. But I will focus on Chipko here because it was this movement that inspired Ramachandra Guha's pioneering study of forest policy and peasant resistance, *The Unquiet Woods* (Guha 1989).

Guha has been a guru not only to me, but to an entire generation of social scientists. The principles and propositions that his work delineated were to define the field of environment and development for many of us. Like other subaltern historians, Guha wrote about peasant resistance but, unlike them, he focused on forests and not agricultural land. Guha emphasized that forests were not abstract objects of value, but had their own specificities—mixed deciduous stands of oak and rhododendron were decidedly different from pine monocultures. By focusing on the Garhwal and Kumaon Hills—not on the Indo-Gangetic heartland or the Cauvery Delta, or for that matter Bengal—the region that continues to claim hegemonic status in the social sciences as representing all of India if not the entire postcolonial world, Guha brought attention to the 'marginal' areas of the country which continue to sustain millions of people. Also introduced was the concept of moral economy (Scott 1976), now firmly yoked to the notion of environmental sustainability. These concepts and concerns were to become the hallmark of engagements with environment and development in India.

If Chipko (and Silent Valley) marked the advent of an environmental sensibility among upper-class urban Indians and introduced a generation to the notion that 'red' and 'green' issues were inseparable, its gains were reaped in the decade of the 1990s with the Narmada Bachao Andolan. The academic challenge to big dams began in a small way with Vijay Paranjpye's critique of the benefit-cost analysis of the Sardar Sarovar and Narmada Sagar projects (Paranjpye 1990). That study showed quite clearly that major decisions were being made on the basis of scant data and dubious assumptions; that the social and environmental impacts of the projects were largely a matter of ignorance and indifference to planners. From examining the project on its own terms, the critique widened to consider the class and region-specific implications of benefits and costs. Is it fair to displace some of the most impoverished citizens of the country in order to benefit those who are already well off? Why are the voices of those adversely affected by the dam excluded from the development debate, forcing them to take to the streets?

Besides issues of equity and political representation, the anti-dam movement also spurred scholars to examine the actual performance of large dams, leading to the realization that many of them had failed to deliver the benefits that they promised (for a survey, see Singh et al. 2000; also Manthan 2005). In turn, this led to a closer consideration of alternatives to large dams, in the form of technological choices for irrigation and power generation, and modes of watershed management that were based on more decentralized, local and regional scale planning. As these wide-ranging issues came into prominence because of the anti-dam movement, there was also a meta-critique that emerged. This meta-critique challenged dominant conceptions of citizenship and development. Drawing on the experience of the millions who had been displaced and impoverished by development projects since Independence, it asked what the dominant model of capital-intensive development had done for the poor. If it benefited the nation, were not the poor a part of the nation too? The lives of hill *adivasi*s in the Narmada Valley testified that there were many ways of relating to nature besides building large dams, and dams submerged this great cultural diversity and autonomy (Baviskar 2004).

More than any other movement, the Narmada Andolan forced us to deal with questions of citizenship and cultural pluralism in the politics of development and environment. The overwhelming opposition that the Andolan and the critique of large dams encountered was revealing. It showed that there were not only crass political and economic interests promoting large dams, which of course there were—huge contracts promise huge kickbacks and commissions, but there was an equally influential factor at work—the power of development as an ideology. The engineers who invoked Bhakra's success and quoted Nehru on 'the temples of modern India' without a sense of irony were not evil men out to swindle the poor. For the most part, they were well-intentioned, patriotic Indians whose dreams of a better world demanded large dams.[2] They imagined that dams would

---

[2] For a brilliant exposition of the cultural politics around the construction of the Aswan Dam in Egypt, see Mitchell (2002).

bring progress and prosperity to all Indians, an amorphous mass that got hazy around the edges where the displaced multitudes lurked. The same power of development as an ideology resonating with nationalist desires informed the Supreme Court's judgement on the Sardar Sarovar case that 'dams are good for the nation'. The reversals suffered by the Andolan due to the effective counter-mobilization of regional sentiments in Gujarat and nationalist ambitions at the Centre remind us of the importance of ideas and ideologies that exceed materialist concerns.

As Ram Guha has pointed out in his subsequent writings, there is a distinctively Indian quality to the critique of development fostered by the Chipko and Narmada movements (Guha and Martinez-Alier 1998). In espousing an environmental ethic that challenges the ideology of industrial development and the class inequalities that sustain it, these movements embody an engagement with European modernity without being defined or encompassed within its terms. By adopting the discipline of satyagraha and struggling for swaraj for ordinary Indians, Chipko and Narmada revived the possibility of imagining alternate utopias. In the project of what Dipesh Chakrabarty calls 'provincializing Europe' (Chakrabarty 2000), perhaps the true inheritors of Gandhi's legacy are the people who sing of Uttarakhand as paradise, the Himalaya as a flower, or those who praise the Narmada as a generous girl bestowing the gift of life on all whom she meets. Re-signified by the context of political struggle, these localized imaginings of sacred landscapes are far removed from monolithic Hindu nationalism and inspire actions in defence of places which have been made meaningful through labour and love.

Achievements and Exclusions

Drawing upon these movements, we have developed a distinctive cultural politics of environment and development and I now want to evaluate the conceptual gains from this process. I have discussed elsewhere why I find the term 'cultural politics' more apt than 'political ecology' for this field (Baviskar 2003b), so I will leave that aside for the moment, and focus on its distinctive attributes.

First, the field of environment and development in India emphasizes holism and interconnectedness. This may be unsurprising, given that any discussion of ecological processes must necessarily do so. But there is also a careful distancing from ecological theories such as homeostasis, and awareness about the dangers of uncritically importing organic metaphors from ecology. The tendency towards holism leads to frequent trespassing across disciplinary boundaries, creating a productive hybridity that is an antidote to the compartmentalized approaches of the past.

Second, we now treat the environment not simply as a set of 'factors of production' but as material *and* symbolic resources, sustaining livelihoods but also life in the larger sense, including a life of the imagination that strives to understand the mundane but also to transcend it through individual and collective projects both secular and spiritual (Kumar 2003).

Third, we respect much more the notion of *ecological* as well as social limits to growth. For generations of Marxists brought up on technological optimism, social relations were the primary constraints on equality and prosperity, for the productive forces of industrialism created the potential of plenty for all. Later, for a post-materialist generation of scholars, especially those influenced by science studies and the social construction of everything, 'objective' ecological constraints were not relevant; what mattered was the discursive production of things.

This focus on perceptions, on how authoritative versions of truth were produced, led to a form of pluralism that emphasized how nature was capable of being appropriated in an infinite variety of ways. What got lost was an appreciation of the biophysical properties of nature, all the elements one cannot get around—that the 'social construction of forests or dams' cannot be independent of the specific properties of forests or rivers in particular locales. It is this respect for the biophysical, for ecological as much as social limits, that is central to the cultural politics of environment and development. Fourth, this approach reintroduces a focused view of the operations of power. The post-structuralist notion of power as diffuse and immanent, while no doubt adding nuance, was not very helpful in addressing social inequality or ecological degradation, or the question that Lenin asked so precisely: What is to be done? This is the question to which the cultural politics of environment and development addresses itself.

This, then, is the critical gap that cultural politics spans. It offers a critique of knowledge, especially that which claims the authority of common sense, challenging the self-evident verities of developmentalism and, now, globalization. At the same time, it remains alert to the power relations that produce hegemonic forms of knowledge as well as the entire set of social practices through which inequality is reproduced. It has tended to concentrate on the workings of state institutions such as forest and irrigation bureaucracies, as well as on the micro-practices of politics within the household and village. These sites of conflict have been more readily available for analysis, often because they have been highlighted by social movements. Research on participatory development fostered by international development organizations has also helped to direct attention to common property resources, perhaps even at the expense of private property, an area for reform that has been off the public policy agenda for a while.

In deriving inspiration from social movements and the many collective struggles taking place across the country, our scholarship has been enriched in manifold ways. At the same time, it has made us less attentive to more low-key issues, the quotidian workings of power that, by their very ordinariness, deflect and disarm our scrutiny. I will discuss only three issues here: markets, middle classes and mobilization across sites and scales, all of which to my mind need to be incorporated more thoroughly into our analyses. Consider the gradual processes of commoditization and privatization that have made incursions everywhere. Spectacular struggles against a Gwalior Rayon factory or a Coke bottling plant extracting and polluting water get noticed. But the gradual infiltration of packaged water and private water treatment solutions like Aquaguard in the lives and homes of the well-to-do represents no less of a challenge, signalling as it does that the rich have abdicated their power to intervene on the issue of water quality as a common good.

The environmental implications of the increasing *segregation* of what used to be common property resources—water, space, sanitation, transport, biodiversity, where the rich are able to buy their way out of scarcity while the poor are condemned to substandard and scant resources, simply have not received enough attention. Could this be because there has been no major social mobilization around these issues? Or take the question of the labour market and how it naturalizes the predicament of poor workers. I quote from an interview with S.P. Marwah, an IAS officer and ex-Labour Commissioner for Delhi, the senior-most official responsible for safeguarding the rights of workers in the city:

Marwah: The main issue of concern before the Delhi government is population—unchecked immigration in the city. This is the basic cause of all problems ... It also results in environmental problems ... The Supreme Court acted on public interest litigation and acted to clean the air. Delhi is the fourth most polluted city in the world.

Interviewer: Has it improved?

Marwah: Oh yes. Recently kids were asked if they could see the sky and stars and they responded that they could see the stars now. It was bad [before], you could not see the sky, only black clouds.

Interviewer: But what about the workers?

Marwah: They were given compensation.

Interviewer: But what about the unorganized labour?

Marwah: Some must have gone back to their villages and others took up [other] jobs in the city. *Water finds its own way.* In practice no workers were laid off or dislocated. There are large-scale development activities ... Overall it seems everyone welcomes the efforts and is happy. Who would want to see dirt and no development?

Indifference about the devastating effect of displacement for the poor is summed up in the Labour Commissioner's remark, 'water finds its own way', naturalizing their trauma as the simple ebb and flow of footloose and fancy-free nomads. The mass of workers displaced by the closing of factories and demolition of squatter settlements in Delhi work in what is euphemistically called 'the informal sector'. There is nothing informal about the systematic exploitation that they experience; a better term to use is 'unorganized' because it is that which defines their conditions of work and limits the possibility of collective resistance and transformation. The loosening of labour laws, however imperfectly applied in the past, and the 'freeing' of the market has only worsened their lot.

Their vulnerability renders workers invisible to all but a few scholars of labour relations or those whose long-term attention to a region gives them the temporal vantage for tracking demographic and livelihood changes. But why do migrant workers have few allies among those studying environment and development? It strikes me that we prefer social groups from whom we can expect the task of sustainable management of natural resources—seeking ecology and equity simultaneously. Those who wind up on the pavements of Delhi and Chennai looking for work have few resources besides their own labour-power and ingenuity. Do we find them less 'interesting' because, in the ultimate analysis, we are concerned more with safeguarding resources rather than promoting the welfare of those whose lives are marked by extreme deprivation?

In looking back at our analyses of the cultural politics of environment and development with the benefit of hindsight, it is apparent that we have neglected a critical section of the population, viz. the middle class, especially that fraction which can be described as the intelligentsia. The middle class has a matter-of-fact hegemonic presence in the life of our nation; its domination has a patina of 'naturalness' that renders it difficult to challenge. Support and mediation by this 'reference public', to use Lipsky's term (1968), has sometimes been a crucial resource for grass-roots movements. But, for the larger part, the intelligentsia's pursuit of the 'public interest' has generally secured its own interests and ensured its own reproduction (Deshpande 1997). Impatient with and disdainful of the messiness of political engagement, the intelligentsia takes recourse to avenues of influence that are more amenable to its power, including the shortcut of approaching the higher judiciary. Revealing a fascination for charismatic authority that verges on the fascist, it acclaims and applauds vigilante judicial action that infringes on legislative and executive jurisdiction.

The Indian experience shows that the bourgeoisie does not safeguard the public sphere, or uphold civil society in a democracy. In fact, as projects of development and conservation make evident, it often works to systematically exclude the poor from citizenship. Access to a *public* sphere of political debate and action is usually predicated on access to *private* resources. For instance, the urban spatialized form of a public sphere, 'the republic of the streets' (Joyce 2003) created by unruly, recalcitrant vendors and itinerant crowds, is marked by great inequality—while the bourgeois citizen can stroll along confidently, others must keep an eye out so that they are not caught in a municipal raid. The poor struggle against the denial of resources, environmental and political, by protesting when they can but, more often, by simply enduring great hardship. Partha Chatterjee (2004) uses the term 'political society' to describe the parallel road to power adopted by those denied access to civil society, but I think what is most striking and poignant about such efforts is that they strive for inclusion *within* civil society, not seek to carve out a domain outside it. It is the role of the intelligentsia in maintaining unequal access to resources that we must examine more closely. The cultural politics of environment and development demand that we make the connections between poverty and the unbridled consumerism of a privileged class, its sense that it can have it all, aspirations that can never be met without sacrificing someone or something. In other words, we need to 'study up'.

Finally, we need to pay far closer attention to how the cultural politics of environment and development mobilizes groups across scales and sites. How, for instance, does the anti-dam campaign bring together disparate entities—caste Hindu peasants and *adivasi*s in the Narmada Valley, environmental and human rights organization in India and abroad, disillusioned engineers and disaffected bureau-crats, unions of public sector employees, metropolitan 'causeratti' and many others to pursue a common cause? This is another taken-for-granted aspect of contemporary movements that scholars shy away from addressing except in general or celebratory terms (Keck and Sikkink 1998; Khagram et al. 2002; Khagram 2004). Accusations about being anti-national and anxieties around authenticity have led many activists and scholars to downplay the importance of solidari-ties across class, region and nation, and the hybridity that marks all creative politics.

To contend with global actors, institutions, ideas and processes, we need counter-flows of transnational support. We need to acknowledge and encourage these coalitions even as we remain alert to the con-sequences of the compromises of power. For instance, a globalized discourse on indigeneity compelled *adivasi*s to perform acts of 'stra-tegic essentialism' so that they were represented as ecologically noble savages. Perhaps the predicament of displaced workers in Delhi has not attracted the sympathy and support of the intelligentsia because, unlike *adivasi*s or distant peasants, they seem to be so totally devoid of ecological virtue. The urban poor are a proximate presence defy-ing projects of Improvement—they come uninvited to cities, have too many children, live in squalor and, the biggest threat of all, they do not know their place. The barely disguised disgust and unease that mark social relations across class in the urban context convey the depth of this cleavage. When we do not study alliances closely and critically, we also miss the opportunity to understand the *absence* of alliances that make progressive political projects possible.[3] Markets, middle classes and multiple scales of action—I urge that we attend to these. And to the intimate connections between the country and the city, places articulated by the above three, places of injustice and suffering but also always places of hope.

I would like to close with the following lines written by Raymond Williams, the great cultural critic, in his classic work *The Country and the City*:

> H. G. Wells once said, coming out of a political meeting where they had been discussing social change, that this great towering city [London] was a measure of the obstacle, of how much must be moved if there was to be any change. I have known this feeling, looking up at great buildings that are the centres of power, but I find I do not say 'There is your city, your great bourgeois monument, your towering structure of this still precarious civilisation' or I do not only say that; I say also 'This is what men have built, often so magnificently, and is not then everything possible?' Indeed this sense of possibility, of meeting and movement, is a permanent element of my sense of cities: as permanent a feeling as those other feelings, when I look down from the mountain at the great coloured patchwork of fields that generations of my own people have cleared ...; or the known living places, the isolated farms, the cluster of cottages by castle or church, the line of river and wood and footpath and lane; lines received and lines made. So that while country and city have this profound importance, in their differing ways, my feelings are held, before any argument starts. (Williams 1973: 5–6)

While surveying the cultural politics of environment and development in India, the roads taken and not taken, I am struck by how vast and exciting the field before us appears. There is so much to do. It is both our privilege and responsibility to contribute to this arena for research, reflection and action.

---

[3] However, there is always the possibility of unintended outcomes. The revolt by Delhi's Residents Welfare Associations against the privatization of water supply and the hike in water rates has gleaned lessons from South Africa and Bolivia. Used to getting subsidized water, middle-class citizens have opposed privatization, but perhaps their initiative might also ensure that water remains affordable for the poor.

References

Baviskar, Amita. 2001. 'Written on the Body, Written on the Land: Violence and Environmental Struggles in Central India', in *Violent Environments*, eds. Nancy Peluso and Michael Watts. Ithaca, NY: Cornell University Press.

————. 2003a. 'Between Violence and Desire: Space, Power and Identity in the Making of Metropolitan Delhi', *International Social Science Journal* 175: 89–98.

————. 2003b. 'For a Cultural Politics of Natural Resources', *Economic and Political Weekly* 38(48): 5051–55.

————. 2004. *In the Belly of the River: Tribal Conflicts over Development in the Narmada Valley*, second edition. Delhi: Oxford University Press.

Chakrabarty, Dipesh. 2000. *Provincializing Europe: Postcolonial Thought and Historical Difference*. Princeton, NJ: Princeton University Press.

Chatterjee, Partha. 2004. *The Politics of the Governed: Reflections on Popular Politics in Most of the World*. New York: Columbia University Press.

CSE (Centre for Science and Environment). 1982. *The State of India's Environment: A Citizen's Report*. New Delhi: CSE.

Deshpande, Satish. 1997. 'From Development to Adjustment: Economic Ideologies, the Middle Class and 50 years of Independence', *Review of Development and Change* 2(2): 294–318.

Guha, Ramachandra. 1989. *The Unquiet Woods: Ecological Change and Peasant Resistance in the Himalaya*. Delhi: Oxford University Press.

Guha, Ramachandra and Juan Martinez-Alier. 1998. *Varieties of Environmentalism: Essays North and South*. Delhi: Oxford University Press.

Joyce, Patrick. 2003. *The Rule of Freedom: Liberalism and the Modern City*. London: Verso.

Keck, Margaret, and Kathryn Sikkink. 1998. *Activists beyond Borders: Advocacy Networks in International Politics*. Ithaca, NY: Cornell University Press.

Khagram, Sanjeev, James Riker, and Kathryn Sikkink, eds. 2002. *Restructuring World Politics: Transnational Social Movements, Networks, and Norms*. Minneapolis: University of Minnesota Press.

Khagram, Sanjeev. 2004. *Dams and Development: Transnational Struggles for Water and Power*. Ithaca, NY: Cornell University Press.

Kumar, Nita. 2003. 'The Ganga at Banaras', in *Waterlines: The Penguin Book of River Writings*, ed. Amita Baviskar. New Delhi: Penguin India.

Lipsky, Michael. 1968. 'Protest as a Political Resource', *American Political Science Review* 62(4): 1144–58.

Manthan Adhyayan Kendra. 2005. *Unravelling Bhakra: Assessing the Temple of Resurgent India*. Badwani, MP: Manthan Adhyayan Kendra.

Mitchell, Timothy. 2002. *Rule of Experts: Egypt, Techno-politics, Modernity*. Berkeley: University of California Press.

Paranjpye, Vijay. 1990. *High Dams on the Narmada: A Holistic Analysis of the River Valley Projects.* New Delhi: Indian National Trust for Art and Cultural Heritage.

PUDR (People's Union for Democratic Rights). 1995. *A Tale of Two Cities: Custodial Death and Police Firing in Ashok Vihar.* Delhi: PUDR.

Scott, James. 1976. *The Moral Economy of the Peasant: Rebellion and Subsistence in Southeast Asia.* New Haven, CT: Yale University Press.

Singh, Shekhar, Raman Mehta, Vishaish Uppal, Asmita Kabra, Bansuri Taneja, and Prabhakar Rao. 2000. *Environmental and Social Impacts of Large Dams—The Indian Experience.* Report prepared for the World Commission on Dams, Indian Institute of Public Administration, New Delhi.

Vohra, B.B. 1980. 'A Land and Water Policy for India', Sardar Patel Memorial Lecture, Ministry of Environment, Government of India, Delhi.

Williams, Raymond. 1973. *The Country and the City.* New York: Oxford University Press.

7

State, Households and Markets in Education

Jandhyala B.G. Tilak

Introduction

As the title suggests, this chapter focuses on three closely related aspects of the financing of education in India: increasing reluctance of the state to spend on education, compulsion to pay for education by families, which, in my view, is mistakenly termed 'willingness to pay' and the role of the market.

The literature on economics of education has considered only two domains, individual and social, in the context of investment decision-making in education (for example, Majumdar 1983). But in my view there are three domains, namely, individual (household domain), market domain and public (social) domain. Investment decision-making in these three domains is influenced by three different sets of considerations, and therefore, I argue that it may not be proper to combine the household and market domains into one category and call it individual or private domain, as many do. Decision-making in the public domain ought to be guided by several considerations. Principal among them are: the public good, merit good, basic need, human rights nature of education, its basic role in promoting equity and nurturing social values. Public approach to education also ought to be guided by human development perspectives.

The long-term interests of society figure prominently in the decision-making process in public domain. Individuals, on the other hand, have a relatively short-term perspective. They are concerned with, apart from acquisition of individual values, mainly with the maximization of their lifetime earnings or at the most their horizon may extend to that of family earnings as a whole. Decisions in the market domain are guided by even shorter-term considerations; in fact, the single most important consideration is profit maximization. Other considerations such as philanthropy and charity were once important factors but they are virtually extinct now. Thus, the distinction between the three domains is quite sharp, and hence they need to be separately analyzed, recognizing, however, at the same time, the interrelationship between them.

State Spending on Education

The state spends on education, in many traditional and modern societies, out of the general revenues, as education is regarded as a:

1. public good, producing a huge quantum of externalities—social, economic, technological, political and cultural;
2. social merit good, whose consumption is good for the individual as well as for society, even if the individual is not aware of it and hence reluctant to consume it; and
3. human right and human development (and also as a freedom in itself, *à la* Amartya Sen).

Besides, education is favoured by the state as it promotes equality of opportunity. Imperfect capital markets reinforce the case for the state's role in this sphere, as does the fact that education is subject to scale economies. Education is also favoured as it is considered a pious responsibility of the state.

The pattern of spending on education during the post-Independence period in India does not indicate that these concerns have been clearly recognized. During this period there has been a significant increase in expenditure on education: in absolute terms it increased about 900 times from ₹55 crore in 1947 to ₹75 thousand crore in 1999–2000. But in real prices it increased at a rate of growth of 6 per cent during the five decades (1950–51 to 1999–2000). The real rate of growth of per capita expenditure on education was 3.8 per cent; and in per pupil terms it was just 2.4 per cent per annum.

The decadal trends in growth in public expenditure on education are indeed interesting to note. During the 1950s a good beginning was made in the growth in expenditure on education; the decade of the 1960s was the most favourable period, as in many developing and developed countries. This might have been the effect of 'the human

investment revolution in economic thought' initiated by Theodore
Schultz (1961). The global disenchantment with education, partly at-
tributable to the growth of educated unemployment on the empirical
scene, and the emergence of screening and credentialism theses on
the role of education on the theoretical front (for example, Arrow
1972; Spence 1973), caused a setback for the growth of expenditure
on education during the 1970s in the Third World. India also has had
a similar experience. The 1980s marked the revival of faith in education. Its role in poverty reduction was recognized. 'Human resource
(led) development' (Behrman 1990) became a favoured theme by the
mid-1980s, and education was regarded as an important component
of human resource development.

Expenditure on education increased during the 1980s at a reasonably high rate, particularly as compared with the preceding decade.
Though there were severe cuts in allocations during the first half of
the decade of the 1990s, following the introduction of economic
reforms, especially stabilization and structural adjustment policies
(Tilak 1996b), the rate of growth rose to some extent. This was partly
due to the global recognition of education as not only a means of
development, but as development itself, as theorised by human development specialists (for example, Amartya Sen and Mahbub-ul Haq).
But on the whole, during the last 50 years, the rate of growth in per
student expenditure on education was a bare 2.4 per cent per annum,
less than the Hindu rate of economic growth (Table 7.1).

**Table 7.1: Annual Real Rate of Growth in Public Expenditure
on Education in India (Percentage)**

	Total	Per capita	Per pupil
1950s	10.17	8.12	2.56
1960s	4.78	2.44	4.03
1970s	4.37	2.20	0.98
1980s	7.47	5.19	3.28
1990–91/1999–2000	8.99	6.94	6.84
1950–51/1999–2000	6.03	3.75	2.44

Source: Based on *Analysis of Budgeted Expenditure on Education, Selected Educational Statistics,* and *Education in India* (various years). New Delhi: Ministry of
Human, Resource Development, Department of Education.

What have been the trends in the relative priority accorded to education after independence?

Share of Public Expenditure on Education in GNP

On the recommendation of the Education Commission (1966), the Government of India fixed in the *National Policy on Education 1968* a target of investing 6 per cent of the national income in education from the public exchequer by 1986. Over the years, this proportion has increased remarkably from 0.6 per cent of GNP at the inception of planning (1951–52) to about 4 per cent by the end of the century, even though the growth has not been smooth. This may seem to be a remarkable increase (Figure 7.1). However, it needs to be underlined that the current ratio is much below:

1. the requirements of the education system to provide reasonable levels of quality education to all the students presently enrolled;
2. the requirements of the system to provide universal elementary education of 8 years for every child in the age group 6–14, as universalization of elementary education in a comprehensive

Figure 7.1: Share of Public Expenditure on Education in GNP (1951–52 to 2001–02)

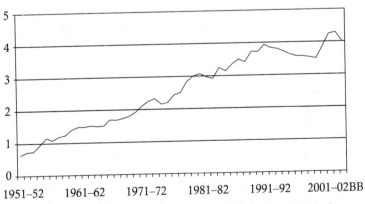

Source: Based on *Selected Educational Statistics 2001–02.* New Delhi: Government of India, Ministry of Human Resource Development, Department of Education.

sense includes universal provision of resources, universal enrolment and universal retention, and consequent growth in secondary and higher education (estimated to be about 8–10 per cent);

3. the recommendations of the Education Commission (1966), the resolve made in the *National Policy on Education 1968*, reiterated in the *National Policy on Education 1986*, the revised Policy (1992) and the promises made by successive prime ministers repeatedly even from the ramparts of the Red Fort to invest 6 per cent of GNP in education and

4. the proportion of GNP invested in education in many other developing, leave alone developed, countries of the world, including those in Africa.

It would be a stupendous task to reach a level of 6 per cent of GNP before the end of the 10th Five-Year Plan, i.e., by 2007, as promised by the Government of India recently, from the current level of about 4 per cent. The goal, originally set to be achieved about two decades ago, is being repeatedly postponed and may get further deferred, though it has little sanctity in view of the increasing needs of the education system.

Share of Expenditure on Education in the Total Budget

Perhaps a more important gauge of what is actually happening is revealed by the priority given to education in the budget. Considering the union and the state budgets together, government expenditure on education formed about 14 per cent of the total in 1970–71. Ever since, the ratio has tended to decline. It has been around 11 per cent in recent years. Even though the share of education in the union budget oscillated frequently, on the whole, it has increased from 1.6 per cent in 1967–68 to nearly 4 per cent by the end of the 1990s, and in the state budgets, it has been around 20 per cent. The total appears to be stabilizing around 10 per cent—declining from 14 per cent in the early 1970s/1980s (Figure 7.2).

With respect to the share of education in total government expenditure, India fares very poorly in comparison not only with advanced countries, but also some of the poorer ones. India has been spending only 11 per cent on education out of total government (union and

Figure 7.2: Expenditure on Education as Percentage of Total Government Expenditure (1967–68 to 2001–02)

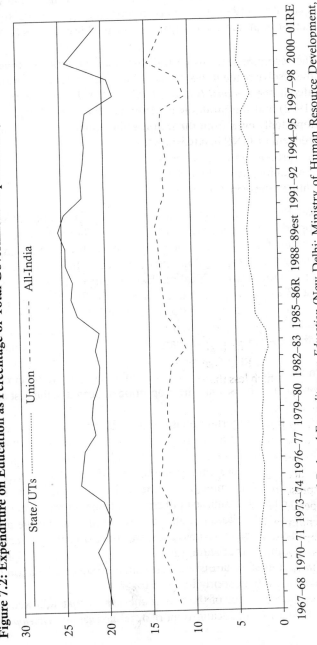

1967–68 1970–71 1973–74 1976–77 1979–80 1982–83 1985–86R 1988–89est 1991–92 1994–95 1997–98 2000–01RE

Source: Based on *Analysis of Budgeted Expenditure on Education* (New Delhi: Ministry of Human Resource Development, Department of Education).

state) expenditure, compared to more than 15 per cent in many advanced countries (1995–97). The corresponding figure was above 20 per cent in several rich and poor, and small and big countries (UNDP 2003).

In terms of these two indicators of the relative priority accorded to education, viz. the share in GNP and the share in total government expenditure, India fared better during the 1980s. But after economic reforms were introduced in the beginning of the 1990s, the shift has been away from the education sector. Public finances for education began to be affected by severe squeezes.

Expenditure on Education in Five-Year Plans

Five-Year Plans are an important instrument of development strategy adopted by independent India. Five-Year Plan outlays set new directions for further development, and hence they assume importance, though they are small in size compared to huge non-plan expenditures in the case of education. Expenditure on education in the Five-Year Plans has shown a rapid rise since the first Five-Year Plan. But its relative importance has declined, from 7.9 per cent in the First Five-Year Plan, to 2.7 per cent in the Sixth Five-Year Plan. It is only during the Seventh Five-Year Plan, and later in the Eighth and the Ninth Five-Year Plans that this declining trend was reversed. The share in the Ninth Five-Year Plan was quite high, above 6 per cent; but it was still much less than the proportion allocated in the first plan (Figure 7.3).

There are three important phases in the allocation of resources to education in the five-year plans. During the first three plans, the allocation to education as a proportion of total five-year plan expenditure was more than 5 per cent. Even though it declined in the second plan, the decline was immediately checked in the third plan. This phase represents the enthusiasm of the government immediately after independence to allocate higher outlays for education; the average expenditure during the three plans was 6.9 per cent. The second phase, consisting of the fourth, fifth and the sixth plans, was characterized by a consistent decline in the relative share of education (to an average of 3.7 per cent).

This is indeed surprising as this is the period that followed the famous Kothari Commission Report on *Education and Development*

**Figure 7.3: Expenditure on Education in Five-Year Plans
(Percentage of Total)**

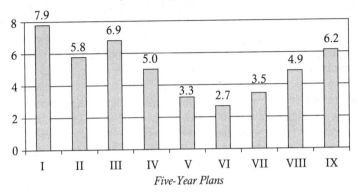

Source: Based on *Analysis of Annual Plan, Education Sector.* New Delhi: Government of India, Planning Commission, Education Division (various years).

that emphasised, inter alia, the need for expansion of education *for* development. The *1968 National Policy on Education* for the first time accepted the 'investment' nature of education. But all these have had little effect on allocation of public resources to education. The Seventh, Eighth and Ninth Five-Year Plans form the third phase when efforts were made to check the declining trend and to substantially increase the allocation to education. This phase of the post-*1986* policy period reflects the positive effect of the policy, with the average of the three plans increasing to 4.9 per cent. Whether the beginning of the century and the 10th Five-Year Plan mark a continuation of the 3rd phase or a new phase is yet to be seen.

The relative allocations to all levels—elementary, secondary and higher education—as a proportion of total plan expenditures[1] have experienced a decline. However, there has been some attempt to increase expenditure on elementary education after the *National Policy*

---

[1] This, namely, the share of a given level of education in total Five-Year plan expenditure, may be a more reliable indicator of the relative priority accorded to a given level of education than the share of a given level of education in the total expenditure on education in a Five-Year plan. The later, which is used extensively, implicitly places one level of education against another level, and causes an avoidable fragmented look at education development.

on Education (1986) was formulated. The share of elementary education in plan expenditure has decreased, on the whole, from 4.3 per cent to 3.2 per cent from the first to the ninth plan. It was at the lowest in the fifth and sixth plans at a ratio of 0.8 per cent. The decline was less pronounced in the case of secondary education. For higher education the share which was a meagre 0.7 per cent in the first plan actually went down to 0.3 per cent in the eighth plan (Figure 7.4)!

National and more importantly international pressures have helped boost the tardy growth in the allocations to elementary education in recent years. International aid also came in handy. In fact, much of the growth in the allocation to elementary education is contributed by external aid and hence it can be described as 'aid-led growth' (Tilak 1999a). But secondary, and more so higher education, has suffered very severely. One notices a significant decline in public expenditures on higher education during the 1990s. Public expenditure on higher education per student declined in real terms by 27 per cent between 1990–91 and 1996–97; it has marginally increased in later years, according to revised/budget estimates, but the increase may not be sustained. The decline might continue.

Figure 7.4: Shares of Elementary, Secondary and Higher Education in the Total Five-Year Plan Expenditure (Percentage)

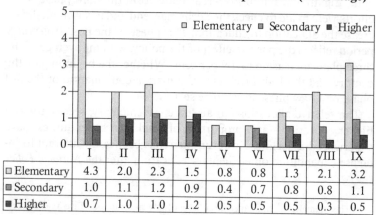

	I	II	III	IV	V	VI	VII	VIII	IX
Elementary	4.3	2.0	2.3	1.5	0.8	0.8	1.3	2.1	3.2
Secondary	1.0	1.1	1.2	0.9	0.4	0.7	0.8	0.8	1.1
Higher	0.7	1.0	1.0	1.2	0.5	0.5	0.5	0.3	0.5

Five-Year Plans

Source: Based on *Analysis of Annual Plan, Education Sector.* New Delhi: Government of India, Planning Commission, Education Division (various years).

A steep decline is noticeable in public expenditure on various items in higher education, such as scholarships, an important measure to promote equity. As a proportion of the total expenditure on higher education of the union government, the amount spent on scholarship that was always small, declined further from about 0.5 per cent to 0.25 per cent between 1990–91 and 2000–01. In absolute terms also one finds a similar decline in real prices.

To sum up, the state's reluctance and unwillingness to invest in education is attested to by several indicators:

- real growth in total per capita and per student expenditure
- trends in relative share of expenditure on education in the budget and in five-year plan outlays
- the relative shares of various levels of education in total five-year plan expenditures
- public expenditure on higher education.

Even as a proportion of GNP, expenditure on education has not shown significant increases. It is rather reluctantly increasing at a snail's pace; currently it is below the 6 per cent norm which was the target set for achievement nearly two decades ago.

The state's unwillingness to invest in education is also clear from the policy statements occasionally made, particularly with respect to, but not necessarily confined to, higher education. For example, following the recommendations of the committees set up by the University Grants Commission (UGC 1993) and the All India Council for Technical Education (AICTE 1994) (Dr Justice Punnayya Committee and Dr Swaminadhan Committee, respectively), institutions of higher education were required to raise at least 20 per cent of the required resources through fees and other sources, implying that government subsidies would be restricted to less than or about 80 per cent of the requirements. Second, the Ministry of Finance (Government of India 1997) in its paper, *Government Subsidies in India*, has stated that 'subsidies to higher education would be gradually reduced to about 50 per cent'. Third, when reformulating the student loan programme in the early 1990s, the government argued that loan programmes would be reorganized so that with the recovery of loans, *higher education would eventually become self-financing.* In case of school education, it has preferred expansion of low-cost and low-quality alternative systems of primary education and literacy to the formal school system. Also revealing is the preference for recruitment of untrained, underqualified and poorly remunerated teachers to those who are fully qualified and reasonably well paid. Last, and tellingly, there is the encouragement and support given to private educational institutions with the almost stated objective of saving public resources. It is difficult not to infer from these the increasing unwillingness of the state to allocate budgetary resources to education.

The question is: Why is the government unwilling to spend on education?

First, there is the general belief that public expenditure has no significant impact upon the development of education, and that its effects on literacy, enrolment rates and achievement levels in school are not pronounced (World Bank 2003).

But this is not necessarily true. As I have tried to show elsewhere (Tilak 1999b), government expenditure on education per capita is the second most important factor (after number of teachers) for the development of education. As budget expenditure on education per capita increases, the rate of attendance of children in schools tends to increase systematically and significantly. The coefficient of correlation is as high as 0.8 (Figure 7.5). Similar strong relationships are found with expenditure on education and other indicators of educational development including the aggregate index of education.

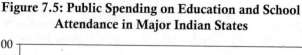

Figure 7.5: Public Spending on Education and School Attendance in Major Indian States

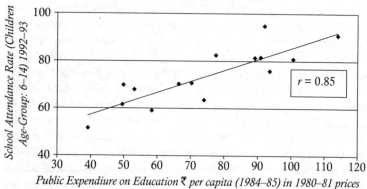

Public Expendiure on Education ₹ per capita (1984–85) in 1980–81 prices

Source: Tilak (1999b).

Secondly, government's reluctance to spend on education is ascribed to the underdevelopment of the economy. One of the most widely held beliefs is that economically poor societies obviously cannot spend much on education and so must be the case in India. Statistical evidence does not support such a presumption.

1. There exists no statistically clear relationship between the level of economic development of states (state domestic product per capita) and their level of spending on education as per cent of state domestic product (SDP). For instance, economically poor states like Bihar and Assam spend a higher proportion of their income on education, and relatively more prosperous ones like Haryana and Maharashtra allocate small proportions to education (Table 7.2).

2. That the levels of SDP vary and hence proportions of SDP do not mean much, may not be tenable, as the weak relationship between economic development and education expenditure holds true with respect to absolute levels of expenditures as well. In other words, this relationship is not confined to the relative proportion allocated to education and SDP per capita.

Table 7.2: SDP per Capita and Expenditure on Education

| | | Education as per cent of SDP (1998–99) | | | |
		High	Medium	Low	Very Low
SDP per capita, 1977–78	High	Nil	Nil	Tamil Nadu, Punjab, Gujarat	Haryana, Maharashtra
	Medium	Himachal Pradesh	Nil	Karnataka, West Bengal	Andhra Pradesh
	Low	Tripura	Rajasthan, Kerala	Nil	Nil
	Very Low	Bihar, Assam	Orissa, Uttar Pradesh	Nil	Madhya Pradesh

Source: Based on *Analysis of Budgeted Expenditure on Education,* and *Selected Educational Statistics* (New Delhi: Ministry of Human Resource Development, Department of Education), and *Economic Survey* (Ministry of Finance, Government of India) (relevant years).

It holds true with respect to SDP per capita and the expenditure on education per capita and many other appropriate indicators as well. The relationship between SDP per capita and expenditure on education per capita is not significant and systematic. For example, among the 18 major states in India, Himachal Pradesh ranks 8th with respect to SDP per capita in 1997–98, but ranks at the top in its spending on education in 1998–99; so is the case of Tripura which ranks 12th in SDP per capita but spends the second-largest amount on education; and the evidence of Kerala is well known: spending the third-largest amount on education, it ranks 10th with respect to SDP per capita. The richer states like Punjab and Haryana (ranking respectively, second and third in SDP per capita) rank poorly (seventh and eighth, respectively) with respect to spending on education per capita. West Bengal figures almost at the bottom (16th among the major states) with respect to spending on education, but ranks 6th with respect to SDP per capita. These are not exceptions; on the contrary, they seem to represent the general rule.

3. There also does not exist any significant systematic relationship between the rate of growth of national income per capita and the rate of growth of expenditure on education per capita in real terms. The simple coefficient of correlation between the two is 0.2, when estimated on the all India time series data from 1950–51 and 2000–01 (Figure 7.6).

But an increase in GNP per capita might lead to an increase in expenditure on education per capita. Government expenditure on education per capita was consistently more elastic to GNP per capita during the first four decades after Independence, though the coefficient gradually declined in value over the years. The coefficient of elasticity was 5.4 in the 1950s, which declined to less than unity (0.8) by the 1990s (1990–91 to 1996–97).[2] The economic reforms introduced in the beginning of the 1990s seem to have affected the relationship considerably.

All this makes it clear that both at the national and state levels economic conditions (as reflected in growth of GNP and the like) do not have a determining effect on allocation to education. Earlier, I

---

[2] The corresponding coefficient was 2.3 in the 1960s, 3.2 in the 1970s and 2.0 in the 1980s.

Figure 7.6: Real Growth in GNP per Capita and Expenditure on Education per Capita

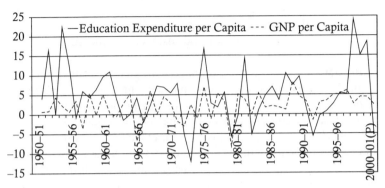

Source: Based on *Analysis of Budgeted Expenditure on Education*, and *Selected Educational Statistics* (New Delhi: Ministry of Human Resource Development, Department of Education), and *Economic Survey* (relevant years) (Ministry of Finance, Government of India.

have attempted to show that allocations for education by the Finance Commission and the Planning Commission to various states are also not systematically influenced by any meaningful criteria (Tilak 1989). Allocations by the Planning Commission might be expected to favour educationally backward states in order to reduce regional disparities. This is, after all, one of the objectives of the plans. Awards of Finance Commissions, on the other hand, might be expected to tilt towards educationally advanced states, since these are mainly meant for maintenance of the system. And larger and more developed educational systems would require more resources. Yet neither set of allocations can be explained with reference to stock or flow indicators on education development or by other economic factors.

Logically, the conclusion is that low levels of state expenditure on education are not due to economic constraints. Nor are they influenced by the level of educational development and corresponding needs. The explanation for the government's unwillingness to invest in education would perhaps lie in misconceptions such as:

- education is not an imperative for economic development, indeed that economic miracles can be achieved without significant educational progress,

- even if education is important for development, higher levels of expenditure do not necessarily improve a population's educational status, and
- internal efficiency in education can be improved through reduced public expenditure and cost recovery measures.

In addition there is the occasional remark that the state is reluctant to increase expenditure on education since the quality of education is poor, teachers do not teach, no worthwhile learning takes place in schools and colleges and universities perform only a babysitting role, etc. It is arguable that these are quite likely the consequence of underfunding. They cannot constitute a case for withdrawal of public resources. A 'conspiracy theory' is also advanced suggesting that elite governments do not want the masses to be educated and are therefore reluctant to invest in it. The most likely explanation for the state's unwillingness to invest in education lies in the lack of 'political will' to accord due priority to education (Drèze and Sen 2002).

Household Investment on Education

'Willingness to pay' has gained ground in the context of growing budgetary cuts on education. It is strongly urged by many that this willingness should be tapped to the maximum so that the burden on the exchequer is reduced. Household spending on education is justified on three grounds:

1. governments lack adequate resources to finance education and therefore households have to contribute at least partly towards the cost,
2. household expenditure through fees will improve the system's efficiency,
3. household spending reflects willingness and ability to pay in education and this should be tapped in full.

These grounds are resisted by counter arguments resting on the following:

1. Household expenditures, more appropriately payment of fees and other user charges, militate against the letter and spirit of

free and compulsory education as enshrined, for example, in the Constitution of India and the Convention of the Rights of Children (1948).

2. Such expenditures perpetuate inequities since they tend to vary directly with household incomes.

3. High levels of expenditure may compel the poor not to opt for schooling, and, hence the demand for education will be distorted.

4. Household expenditures are actually a reflection of the state's inability and inefficiency in providing education.

5. Household expenditure on education is inconsistent with the nature and philosophy of education and reduces it to a 'commodity' that can be bought.

However, household expenditures on education in India are substantial and they have increased over the years. According to the *National Accounts Statistics*, household expenditure (private final consumption expenditure) on education in India was of the order of ₹15.7 thousand crore in 1996–97. This is indeed sizeable, forming more than 1 per cent of gross domestic product (GDP). It increased nearly 100 times in 36 years from ₹159 crore in 1960–61 to ₹15.7 thousand crore in 1996–97! In real terms the growth has been seven times between the same periods and in per capita terms the real increase has been 3.3 times.

The overall rate of growth in household expenditure on education per capita in real prices was 3.4 per cent per annum during 1950–51 to 1996–97, but the growth has not been smooth over the decades. While the first two decades after the inception of planning, i.e., the 1950s and the 1960s registered a reasonably high rate of growth, the economic problems of the 1970s in terms of high inflation, adversely affected total household budgets and allocations to education. Accordingly, the rate of growth was as low as 1.2 per cent per annum in the 1970s. Though in the 1980s there was some reversal in the trend, the situation in the 1990s was not favourable to education. During 1990–91 to 1996–97, the real rate of growth has been only 2 per cent per annum (Table 7.3).

Analyses of the 42nd and the 52nd rounds of the National Sample Survey data that refer respectively to 1986–87 and 1995–96 (Tilak 1996a; 2002b) and the National Council of Applied Economic Research (NCAER) surveys on human development (Tilak 2002a)

Table 7.3: Rate of Growth in Household Expenditure
on Education

	Total	Per Capita
1950s	7.1	5.1
1960s	9.1	6.8
1970s	3.5	1.2
1980s	4.8	2.6
1990s[a]	3.9	2.0
1950–51 to 1996–97	5.6	3.4

Source: Based on *National Accounts Statistics* (various years) (New Delhi: Department of Statistics, Planning Commission).
Secondary Source: Tilak (2000).
Note: [a]1990s: 1990–91 to 1996–97.

highlight certain interesting features relating to household expenditure on education. We shall take note of a few of them.

Households incur huge expenditure on education of their children. According to the National Sample Survey (1995–96), on average a household has to spend ₹500 per child per annum on primary education. For upper primary education, the expenditure increases to about ₹900; it further increases to ₹1,577 in secondary schools and to ₹2,923 in higher education. These figures refer to 1995–96. A quick comparison with the earlier set of estimates shows that there has been a steep increase in the levels of household expenditures between 1986–87 and 1995–96. The expenditure on primary education per student in 1986–87 varied between ₹84 in government schools in rural areas and ₹569 in private schools in urban areas (Table 7.4).

Systematic patterns are discernible with respect to household expenditures on education. Household expenditure on education is highly elastic to income levels. Rich households spend more than low-income households on education. According to the 52nd round of the National Sample Survey, average household expenditure of the top expenditure quintile on education is about six times that of the bottom expenditure quintile.

The 'wealth effect', defined simply as a ratio between the expenditure of high and low income households minus one, is more pronounced in private schools than in government schools. Further,

**Table 7.4: Average Annual Household Expenditure per Student
(Age Group: 5–24), 1995–96**

(in ₹)

	Rural	*Urban*	*Total*
Primary	297	1,149	501
Middle	640	1,529	915
Secondary	1,180	2,219	1,577
Higher	2,294	3,304	2,923
All	570	1,686	904

Source: National Sample Survey Organisation.
Secondary Source: Tilak (2000).

**Figure 7.7: Household Expenditure on Education: Wealth Effect
on Education**

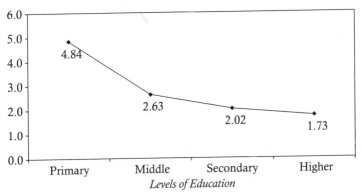

Source: Based on National Sample Survey.
Secondary Source: Tilak (2000).

more interestingly, the wealth effect is quite pronounced in primary
education, and declines with the level of education (Figure 7.7). In
a sense, the present system of financing seems to be more equitable
in higher education than primary education. This pattern may significantly change with the rapid growth in high fee charging private
colleges. Consequently, the wealth effect could become equally, if not
more pronounced in higher education.

As a proportion of household income, poor households spend consistently more than the rich. Bottom income households have to spend, according to the NCAER survey (Tilak 2002a), 6.9 per cent of their total income on education and this proportion declines consistently with increasing levels of household income, as one would expect. It is only 0.6 per cent of household income that top income households have to spend on the education of children. This holds for all groups in the population—caste groups including scheduled castes, scheduled tribes and others; religious groups including Hindus, Muslims and Christians; boys and girls and among different landowning groups. Further, it is found to hold in all states with almost no exception. The poor households have to spend a larger proportion of their meagre incomes on education than richer households.

The coefficient of elasticity of household expenditure on education to total income (in fact, expenditure) of the households between 1950–51 and 1996–97 is positive, and greater than 1; it is 1.5. These are based on *National Accounts Statistics*. It means that household expenditures on education are elastic to household income. A 1 per cent increase in total household income would result in a 1.5 per cent increase in household expenditures on education. When the figures are considered in per capita terms, the coefficient of elasticity is much higher at 2.1. If household income per capita increases by 1 per cent, household expenditure on education per capita increases by 2.1 per cent. This suggests that household expenditures on education change considerably and positively to changes in household income (or expenditure) levels.

In terms of the coefficient of elasticity of household expenditures on education per capita to total household expenditure per capita, the 1950s were a good decade (with the coefficient being 3.0), the decade of the 1960s being the best period, with the highest coefficient of elasticity (5.9); 1970s the worst period (the coefficient was 0.24) and 1990s not much better than the 1970s (the value of the coefficient was 0.78); during the decade of the 1980s it was marginally better (1.0). The spiralling inflation and other economic problems of the 1970s seem to have weakened the relationship between household income (or total expenditure) and expenditure on education over the decades. More basic needs like food and other items might have been given higher priority than education and accordingly increase in incomes might not have caused increase in expenditures on education to any noticeable extent. The relationship did not improve much during later periods.

The values of the coefficients of elasticity of household expenditures on education to household income (or expenditure) are higher than the coefficients of elasticity of government expenditures on education to total government expenditure. This means that households respond to education needs more favourably than governments. A 1 per cent increase in household incomes would result in a more than proportionate increase in expenditure on education, which is much higher than the response of government expenditure to a similar 1 per cent increase in income (or total expenditure) of the government.

Average household expenditure on education per student in a state shows some relationship to the SDP per capita. Economically prosperous states/union territories like Delhi, Chandigarh, Punjab and Haryana figure at the top of the list in household expenditure on education per student with backward states like Madhya Pradesh, Assam and Bihar at the bottom (Figure 7.8). For example, households in economically advanced states spend more than the households in economically poor states. The simple coefficient of correlation between SDP per capita and household expenditure on education in 1995–96 was 0.6. Household expenditure is also inversely related to poverty level in the state, the coefficient of correlation being –0.45.

Quite strikingly, according to the 1995–96 National Sample Survey, there are no significant differences in household expenditures on education by gender, i.e., between girls and boys (Table 7.5). In fact, except for a small difference at the primary level, the differences favour girls in other levels of education. This is particularly true in rural areas and for India as a whole. In urban areas, the differences are against girls in all levels of education but the differences are marginal.

Table 7.5: Household Expenditure on Education per Student, by Gender, 1995–96

	Boys	*Girls*	*All*
Primary	507	494	501
Middle	904	933	915
Secondary	1,552	1,619	1,577
Higher	2,879	2,995	2,923
All	919	882	904

Source: National Sample Survey.
Secondary Source: Tilak (2000).

Perhaps the importance of girls' education is being increasingly recognized by the households, and accordingly they do not discriminate against girls in spending on their education—a welcome feature.

Why are households 'willing' to spend on education? In general, employment and economic returns, including not only employment-related earnings but also factors like dowry, may exercise considerable influence on investment decisions by households in education. This is particularly true with respect to higher education. But why do households spend even on elementary education that is (expected to be) provided free by the state? Households are found to be spending considerable amounts on their children's primary education. As noted earlier, according to the National Sample Survey (1995–96) estimates, on average a household has to spend ₹500 per year per child on acquiring primary education, and about ₹900 on upper primary education. Even poor households (bottom quintile) spend nearly ₹200 on primary education per annum per child. Households from even lower socio-economic backgrounds—scheduled castes, scheduled tribes, households whose primary occupation is not high in the occupational hierarchy—all spend considerable amounts on acquiring education, including specifically primary education. About 30 per cent of the expenditure on primary education goes in the form of fees—tuition and other fees, one-fourth on uniforms, another one-fourth on books and stationery and a sizeable amount on private coaching, all of which are expected to be provided by the state. Apart from free education, learning/instructional material like textbooks, stationery and other incentives such as uniforms and noon meals are received free only by a small fraction of the students.

In addition to the expectation of attaining a higher social status, households may also spend on education to ensure that their children excel others in the race for ranks. Rich households tend to 'buy' quality education for their children, which is not affordable by the poor households. This means that the households perceive perhaps rightly that public resources are not adequate to ensure 'good quality' education for their children. 'Good' quality may be defined at the bottom as *reasonable* quality or *tolerable* level of quality. Households tend to equate, in the absence of any other information, high costs with high quality.

What I wish to argue is, it is not necessarily the *willingness* of the households, but the *compulsion* they feel which makes them spend on education. Households may feel compelled to invest in education, if

Figure 7.8: Household Expenditure on Education per Student, by States (1995–96)

(in ₹)

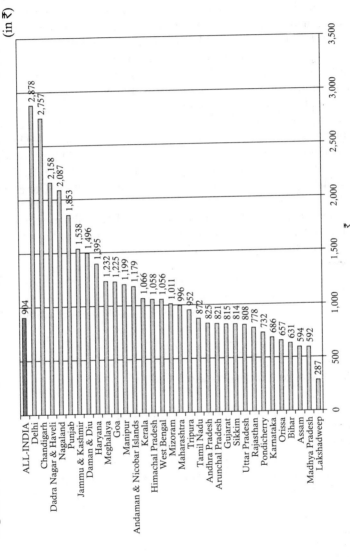

₹

ALL-INDIA 904
Delhi 2,878
Chandigarh 2,757
Dadra Nagar & Haveli 2,158
Nagaland 2,087
Punjab 1,853
Jammu & Kashmir 1,538
Daman & Diu 1,496
Haryana 1,395
Meghalaya 1,232
Goa 1,225
Manipur 1,199
Andaman & Nicobar Islands 1,179
Kerala 1,066
Himachal Pradesh 1,058
West Bengal 1,056
Mizoram 1,011
Maharashtra 996
Tripura 952
Tamil Nadu 872
Andhra Pradesh 825
Arunchal Pradesh 821
Gujarat 815
Sikkim 814
Uttar Pradesh 808
Rajasthan 778
Pondicherry 732
Karnataka 686
Orissa 657
Bihar 631
Assam 594
Madhya Pradesh 592
Lakshadweep 287

Source: National Sample Survey.
Secondary Source: Tilak (2000).

public efforts, as reflected in the quantity and quality of physical and human infrastructure (teachers) available in schools are perceived to be inadequate. Under such circumstances even poor households would spend on education out of compulsion. Therefore, the poorer the quality of infrastructure and other facilities in public schools, ceteris paribus, the higher could be the level of expenditure of households on education. The quality of school infrastructure could be measured in terms of a large number of indicators, such as its availability within the habitation or at least within walking distance, type of school buildings, quality and number of teachers, etc. The quantity and quality of school facilities could as well be measured in terms of public expenditure per student. A decline in public expenditure per student is accompanied by an increase in household expenditure on education. If the facilities in public schools were better, families would perhaps not feel the need for incurring expenditure. Therefore, I argue that it is wrong to suggest that families are *willing* to spend on education; they are in fact *compelled* to do so. The 'willingness to pay' is also measured in terms of the amount of fees paid to the schools and other expenditure incurred by households. This may reflect the ability to pay to some extent; in some cases it may not even represent the true ability to pay (as the expenditures might have been incurred by borrowing, and even mortgaging their small fixed assets or their own future earnings), but this does not necessarily reflect 'willingness to pay'.[3]

Role of Markets in Education

The private sector in education is not a new phenomenon in India. Role of private sector in education is favoured essentially to meet 'excess' and also 'differentiated' demand for education. Excess demand refers to the demand unmet by the public sector institutions. Differentiated demand refers to demand for a particular type and quality of education (for example, religious education, English medium

---

[3] The hollowness of the concept of 'willingness to pay' becomes clearer in the context of health care, where also the concept is used almost synonymously. A person will be ready to incur large expenditures, as he/she knows that the alternative could be fatal. Can this be described as 'willingness to pay'?

education and high quality education), different from what is provided in public institutions. I have argued elsewhere (Tilak 1994) that, in India, differentiated demand might explain growth in private education at school level whereas excess demand may be the main factor for growth in private higher education. The private sector is also favoured by the government as it can tap the untapped resources available in the society for the development of education and correspondingly the government can reduce its expenditures. Many other claims that are made in this context, such as that the private sector will contribute to increase in access, quality and equity in education, etc., are, to my mind, to a great extent untenable and even false. In an international comparative analysis, I have tried to explode many of these and related myths on private education (Tilak 1991).

The private sector founded several schools and colleges in India before and immediately after Independence. The motives of the private sector of the 1950s and the 1960s were to a considerable extent, philanthropy, charity and education development to meet excess and to some extent, differentiated demand. Many of the institutions established during this period willingly subjected themselves to state control and regulation in all respects and even accepted state financing with all its conditions. Profit was not the main consideration. Hence, they cannot be equated to the private institutions that have sprung up in the last quarter century, and more particularly after 'marketisation' of education became the buzzword. That the earlier kind of private institutions—state-aided private institutions that can be aptly described as *pseudo* private institutions—led to distortions in allocation of public resources is a different matter (Tilak 1994).

Private institutions born in the era of marketization are solely guided by the market principle, viz. profit maximization. They are also self-financing, and tend to defy or at least resist state regulation of any kind, necessitating judicial intervention very often. Student fees, charged not necessarily in proportion to costs, are often the only source of funds for such institutions. Investment by the private management is very limited, and, if any, is confined to capital investments in the initial years, which are also recovered in a short period.

The growth of this modern private sector in education is a response to the lack of a clear government policy on the role of the state and markets in education. The historic judgement of the Supreme Court in 1992 that practically banned capitation fee colleges, stating that capitation fee is 'patently unreasonable, unfair and unjust' was followed

by another historic judgement in 1993 that paved the way for the
growth of the very same capitation fee colleges, under the name of
self financing colleges. Elaborate mechanisms were developed by the
state that helped in the proliferation of self-financing fee colleges. For
instance, in Andhra Pradesh, such colleges have increased in number
from almost nil in the early 1980s to 450 by 1996–97 (Table 7.6). Today such colleges offer not only engineering and management education, but also arts and sciences and outnumber public institutions, by
several times. In fact, in absolute numbers, and also as a proportion of
the total, government colleges turn out to be negligible. For example,

Table 7.6: Growth of Colleges in Andhra Pradesh

| | Government | Private | | | Total |
		Aided	Unaided	Total	
1969–70	40	80	0	80	120
1979–80	64	147	1	148	212
1984–85	133	181	9	190	323
1989–90	147	182	33	215	362
1993–94	156	182	88	270	426
1996–97	167	187	450	637	804

Source: *Performance Budget of Andhra Pradesh, 1997–98* (Hyderabad: Government of Andhra Pradesh).

in Andhra Pradesh there were 95 private self-financing engineering
colleges, compared to 11 government colleges; similarly, there were
303 self-financing medical colleges, compared to 25 government colleges (2000–01) (Figure 7.9). The casualty is not just equity, which
is well known, but also quality of higher education. Gresham's law
of money seems to operate in education: private (bad) colleges drive
away public (good) colleges out of circulation.

The *Private Universities Bill*, introduced in the Rajya Sabha in August 1995, with a view to providing for the establishment of self-financing universities is still pending in Parliament. It is widely felt that
the Bill was not processed and passed in the Parliament, not because
the government was not keen on privatization of higher education
in India, not because the private sector is not interested in the Bill,

Figure 7.9: Growth of Private Sector in Higher Education in Andhra Pradesh

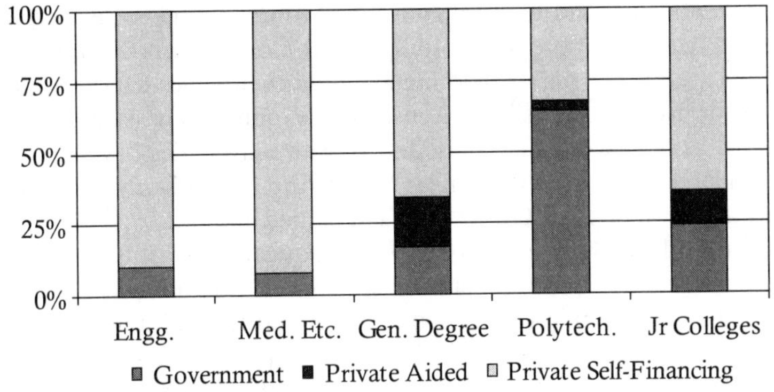

■ Government   ■ Private Aided   □ Private Self-Financing

Source: Performance Budget of Andhra Pradesh, 2001–02 (Hyderabad: Government of Andhra Pradesh).

but probably because the latter was not happy with several clauses in the Bill. For example, the Bill requires formation of a permanent endowment fund of ₹10 crore, provision of free-ships to 30 per cent of the students, and for government monitoring and regulation of the system.

Though the *Private Universities Bill* has not yet been passed by Parliament, and the recommendations of the Ambani–Birla Committee report (Prime Minister's Council on Trade and Industry 2000) were *per se* not accepted, several initiatives taken by the government suggest that higher education is getting rapidly privatized. Perhaps there is no need for the bill. For example, a few private institutions of higher education have been virtually given the status of universities, by recognizing them as 'deemed universities'.[4] Universities (for example, the Guru Gobind Singh Indraprastha University in Delhi) are created, that consist of only affiliating private self-financing colleges. A few other private institutions (for example, International Business Schools and IIITs) are allowed to operate almost as universities or their equivalent offering degree/diploma programmes. All this is in addition to allowing rapid growth of private self-financing institutions at college level,

---

[4] In the last couple of years, there has been a big jump in the number of deemed universities, mostly private, which led the UGC to feel the need to review their working.

and conversion of government-aided private institutions into private self-financing (unaided) institutions in several states.

The private sector found it convenient to remind the state governments that education is, according to the Constitution, a *concurrent* subject, and that state governments could themselves enact legislation for private universities.[5] Consequently, quite a few state governments have enacted such bills, and private universities have sprung up in large numbers, almost in no time, without necessarily obtaining any approval of the UGC or other concerned authority.

Currently, we have a variety of private educational institutions, private universities, private institutions deemed to be universities and self-financing (capitation fee) colleges, in addition to hundreds and even thousands of unrecognized ones such as teaching shops, 'parallel colleges' and coaching centres—all working within the market framework with the sole objective of profit maximization. Such institutions are rapidly increasing in number. State-aided private schools and colleges operate within a different framework. But their growth has come to a standstill, if it has not declined.

These trends of privatization are already producing serious effects on various dimensions of the educational system and society at large. These include effects on quantity, quality and equity in education, research, supply of teachers and 'balanced' development of higher education, as I have described elsewhere (Tilak 1999c).

Since there exists 'excess demand' for higher education, it is possible to argue that demand for higher education in India is rather inelastic to changes in fees. But the coefficient of elasticity may not be zero; it is not in fact less than unity or inelastic for all levels/types of higher education. For example, it is already noted that steep increases in fees at post graduate and research levels in the Indian Institutes of Technology have been counterproductive, leading to a decline in enrolments by more than 37 per cent in the mid-1990s.

One of the most important problems is of ensuring equity in higher education. While the government can, to a great extent, make sure that protective discrimination policies are followed in government and government-aided private institutions, resistance to such policies

---

[5] Interestingly, the concurrency clause was conveniently not remembered by any state government, when the bill to make elementary education a fundamental right was pending before Parliament for more than five years, before it was finally passed in December 2002 as the 86th Amendment.

is much higher in private institutions. The overall fee elasticity of demand for education may not be high but it could certainly be so for economically weaker sections. In other words, with privatization, even if the size of total enrolments does not change, the composition might change in favour of better-off sections with the poor getting completely marginalized.

The government's inability to control the quality of education in private institutions is also being increasingly felt. Even strong proponents of private higher education systems somewhat paradoxically argue that the state should take responsibility for regulating quality in private education. But given the social and politico-economic milieu, the government seems to feel severely handicapped in maintaining quality in these institutions. Generally, once recognition is granted to a private institution (and that is not found to be very difficult) the government cannot enforce any of its conditions. This is true to some extent even of state-aided private colleges. State grants are not usually stopped or delayed for any reason. Massive erosion of quality in private colleges might push down the quality of higher education as a whole.

Further, conflicts between national manpower needs and short-term market signals that influence private higher education institutions can be serious and in the long run might produce serious manpower imbalances—both shortages and gluts. This is evident from the estimates and corresponding recommendations made by professional public bodies like the AICTE and the Medical Council of India with regard to the required number of colleges and manpower which are least taken note of by private colleges, operating in collusion with the government.

All these problems are with respect to 'recognised' private institutions. Emergence of 'fake' national and foreign universities and ghost institutions imparting 'education' and awarding obviously fake degrees is also a problem that is coming to surface. As these institutions are not even 'recognised', the role of the government is practically nil. Occasionally, the UGC or the Association of Indian Universities makes public announcements listing fake universities and ghost institutions, to warn students and parents to be cautious.

In case of school education, even such an arrangement does not exist, though it is well known that there are a large number of private institutions that the government does not recognize. In fact, they cannot be recognized. Many of them were opened under the *Registration of Shops Act* relating to shops and commercial establishments (Deshpande 1991). Unfortunately, no quantitative information is available on such institutions, though it is known that they are booming. Such institutions range from teaching shops to new centres offering computer literacy and training, management institutions, institutions of fashion design and what not. They are run completely on a commercial basis, and pubic educational bodies have no control over them.

The most important apprehensions, which are proving true, relate to vulgar commercialisation of education, and playing on the anxieties of 'gullible parents', charging exorbitant fees formally and informally, starting from application fee to examination fees, fee for grade sheet and fee for attestation by the universities. The unparalleled greed of private enterprise in education in India has been unravelled. The 'carnal lust' (Neave 1996: 20) is visible to the naked eye. Education is being viewed by private enterprise as a very lucrative investment to make huge and quick profits. Students who pay exorbitant fees obviously cannot be involved with consideration for national interests such as public service, service in rural areas, service of the poor, etc. The sole objective of these students, whether it is actually realised or not, is to emigrate to greener pastures. No wonder, the products of the carnal lust cannot be expected to be otherwise. This would be the most harmful effect of marketization of education on the society.

The many legal battles being fought in the high courts and the Supreme Court and the detailed instructions that the courts issue frequently to public bodies suggest a serious malaise with private educational institutions in the country that have little concern for equity, efficiency, norms of educational excellence and most importantly cherished national goals and ideals. Yet they are increasing in number, as there exists a nexus between them and the seekers of profit, seekers of political power and influence. The casualty is education. As Kothari (1986: 596) noted, with the growth of these institutions, 'The objective of equal opportunities for education would be jeopardised in a big way. The overall effect would be to convert education into a force for reinforcing the existing stratification of the society.

All this indicates that markets are highly imperfect and incomplete in India, like in many other developing countries (Stiglitz 2002), and fail to perform any normative role in the development of education, and hence any significant reliance on them would be counter productive.

Concluding Remarks

I have focused, in my lecture, on three closely related aspects of financing of education in India, viz. the unwillingness of the government to spend on education, compulsion on households to spend on education and exploitative markets in education. The government is increasingly unwilling to spend on education; households have little choice but to spend huge amounts even on elementary education that the state is expected to provide free. And markets are taking advantage of the situation.

The unwillingness of the government is related to attitudes and policies towards education. The two other phenomena, viz. increase in household expenditure on education and the rapid growth of private sector in education are direct outcomes of government policies and attitudes. They are also mutually related to each other. Rather than perceiving increase in household expenditure as a negative reflection on its inadequacy, and feeling guilty and ashamed of the same, governments are actively encouraging this trend. There is a formidable constellation at work: absence of a coherent long-term policy on education, and lack of clarity regarding the respective domains of households and markets. This has enabled the private sector to hold the state and households to ransom.

The best answer is provision of good-quality education by the state to all its citizens, financed out of tax and non-tax revenues. I have examined earlier (Tilak 1997) alternative methods of financing education, and concluded that, of all, state financing remains unequalled. It is not households but the government that should feel socially, economically, educationally and ethically compelled to invest in education. After all, this is the practice in most civilized societies of the world.

References

AICTE. 1994. *Report of the High Power Committee for Mobilization of Additional Resources for Technical Education* (Dr Swaminadhan Committee Report), All India Council for Technical Education, New Delhi.

Arrow, Kenneth J. 1973. 'Higher Education as a Filter', *Journal of Public Economics* 2(3, July): 193–216.

Behrman, J.R. 1990. *Human Resource Led Development? Review of Issues and Evidence.* New Delhi: ILO-ARTEP.

Deshpande, J.V. 1991. 'Boom in Teaching Shops', *Economic and Political Weekly* 26(30, 27 July): 1787.

Drèze, Jean, and Amartya Sen. 2002. *India: Development and Participation.* Delhi: Oxford University Press.

Education (Kothari) Commission. 1966. *Education and Development.* New Delhi: Government of India, Ministry of Education.

Government of India. 1997. *Government Subsidies in India.* New Delhi: Ministry of Finance.

Kothari, V.N. 1986. 'Private Unaided Engineering and Medical Colleges: Consequences of Misguided Policy', *Economic and Political Weekly* 21(14, 5 April): 593–96.

Majumdar, Tapas. 1983. *Investment in Education and Social Choice.* Cambridge: Cambridge University Press.

Neave, Guy. 1996. 'Higher Education in Transition: Twenty Five Years On', *Higher Education Management* 8(3, November): 15–24.

Prime Minister's Council on Trade and Industry. 2000. *A Policy Framework for Reforms in Education* (Mukesh Ambani–Kumaramanglalam Birla Report). Report submitted by special subject group on Policy Framework for Private Investment in Education, Health and Rural Development, Government of India, New Delhi. http://indiaimage.nic.in/pmcouncils/reports/education.

Schultz, Theodore W. 1961. 'Investment in Human Capital', *American Economic Review* 51(1, March): 1–17.

Spence, A.M. 1973. 'Job-market Signalling', *Quarterly Journal of Economics* 87(3, August): 355–74.

Stiglitz, Joseph. 2002. *Globalization and Its Discontents.* London: Allen Lane/ Penguin.

Tilak, Jandhyala B.G. 1989. 'Center–State Relations in Financing Education in India', *Comparative Educational Review* 33(4, November): 450–80.

———. 1991. 'Privatization of Higher Education', *Prospects: Quarterly Review of Education* (Unesco) 21(2): 227–39.

———. 1994. 'South Asian Perspectives (on Alternative Policies for the Finance, Control, and Delivery of Basic Education)', *International Journal of Educational Research* 21(8): 791–98.

———. 1996a. 'How Free is "Free" Primary Education in India?' *Economic and Political Weekly* 31(5, 6; 3 and 10 February): 275–82, 355–66.

———. 1996b. 'Higher Education Under Structural Adjustment', *Journal of Indian School of Political Economy* 8(2, April–June): 266–93.

———. 1997. 'Lessons from Cost Recovery in Education', in *Marketising education and health in developing countries: Miracle or mirage?* ed. C. Colclough, 63–89. Oxford: Clarendon Press.

Tilak, Jandhyala B.G. 1999a. 'National Human Development Initiative: Education in the Union Budget', *Economic and Political Weekly* 34(10–11, 6 March): 614–20.

———. 1999b. 'Investment in Human Capital in India: An Inter-state Analysis of Stock and Flow of Human Capital', *Journal of Indian School of Political Economy* 11(January–March): 39–75.

———. 1999c. 'Emerging Trends and Evolving Public Policies on Privatisation of Higher Education in India', in *Private Prometheus: Private Higher Education and Development in the 21st Century*, ed. P.G. Altbach, pp. 113–35. Westport: Greenwood Publishing.

———. 2000. *Household Expenditure on Education in India: A Preliminary Examination of the 52nd Round of the National Sample Survey*. New Delhi: National Institute of Educational Planning and Administration.

———. 2002a. 'Determinants of Household Expenditure on Education in Rural India', Working Paper No. 88, National Council of Applied Economic Research, New Delhi.

———. 2002b. 'Education Poverty in India', *Review of Development and Change* 7(1, January–June): 1–44.

UGC. 1993. *UGC Funding of Institutions of Higher Education,* Report of Justice Dr K. Punnayya Committee, 1992–92. New Delhi: University Grants Commission.

UNDP. 2003. *Human Development Report.* New York: Oxford University Press.

World Bank. 2003. *World Development Report.* New York: Oxford University Press.

8

Development as a Human Right or as Political Largesse

Upendra Baxi

Notions of Development

The notions of development are articulated at many different sites, in many different statist and subaltern languages, and in vastly different contexts of consensual and violently imposed social, economic and political transformation. Many questions arise and, I suggest shortly as many as 12 such questions. However, at the outset may I raise a most crucial question: *Who thinks inside our head when we think 'development'?* I believe that other 'minds' dwell in ours and preside over our thinking and that posing this question is a way of being more reflexive concerning our acts/performances of thinking. Of course, I here hint at but do not develop further any epistemological analysis: suffice it to say, by way of example, that a great contribution of feminist and pluri-cultural 'theory' has been to expose the fact that all too often the Pantheon of 'Dead White Men' think through our heads and this has triggered some stunning new ways of thinking.

The European Enlightenment Idea of Progress (hereafter 'Idea') has shaped much thinking concerning 'development'. We know now that the European Enlightenment was not monolithic and the Idea itself was variously articulated. We also know a great deal today concerning the 'dark side of modernity' that marked the progress of the Idea. Yet, for our purposes, it remains, more or less, true to say that the Idea installed the following founding 'truths':

1. Human agency and responsibility, rather than Divine Will or Reason, presides over definitions of 'progress'—the Idea is thus

presented, and resented, as essentially secular/secularizing; crucially, politics no longer remains presented as *destiny* willed by Gods but as a human enterprise, often directed towards 'emancipation' from tyranny and domination.

2. The image of 'law' consequentially emerges as a human artefact, rather than a divine commandment, concerned with 'appropriate' [read 'sustainable'] distribution of human freedoms and rights within the incremental modification of the doctrine of the Reason of the state.

3. Progress stands variously constructed in terms of the march of 'Universal Reason', which in turn envisages 'civilization' in terms of 'mastery' over nature, both natural nature and human nature and in which faith in science is said to replace faith in God.

4. 'Universal reason' entails violent penetration of the non-European societies, cultures and peoples as a 'necessary' step for promoting diverse versions of the Idea enacted by the forces of colonial capitalist/imperialist, socialist domination and now of globalization.

5. Progress emerges as a material rather than a spiritual idea; thus religious traditions remain important primarily in terms of their relation to economic growth and development; witness the enormous contention spawned concerning Weber's thesis concerning the relationship between 'Puritan Ethic' and the growth of capitalism, and Marx's critique of capitalism in which form religion appears, and this needs *full emphasis*, *not* just as the 'opium of the masses' but *also* as the 'sigh of the oppressed'.

6. Governance becomes at once a matter of deliberative politics and of expertise; the relationship between trust in expert systems and trust in representative power complicates the Idea.[1]

7. Sustained critique of the Idea begins more poignantly to emerge with the Holocaust that converts 'the Camp as Nomos' of governance,[2] though curiously at the same moment cruelly bereft of any reference to Hiroshima–Nagasaki holocaust.

8. Governance by death and 'democidal' governance (Rummel 1997) emerge as the concretization of the Idea during the many

---

[1] Boaventura de Sousa Santos thus names this as 'the pillar of regulation' and 'pillar of emancipation'. See: Santos (2002, 1995). See also, Baxi (2006a).

[2] See, in particular, Agamben (1998) and Badiou (2001).

phases of the Cold War that celebrate Gulag techniques of governance on both sides of the superpower rivalry.

9. Amidst all this in turn arise the languages, logics and paralogics of contemporary inclusive human rights that seek the impossible—to imbue the art and craft of governance with human rights based responsibilities—and in the processes generate diverse forms of politics *of*, and *for*, human rights,[3] ways that redefine the contest over the redefinition of the Idea of Law and the relation between the Rule of Law for some with the Reign of Terror for others.

10. As in the period of mercantilist regimes of colonial governance, contemporary economic globalization all over redefines the Idea under whose auspices politics becomes commerce and commerce becomes politics.

I apologize for this schematic presentation of the Idea, and that too without reference to munificent sources. In the same vein, I may further mention that this presentation of the Idea by the 'masters' of European/Western thought finds an inaugural critique in the three 'Masters of Suspicion'—Marx, Nietzsche and Freud. These lineages of thought have in turn further cross-fertilized postcolonial and post-socialist, even post-feminist, confrontation with the Idea of Progress; they have exposed not just the inner contradictions of the Idea. The fecund corpus of Frantz Fanon, Edward Said, Noam Chomsky, Gayatri Spivak and more recently Eduardo Galeano,[4] critiques the Idea as racist, patriarchal, imperialistic and even genocidal, especially in its colonial and imperial imposition on the non-European peoples.

The dominant discourse concerning development translates the Idea of Progress as a universal, in which form 'development' emerges as a master frame which is context-independent, transhistorical, acivilizational notion. It renders marginal all pre-existing traditions of thought concerning development. Thus, we think with Kant, Hegel, Marx, not a Buddha or Thiruvalluvar. The Buddha presented, summarily put, development as a universal ethic addressed to the elimination

---

[3] Baxi (2006a), n. 1, presents this distinction variously.

[4] Because his work is still so little known to English-speaking audiences. I invite your attention to the inspiring work by Fischlin and Nandorfy (2002).

of the *dukkha* (suffering) outside the means of institutionalized religion and politics[5] and Thiruvalluvar, who composed the epic Tamil Vedas, the *Thirukkural*, educates us all profoundly into two kinds of development as offerings to *Mudevi* (the Goddess of Adversity) and *Lakshmi* (the Goddess of Wealth/Prosperity).[6]

In sum, 'we' think development in two ways: as a *universal idea* and also as a *universalizing project* fashioning global hegemony for the careers and itineraries of messianic, imperial/colonial/racist/patriarchal, and often genocidal domination by the 'West' of the 'Rest'. This universalizing project differentiates itself in the imageries of several complex and contradictory processes—'Westernization' (whether as 'Anglicization' or 'Franco-phonization') 'Modernization', 'McDonaldization' (Americanization) and now 'Globalization'. Thus, development emerges as constitutive of variety of diverse forms of Eurocentrism, indeed a coat of many colours as Zizek (1999) now demonstrates via the troubled threshold distinctions between 'progressive' and 'regressive' forms of Eurocentrism; and all this has been further deconstructed in some histories of caricature from Voltaire to Swift and beyond.[7] We also know full well how *vikas* (development/progress) has always entailed its other—*vinash* (developmental destruction/violence). Always at stake in 'development' is this dialectic play and war between 'development' as progress and 'development' as regressive destruction.

It may be said with justification that the founders and forerunners of Eurocentric thought necessarily sit inside our heads because they created some global histories of the modern world; they thus compel troubled negations/negotiations in the diversely constituted, and radically heterogeneous, postcolonial/post-socialist moments

---

[5] See, for a most remarkable contemporary achievement, Mishra (2004). See also, Ikeda (1998); Pyong-Jik (1979: 13–18); Dallmayr (1998) and Tirumallar (1991). And, for a wider context, see also Settar (1990). I must also here invite specific attention to the writings of Ananta Kumar Giri, a valued colleague at the Institute, which resituate 'modern' Indian political thought in relation to high Euro-American traditions of political thought concerning development.

[6] Incidentally, Lloyd and Susanne Rudolph aptly named their magisterial analysis of Indian development as *The Political Economy of Lakshmi* (Chicago: Chicago University Press, 1986).

[7] Most poignantly narrated by the remarkable 'novel' of Steven Lukes (1995), *The Curious Enlightenment of Professor Caritat: A Comedy of Ideas*.

(Dalmia 2003; Leiten 2004: 1–24 and Young 2001). True as this is, one may still ask whether it would make any difference were we to let some alternate figurations from the other histories of the Enlightenment (described poorly as the non-European Enlightenment) sit inside our heads/minds when we think development. On my part, allow me here, without further elaboration, to say that this would make a decisive difference.

One must add a 'dangerous supplement' to all this heads/minds type talk. Always, development talk presents the Idea in terms of over-rationalized conceptions of self, society and culture. It emerges as a project of rationality reform for state and civil society. In the process, stand ignored the role of sentiment and feeling, and the politics of insurgent passion. It regards protest at the itinerary of the Idea as signifying *anomie*, a state of affairs to be redressed by persuasion where possible, and force when necessary, by *normative/normalcy restoration*. However, this restoration is profoundly patriarchal because it presents Reason as hard and male, and its Other Unreason as soft and female. In un-/rethinking development, 'we' need to constantly return/revisit the feminist thinkers who have exposed and critiqued this phallic *habitus* of development theory and practice and found ways of rethinking development as other than the celebration of political rape culture. Feminizing conceptions of development remains an urgent necessity of contemporary historicity.

The tasks, however, remain difficult even to outline because even decent men and women 'spontaneously' offer and stand otherwise asked, even required, under the banner of civic patriotism to support the violence of the global politics of 'regime change' and the endless 'war *on* terror' that Kofi Annan now presents as combating 'catastrophic terrorism'. Thus, emerges a new politics appropriating passion in the pursuit of collective human security; this itself becomes a universalizing form of politics, and politicking that fully legislates the daring of the production of expedient regime—serving political truths in the service of some messianically ordained human futures everywhere. Clearly, impassioned politics conscripts feeling and sentiment differently than the feminist 'project'.

Further, in some dialectical modes, contemporary human rights activist, and the New Social Movements, praxes seek to engage politics of redefinition of 'development' by reimagining the Idea of Progress more recently represented by the World Social Forum motto: 'Other Worlds Are Possible.' Both these forms entail the celebration of passional logics, and rhetorics, concerning 'development' and pit against the Reason of Globalization the Unreason of Human rights and the aspiration for global redistributive justice.

I remain fully aware that the foregoing observations require fuller enunciation—a task, perhaps, of another conversational occasion with the Institute?

Development as Developmentalism

The enormous labours of theoretic welfare/social choice economists aspire to eschew 'ideological' politics of Unreason. They, in the main, outline 'development' in terms of 'welfarism'—a theoretic stance with its insistence on the Pigou–Dalton Principle, with all its further equity-imbued reworking, that 'social policy should be based solely on individual well-being with no reference to "fairness" or "rights"'.[8] All this, as we notice towards the end of this address, hugely complicates my presentation of development as exercises in political largesse.

Regardless, for the present moment, it remains worth noting that this genre remains concerned with drawing some necessary, and manageable, distinctions between 'development' as a multidimensional and ubiquitous process of social transformation and 'developmentalism' as a dominant ideology, or as several histories of mentality, of directed social change.

Developmentalism may be broadly described as the discourse of power, that is the official mindset of key globally networked policy and political actors dedicated to the pursuit of economic growth. It is a complex 'regime of representation' (in terms of Escobar [1985]) in which relevant knowledges and languages produce the 'truths' of development. Such truths or truth-claims include the following:

- Economic growth is a sine qua non for development, even when its indicators and benchmarks remain subject to contestation/molestation among the erudite knowledge producers.

---

[8] See for a most recent exposition, Alder and Sanchirico (2006). Even a lay reader of this overview and reconstruction of 'welfarism' stands to benefit by wrestling with some languages of formalized economic theory. Much 'real' thought thus presented suggest, after all, the extraordinary difficulties of insinuating the languages of justice and equity in everyday developmental choice-making by governmental/intergovernmental policymakers, whether elected officials or the more radically unaccountable ones.

- Such growth occurs 'best' in conditions of 'free market' institutions and processes, fully respecting the sacrosanct rights of property and contract.
- Economic growth as development requires as free, as humanly possible, movement of global capital (via international trade and commerce and facilitation of the flows of direct foreign investment).
- Such growth facilitates, in the eye of comparative history, human and social development because it contributes to the progressive elimination of substantial 'unfreedoms', an insight first developed by Karl Marx via the contradictory emancipatory passage of labour 'from iron cage to silken chains' and further differently elaborated by Amartya Sen (1999) notably in his *Development as Freedom*.
- The state, and its laws, ought to serve primarily the purpose of 'wealth-maximization' (the programschrift of the law-and-economics Chicago School of thought).
- Legal and even human rights should be accordingly conceived as 'factors of production' always sensitive to the problems of 'transaction costs' (a genre pioneered by Ronald Coase).
- Legal and human rights thus emerge as powers of some to *inflict lawful harm* on others, subject to state/law invigilation directed to preserve 'free' market and 'fair' competition.
- The relatively autonomous adjudicative power remains charged with responsibility to provide ways and means of 'rational'/'well-ordered' adjustments of conflicted interests of the fractions of capital as so many forms of negotiating the wider landscape of class conflict between 'capital' and 'labour'.
- The province and function of a relatively autonomous adjudicature—interpretation and implementation of constitutional and international human rights values, standards and norms—must be disciplined; that is, judicial policy/lawmaking ought to respect macroeconomic development decisions/choices made by the supreme executive and judicial activism ought to be so *structurally adjusted* as not to pose any terminal challenge to the free flow of capital across state borders and boundaries.[9]

---

[9] I name this as marking transition from the Universal Declaration of Human Rights paradigm to the trade-related, market-friendly human rights paradigm. See, Baxi, n. 1, at 235–75.

- Likewise, even the corrupt sovereign must always and everywhere remain possessed of wide and vast militarized powers to hold in check the power of protest and mobilization by the 'Old' (primarily trade union) and the 'New' social movements (primarily human rights and identity/autonomy/secessionist movements).

I do not suggest by any means that developmentalism which thrives on erudite knowledge production stands always geared to serve the orders of hegemonic dispensation, or that it necessarily entails any consensus concerning the ends and means of development. Thus, some large dissenting histories of developmental theory and practice remain precious. These need to be taken more seriously, I believe, than is actually the case, particularly with some postmodernist, and some easy-minded activist, critiques that condemn all development thought and practice as comprising projects of radical evil.

Both the extremist celebration of developmentalism and its critique, however, seriously pose the issue of redistribution of agency, rights and capabilities, and recognition enriching in the process the revisability of the 'new' conceptions of development. This stands often compendiously described in terms of 'sustainable development'. In part, this notion signifies complex legacies of some tormented itineraries—'Another Development', 'Alternative Development'. More recently, the 'post-development' talk re-crafts and retools the 'sustainable development' talk. These, at the end of the day, or rather the long night, resonate well with the Eurocentric critiques of development or the 'dark side' of modernity but do not at the same moment altogether escape the Eurocentric inheritance.

To wholly suddenly switch contexts, may I invite your attention to the magisterial work *Global Business Regulation* by John Braithwaite and Peter Drahos (Braithwaite and Drahos 2000) view the Penelope's Web—'webs of coercion' and of 'persuasion'—entailing many a conflict between developmental actors and developmental principles. Indeed, they caution us against macro-conceptions of development that disregard the dynamics of painstaking resistance to, and renegotiation of, the on-the-ground policies and measures of development.

In evoking this very large thematic, I here suggest, perforce without any further benefit of elaboration, that this cognitive dissonance in the developmentalism talk/discourse remains still anchored in some *magical* belief systems resting on the first premise that development as growth is a good 'thing'. It is said to assure some trickle-down equity change, based on a 'theory that "a rising tide lifts all boats"'.[10] However, the jury it still out on such claims as even the United Nations Millennium Development Goals and Targets so poignantly demonstrate; indeed, the most impoverished continue to suffer and die both in the short and long run, even as their unconscionable suffering continues to provide the grist to the mill of the developers.

The achievement of that good 'thing' proceeds through a new principle of classification and epistemic consolidation that divides the human species in two broad globalized classes: the *developers* and the *developees*. The developers and the developees, we ought to note, remain internally, and often radically, heterogeneous. How far reductive critiques of developmentalism may serve their stated purposes remains an open question.

Yet it does come to pass that most developees often stress that developmentalism conceived as economic growth dreadfully clones the ideology of a cancer cell! The developees thus often regard developmentalism, conceived as growth for its own sake, as the unfoldment of destruction of autoimmunity, a genre that Jacques Derrida, in his later writing, has so presciently narrated for us (Derrida 2003: 95–96).

In some responsive ways the practitioners of development expertise begin to speak to us concerning economic 'growth' with 'equity', providing some stunning examples of welfare economic type knowledge production. This genre seriously urges governmental policymakers to remain equally concerned with the winners and losers of developmental policies. Dominated by some profoundly vexatious issues concerning ex ante/ex post welfare functions and of distributional equity for the losers, this esoteric-looking discourse moves at least seriously towards a 'humane economics'. The issues thus raised remain crucial for any serious pursuit of this combinatory, and inherently mildly redistributive, 'developmentalist' conceptions.

Developmentalism also furnishes some archives of mortal combat between the actually existing classes of the developers and the developees. Surely, in the contemporary conjuncture, we all know how the internally differentiated, and radically heterogeneous classes, of

---

[10] I derive this expression from an article by the Chilean Ambassador to India. See Hein (2006: 8).

developees contest, often violently, the three 'Ds' of contemporary economic globalization: denationalization, disinvestment, and deregulation.[11]

Notions of Development: Twelve Questions

In a minimal sense, development begins when the developers make judgements that the existing state of affairs needs improvement. This at once raises difficult questions concerning the standpoint from which the existing state of affairs may be described as 'bad', or even 'evil', and how the 'good' of 'improvement' may be conceived. Improvement may mean simply bettering the bad or it may signify praxes of transformative thought directed to substantial, if not massive, redistributive social change. All too often, in real life, improvement remains grudgingly ameliorative rather than radically transformative at least from the perspectives of the worst-off.

Developmentalism valorizes the Idea of Progress in ways that in the past 'justified' the barbarity of *insufficiently* civilized European world in their practices of 'civilizing' the already *sufficiently* civilized nations and in the present through a similar destruction of Thirdworldism, as an alternate way of envisaging progress (Baxi 2006b: 713–25). In any event, the previously more sufficiently civilized nations and peoples now remain threatened with rhetoric, and the reality, of extinction by the managers, agents and forces of 'globalization'. I will have to forego here the privilege of further unpacking this dense formulation but I continue to hope that *saharadyi pathak* (literally meaning *readers with a heart*, a notion constituted by some pioneers such as the twelfth-century Kumarila Bhatt, in the early Indian hermeneutic tradition that stressed acts and performances of empathetic reading) may intimately grasp this. Allow me to pose then in this context at least 12 questions concerning 'development', in ways that obviously excite further refinement.

First, the *constructive arena:* how best may the existing 'order of things' be problematized: *merely* as contexts facilitating governmentally informed change decisions? And what may indeed count as 'change' in the *short* as well as the *long* run? Of course, there often

---

[11] See Baxi, n.1, Chapters 8 and 9. See also, Randeria (2003: 305–28).

exists a broad agreement amongst the policy winners/losers concerning 'evils' that need to be remedied both by state and social action: for example, illiteracy, female foeticide, lack of primary health care, infant mortality, indifferent maternal health, lack of access to means of articulating grievances in ways that may possibly ameliorate structural/distributional injustices. However, often enough the policy losers disagree with *state-ways* that entirely marginalize the *folkways* in the designation of some 'bads' and the ways and the 'best' means for moving ahead. Thus arise some extraordinary dilemmas concerning 'pluralist' visions and pursuits concerning development.

Second, the *agency/representation question*: Who may and with authority make both symbolic and instrumental change decisions? *Who may develop whom*? Who may constitute themselves as *developers* and how may the classes of the *developees* be constructed? Is this a question primarily of *representation*, the distribution of political and legal authority to enunciate legislation of contexts of improvement? Or, is it an ethical, even a spiritual, question going beyond the constitution of the sources of external authority and relating to power of the development of moral/communitarian 'sources of self' resisting domination?

Third, the *relative autonomy/dependency question*: How far in an increasingly interdependent/networked world, may the change-*agents* remain relatively independent in arriving at change *decisions*? When may dependence on external contexts justifiably influence/dictate the situation of *choice* within which the change agents may then proceed to make *decisions*?[12] Contrary to some common understanding, the problem of autonomy/dependence haunts not just the governmental change actors but also social change actors, including specifically human rights and development NGOs.

Fourth, the *distributional question*: What 'primary moral goods' may thus be distributed? And how may we conceive these? How best equal concern and respect for all be assured within the aggravating as well as finally un-redressed asymmetrical *distribution of material resources*? Further, the distributional question raises the issue: How are the opportunities for, and burdens of, change to be equitably apportioned between the *developers* and the *developees*?

---

[12] Note the folk saying which translates the sovereignty of consumer choice as follows: 'free' markets agents *decide* what the consumers then proceed to *choose!*

The Indian constitution sought to develop a tolerably clear response to this distributional question entailing conflict between liberty and equality through the device of directive principles of state policy which prescribe such organization of community resources that best subserves 'common good' and avoids 'common detriment'. Of course, the crystallization of these notions was left in trust for the further constitutionally informed practices of governance. These have more often betrayed this vision of development as a process which *disproportionately benefits the Indian impoverished*. In 1950, the Directive Principles of State Policy mandated governance solicitude for the 'weaker sections of society'. However, after 50 plus years of the Indian developmental experiment, these 'weaker sections' have been progressively and variously *further weakened*![13] How justifiably may the developers ask of the developees (peoples and communities affected by development measures) that they willingly bear some 'costs'—in fact, intensely disproportionate burdens—here and now arising, in the expectation that this may make more secure a 'better future' for future generations?

Fifth and related, the *time dimension*: The 'time' of the 'development' remains elusive unless further categorized; we may speak of it variously as 'enduring time ... deceptive time ... erratic time ... cyclical time ... retarded time ... time in advance ... alternative time'.[14] Much developmentalism discourse thinks that the accelerated time (time in advance) also constitutes the enduring time of development. However, the latter temporality is differentially constructed for some worst-off developees; theirs remains the lived and embodied estates of 'retarded', 'cyclical', 'erratic' and 'deceptive' time. Crucial also remain incommensurate the notions of 'alternate time'. The cosmologically constructed Brahminic time thus profoundly contests the Article 17 constitutionally ordained time that so articulately outlaws the imposition of discrimination and disability on the ground of 'untouchability'. The assimilationist constitutional time of 'development' provides little room for any fuller recognition for the cosmologies of indigenous peoples of India, so crudely and expediently

---

[13] At the level of history of ideas, the Indian constitution-makers uncannily and presciently anticipated the genius of John Rawls who later invents the famous *difference principle* (roughly put, inequalities are justified if and only if they advance the expectations of the well-being of the worst-off).

[14] Here to borrow the insightful contribution of Gell (2001).

summated as the 'scheduled tribes'. Likewise, the rate of *accelerated historic change*, under the current zodiac of Indian globalization furiously enacts new constituencies of rightless human beings.[15]

Sixth, the *spatiality concerns:* How may the developers and developees construct, together and separately, the spaces for development? How far may the developees justifiably say that in a political economy of combined and uneven development, 'development' always constitutes the *geographies of injustice*? Is Indian federalism, both in its constantly reworked principle, design and detail to be after all read as mapping the practices of internal colonization, or what Andre Gunter Franck in an international context famously named as the *'development of underdevelopment?'* How far may one situate the discourse naming the BIMARU Indian states (sick or failed states within the Indian federation, originated by the demographer Ashis Bose) in terms of internal colonization that diverts the proceeds of natural resource monopolies in the federating units to the tasks of national economic development via a quiet but by no means a gentle disregard of felt distributional injustices? How far may we read the historic consequences that foment some distinctive Indian insurrectionary spaces which protest differential development or maldevelopment and often seek violently to install new conceptions of human and social development? How may developmental talk fully address these types of concerns?

Seventh, the *directionality concerns:* How may development conceptions define and redefine, imagine and reimagine some collective national and infra-national human futures? I use the term 'infra' rather than 'sub' national futures with a view to rupture the hegemonic character of the contrast. Sub-national descriptions employ federalist constructs of developmentalism. In contrast, 'infra-national' directs attention to the millennial losers of postcolonial development articulated, for example, in India by the victims of the Bhopal catastrophe and the Narmada Bachao Andolan and elsewhere, for example, by Ken Saro Wiwa for the Ogoni peoples and the Zapatista Movement.

This innocuous posing of the question raises a cornucopia of developmental concerns. First, this poses interrogation of the imagination of the national and infra-national human futures. Second, it poses the sovereign concern of 'justice' of development, in which

---

[15] See, generally, Baxi (2006c: 263–84) and the materials there cited.

distribution of rights with accompanying human freedoms contend both with 'welfarism' and 'order' conceived in terms of the tasks of the promotion of collective human security. When human rights and freedoms stand inequitably distributed, when 'welfare' remain wholly constituted by regimes of political largesse, the impoverished masses always carry the potential of collective political violence, which in turn stands represented as a threat to collective human security.

The developers ask of the developees some tenacious order of historic patience in 'negotiating' some perpetually fostered political and structural injustices. When the latter fail to display this exemplary virtue, the developers insist that collective political violence 'distorts' development and deploy the might of the armed violence of the state against the impoverished. How may all this be fully situated within the development talk? Put another way, how may the visions of a just social order for the present and future generations coequally address the rights/freedoms questions alongside with order/security concerns? This poses a serious concern now amidst what I name as two contemporary 'terror wars': the 'war *on* terror' and the 'war *of* terror' (see Baxi 2005a: 7–43). Third and contentiously broadly put, we arrive at the doorstep of definitions of development that 'legitimate' some ineluctable orders of the production of human rightlessness as its necessary prerequisite.

In turn, the *eighth* question concerns *the violence of developmental judgements/decisions*: that is, the question of coercively imposed drastic transformation, as against fashioning participatory consensual measures for attaining 'improvement'. The figure of a fasting Medha Patkar protesting the wholly arbitrarily revised height of the Narmada Dam without the least concern for the plight of dispossessed peoples alongside with the Bhopal violated Indian humanity still struggling for justice, in the 21st year of their catastrophic suffering, narrate to us, even as I write/speak, a contemporary moment of this poignant dramaturgy of development.

Ninth arises the rather complex question of *militarization of governance practices*. The Indian constitution singularly inaugurates this tradition of governance. It encodes people's right to life and liberty (Article 21) alongside with same awesome powers of 'preventive detention' (Article 22) continually and cruelly, redefined by dragnet security legislation. As I demonstrated in my *Crisis of the Indian Legal System*, the exponential growth of paramilitary forces has resulted not just in an expansion of the rather awesome might of the Indian state but has also generated new classes of rightless Indian 'citizens'. Since then, many insightful observers have further demonstrated the anti-democratic dimension of this development.[16]

'Militarization' of Indian governance remains a descriptively complex affair because while governmental developmental decision-makers regard militarized state response to collective political violence as rectifying distortions in the course and the career of Indian 'development', insurgent social actors regard such recourse as putting humane governance/development, as it were, back on its course. They suggest that organized civil society collective political violence serves better the cause of 'development' than developmental state violence. They seem even to further suggest that assorted New Social Movements only provide new fig leaves, further mystifying developmental dominance and hegemony. The question, then, is: How may we best read/narrate organized insurrectionary political violence within the contexts and conjunctures of the Indian development?

In this context at least partially emerges by no means any effete concern with the *tenth* question concerning *orders of reciprocal respect* between 'governmental' and 'social' change agents, the problem of deference towards dialogical pluralism, going beyond mutual paranoia and informing the tasks of evolving social cooperation towards consensual social transformation.

Eleventh, we also confront some *learning curve type issues* concerning the prospects of cumulatively benign accumulation of social and governmentally shared understandings, both from the fairy tales and horror stories concerning experiments in, and experience of, development. Surely, we must ask of development experience everywhere how such cumulative learning may ever occur and indeed be put to some 'wise use' by developers and developees alike. I sincerely hope I remain wrong in saying that the Indian development experience plots such a learning curve, to say the least, rather indifferently.

Twelfth, (without being exhaustive) the *reversibility dimension of development*. Often enough the disagreements concerning the idea of development and the means to achieve it run so deep that some dominant notions of development stand perceived by other individuals and groups as constituting 'regression'. 'Regression' of course remains a value-loaded conception but so remains 'development'. I do

---

[16] I have in view especially the valued writings of A.G. Noorani and Ujjwal Kumar Singh; see, more recently, Khalidi (2003).

not think that one may make much sense of development without its other—'regression'.

As early as 1982 in my *Crisis of the Indian Legal System* (Baxi 1982), I suggested that we distinguish the notion of *regression* from that of the *lack* or *failure* of development. I there offered, via a detailed narrative of the Bhagalpur blindings situation, reading regression as a situation in which the proclaimed values of development suffer annihilating devaluation by conjoint exertions of governmental and civil society actors alike. Revisiting 'regression' since then furnishes an even more tormenting register. If we were to read the valiant struggles waged by the Narmada Bachao Andolan as pre-eminently protesting failure of development, surely the situations of 'ethnic cleansing', Indian-style, that enact, with grave impunity, for example, the 1984 Sikh Massacre and recently Gujarat 2002 epitomise regression. Both the situations of politics of regime-sponsored/tolerated human abuse and human rights violation and mass cruelty were represented, with active participation of dominant civil society actors, as situations of *misfortune*, not *injustice*.[17] In both, genocidal/democidal practices were presented as events of political *misfortune*, not as structurally inscribed/embedded organized political injustice. In both the residues of injustice stood unredeemed, so much so that the Gujarat still remains celebrated in terms of a paradigm of overall *good governance*![18]

Forgive me for mentioning in this context the first dreaded 'M' word. The Marx of *Capital, Volume One* carries an enduring message: the bourgeois (and one may now add also the socialist, and now hyper-globalizing) notions concerning the *rule of law* remain accompanied always by the *reign of terror*, and may even remain inconceivable outside this contradictory relationship. For the present moment, allow me to suggest that regression occurs when 'development' policies seek to escalate the *reign of terror* both as a *necessary* and *sufficient* condition for the attainment of the *rule of law* pursuits. For this reason alone, I have always maintained that the world will be a less unhappy place for the politics of human hope when it acquires per a thousand theorists of development even 10 theorists of regression.

---

[17] To here evoke the germinal distinction offered by Judith Shklar in her *Faces of Injustice* (Shklar 1990). See also, Baxi (2005b: 332–83).

[18] On a different register, the gifted and agonizing corpus of Mahasweta Devi in her deeply poignant remains deeply relevant for understanding the several moments of the Indian regression. I have particularly in view her *Bashai Tudu* (Devi 1990) and *Choti Munda and His Arrow* (Devi 2002).

Some Distinctive Itineraries of Indian Development

This cluster of 12 concerns/considerations stands variously cognized in different itineraries of the Indian development vision and experience. How I wish that all of us on this public occasion enjoyed the resources of time, tenacity and synergy to more precisely relate each of the 12 questions to these distinctive itineraries!

Regardless, please allow me to archive these in rough and bold, but not hopefully indifferent, strokes because the Foundation Day Lecture provides no scope for monographic analysis, which must await labours of another day. What follows is rather a crude summation of several large histories of decisive moments of rupture/fissure within the Indian development talk/discourse. I may by way of a prefatory observation say that that these 12 concerns remain differentially distributed in these moments.

The Mohandasian Conceptions

At the outset, then, I believe that it remains necessary to retrieve the Mohandasian legacy concerning development ethic.[19] As one more largely drawn to Ambedkar, I find it somewhat difficult to do full justice to the Mahatma legacy (Baxi 1995: 122–49).

Even so, I must summarily note here that India was fortunate to have the Mahatma of the *Hind Swaraj*, who critiqued development as mindless Westernization. He regarded as toxic the Western liberal political institutions, processes and principles, and suggested in their place the institution of communitarian collective self-governance based on fraternity and non-injurious exercise of freedom and rights. Precisely because of this daring, his name may only be recalled in the safety of an empty ritual on two occasions: the day of his birth and the day of his assassination. For each of the remaining 363 days each year since the Independence, his political successors function and flourish blithely as assassins of his memory. In a deep irony, his

---

[19] I use the term Mohandasian, because his last name has since long become a political trademark and his middle name was appropriated by the popular Doordarshan espionage serial named *Karamchand*! Regardless of all this, I commend to interested readers the eminent corpus of Professor Thomas Pantham, which offers some remarkable ways of reading Mohandas. See also, Rudolph and Rudolph (2006).

name is soiled in each and every moment of transaction of the Indian rupee notes; the Mahatma who protested wealth acquisition now translates into an icon constituting a 'legal tender' for an independent India, which has otherwise fully relegated his luminous memory to constantly refurbished political dustbins.

Arthur Koestler (1960) in his *Lotus and the Robot* naming all this as 'Bapucracy' said witheringly that if the 'West' was thus toxic, the Mahatma after all installed as his political heir Jawaharlal Nehru, as a 'chief poisoner'! I will have to, for lack of time, forego some enormous public pleasure of deconstructing Koestler! But it remains pertinent to note that this legacy was further enacted by Acharya Vinoba Bhave and Jai Prakash Narain at national level and remains still nurtured at micro-levels of invisible politics by a whole variety of endangered species comprising minuscule and live Mohandasians.

In this vision, *development* talk may not be divorced from tasks of *justice*. For Mohandas, justice stood defined by forms of peaceful, non-violent struggles; the idea of *justice as struggle* remains a most distinctive contribution of Mohandasian theory and practice of people-centred development. Justice as a virtue of solidarity in struggles of the suffering peoples always signified concerns for justice as redistributive, or *not at all*. In Mohandas, justice as struggle emerges both as a concern of the ethics of participation and as a substantive ethics of *sarvodaya*, the equal development of all, in which ownership of means of production in a few hands constitutes a sacred trust for all.[20]

The notion of trusteeship was Mohandas' answer to violent socialism; the capitalist was entitled to accumulation of profits only because he served, finally, the ends of socially just distribution. This meant, then, both the capitalist and the working classes owed collective fidelity to development, oriented to improving the plight of the rightless, dispossessed, disadvantaged and deprived masses of the Indian impoverished conjured by the image of governance as *daridranarayan*, a secular incarnation which so richly conceptualized an alternative to the paradigm of state 'welfarism'.

Lest all this may sound quaint to some Chennai, and Indian, hyperglobalizing ears, it needs saying that Mohandas presciently prefigured

---

[20] It is another matter that an eminent Gujarati Marxian, Dinkar Mehta witheringly caricatured Sarvodaya by the maxim: 'Let an ant double its size and so let the elephant!'

much contemporary discourse concerning ethical and human rights entities, passing currently in the languages of corporate social responsibilities of multinational corporations and related business entities (Baxi 2006a: 276–302). For Mohandas, development ethics remained *inconceivable* outside the development of business and professional ethic. In this regard, the Nobel Laureate Amartya Sen remains an unconscious and partial heir to Mohandas when he re-codifies, in *Development as Freedom*, transparency and accountability obligations of the agents and managers of liberal 'free' market processes and institutions!

More crucial, I believe, remains the Mohandasian legacy concerning development as a *form of praxes of non-violent social change*. This is no doubt a very complex inheritance, because it speaks to violence in all its habitats, in civil society as well as state formative practices. In a broad outline, we may read this as an aspiration to promote a political and moral economy of consensual rather than force-based pursuit of developmental tasks and decisions. In a contemporary idiom, this signifies practices of participatory, self-determinative pursuit by human beings as *subjects* rather than *objects* of development. It counsels wise avoidance of recourse to coercion, force, fraud, corruption and even terror in the wielding of state power and prowess in the enforcement of developmental decisions.

In sum, it at least advocates, as a political virtue, citizen immunity from militarized practices of self-styled 'good governance'. Further, it disarms militant forms of protest that have as its aim, or its effect, caused large-scale destruction of public property and wanton annihilating insurgent violence against human beings.

No votary of *unjust social peace*, howsoever constructed/imposed, Mohandas exemplified the deployment of his spiritual body (and the bodies of some of his ardent followers) as a site of struggle against colonial imperialism; he invented an entirely ethical 'technology of the self' (to here adapt Michael Foucault's luminous phrase) in protest against structurally imposed/adjusted forms of political injustice. For him, the *suffering of the just* (a phrase deeply beloved of Saint Thomas Aquinas) always provided a fecund site for resistance and struggle directed to disinvestment of the authority of authors of conceptions of development and their development *telos* conceived merely as planned social change from the above. Citizen insurrection, in Mohandas, is a form of civil disobedience that always contests 'development' by *molestation* (to borrow a phrase from Edward Said) of the 'authority of authority', indeed historically most productive when accompanied by conscientious adoption of pacific means. Mohandas promoted a truly republican and deeply communitarian understanding of 'development' contrasted with the rather ethically indifferent flourishing of the vestiges of the Indian plebiscitary democracy. He emphasized, Aristotle-like, the heavily burdened notion of citizen as a being who knows both how to *rule* and how to be *ruled*. For him, then it is never ethically *enough* to contest regime-based development decisions (these indeed may not be *otherwise!*). Rather, citizen protest at developmental decisions ought always to weigh the alternate choices they may feasibly pursue in an imagined situation when they, in turn, occupy the commanding heights of governance powers.

Mohandas thus developed a difficult encoding of the ethic of citizen protest, an ethic of responsibility burdening social movements with the Herculean tasks of installing blueprints of just governance and just development; for him, social and human rights activism necessarily had to transcend pyrrhic satisfactions arising from state-basting.

In this, he thus anticipated almost a century earlier John Rawls' notion of the 'original position' as an envelope for social contract between the rulers and the ruled. I may not belabour this obvious point save noting that with Mohandas this social contract requires everyday negotiation/renewal by conscientious citizens, as the would-be-rulers, not just as habitually protestant actors thriving on exposé of the quotidian pathologies of state power, and yet also burdened finally as well with all the excesses of state mandated/managed measures, means, methods, moods and messages concerning 'development'.

The Nehruvian Mediation

I name the Nehruvian model of development as 'mediation' because it creatively adapts the Mohandasian legacy in terms of presenting an inaugural postcolonial version of the idea of progress both within and beyond the framing discourse of the European Enlightenment. In a sense, the contrast cannot be greater or more poignant. Mohandas insisted not on just *freedom* but on *just* freedom. In contrast, when coerced by Andrew Marlux to produce a one-liner, Jawaharlal defined the problematic of the Indian development as building a *strong state with just means,* not a *just state with strong means.*[21]

This remarkable feat included diverse features, which may only be here presented with the epistemic violence of Microsoft—induced notorious bulleted presentation, here straddling the 12 concerns of, and for, development:

- The pursuit of economic growth placed emancipatory faith in big science and high technology, and the vaunted celebration of the diffusion of 'the scientific temper' amongst the developers and developees alike.
- The syncretic configuration combining the 'best' elements of classical liberalism with those of 'scientific socialism'.
- The development of constitutional secularism as gateway for inclusive and rational politics, facilitating individual and social excellence through *achieved* rather than *ascribed* identities; thus already anticipating the newly fangled languages of contemporary multiculturalisms.
- The notion of directed social transformation through national five-year plans, having among their principal aims the achievement of accelerated self-reliant growth infused with homeopathic doses of social equity.
- The recasting of the Indian National Congress, and its postcolonial imagination, along what Antonio Gramsci famously named as the 'Modern Prince'.
- The penchant for safeguarding executive supremacy, via the already historically superannuated notion of parliamentary sovereignty, from expansive judicial review process and power and within this the inculcation of the principle of Cabinet responsibility wholly consistent with an aristocratic and oligarchic role and function for the office and authority of the Prime Minister.
- Nurturance of the broad principle of federalism, though held within the expedient detail inscribed in the constitution, always animated by the 'sprit of reform': in sum, a creative attempt to hold within the logics of centralization some enclaves of democratic decentralization.

---

[21] I have elaborated this in my two essays in Dhavan and Paul (1992).

- Accentuated emphases on the third tier of federalism via institutions of *panchayati raj* institutions and schemes for community development, further fostered by the flows of Prime Ministerial communicative power over and across the installed hierarchies of the federal principle and detail.
- Endeavours at 'nation-building' through broad political consensus where possible and recourse to some awesome powers of preventive detention and militarized governance where necessary.
- The development of ethical diplomacy through leadership of the non-aligned movement, within and outside the United Nations, that endowed the voice of Indian 'civilization' to be powerfully heard across the cacophonic and cruel pursuits of the Cold War global politics.
- The articulation of a world-remarkable, and non-Eurocentric, *jus cosmopilticum* hospitality for South Asian enforced diasporic communities.

Clearly, we travel a very great distance from the quintessential Mohandasian legacy of human and social development which at the same moment still remains somehow not entirely disloyal to it. This form of hybrid 'loyalty' entailed both a reconstruction and placing at the margins of state formative practices some resurgent re-articulations of the Mohandasian legacy.

The Post-Nehruvian Moments

The post-Nehruvian unfoldment of notions of development theory and practice remain most difficult to decipher, outside perhaps in terms of similar strains and forms of hybrid disloyalty to the Nehruvian legacy. But some rich narratives remain available in their formative elements, as it were. These include variously:

- The recasting of the Indian state as state finance capitalist in Indira Gandhi's accession to power via the abolition of privy purses and the nationalization of banking and insurance markets with a stated yet inadequately realized lofty aim of empowering the Indian impoverished.
- The increased tendency towards undemocratic centralization of state power, already immanent in the Nehurvian paradigm

but never before the Emergency of 1975–76 presenting state authoritarianism as the best possible way of redeeming constitutional pledges for the Indian impoverished.

- The several post-Emergency moments that further reinstall and accentuate democratic good governance as a superior ethical mode servicing the goal of 'growth with equity'.
- The imagery of development as an affair and a project of *technopolitics* in the Rajiv Gandhi Era, during which Indian development truly becomes a 'pilot project'.
- The eclipse of notion of agrarian land redistribution that gets subsequently translated/diffused by political regimes into national and regional politics of expansive regimes of affirmative action.
- The simultaneous emergences of a radical/reactionary growth of the *Hindutva*, more specifically *Moditva*, generated politics of identity, which seeks to redefine development in terms of new forms of protection of the rights of 'Hindu' dominant majority.
- The further emergence of development, especially since the late 1980s, as a discourse placed primarily at the service of the human flourishing and well-being of the dominant hyper-globalizing new Indian middle classes.
- The creeping transformation of new social and human rights *movements* into *markets* which while marshalling the power of Indian globalizing print and electronic media, challenge governance legitimation (via social action/public interest advocacy networks) also ultimately recuperate the statist narratives of 'development' as 'progress'.
- The globalizing conscription of transactional relations of solidarity via translational advocacy networks (TANs) that somewhat uneasily negotiate/straddle social action for global justice.

Since then, and I beseech your forgiveness for an enormous encapsulation, the extraordinary passage from the Mahatma to (to mark now an enormously signifying practice of a third 'M' word) Manmohan enact with some cruel poignancy the prowess of instrumental reason legislating politics of interests, fully disregarding the utopic conflict of visions (politics of values).

Even if some of us may want to rest content by saying that there is simply no way to bridge whole continents of dissensus concerning the meanings of development, yet an order of *sovereign difference*, does after all emerge, a difference that marks off and sets apart altogether two different obsessions. On the one hand, the magnificent obsession constructing development as an affair of social justice and human rights and on the other the meagre, the lean and mean, obsession with development as an affair of technopolitics of 'good governance' in a hyper-globalizing India whose ultimate ambition is to make India a safe harbour for the flows of direct foreign investment subserving some incipient future histories of India as a global player/power.

The Right to Development Talk

The United Nations 1985 Declaration on the Right to Development globalizes in some profound ways the message of the Mahatma, in an adaptable and globally portable version. The right to development accrues both to nations and to 'individuals who make up nations'. It asserts that human beings ought never to be regarded as *objects* of development; rather, the human person is the 'central subject of development process' which should make 'the human being the main participant and beneficiary of development'. Development itself stands described in terms of 'appropriate policies which aim at constant improvement' and 'well-being of the entire population and of all individuals'. Such improvement may only flow when the political order ensures 'active, free, and meaningful participation' of all individuals. Participation stands construed as human rights-based in two distinct ways: first, all individuals should have available to them internationally defined human rights norms and standards and second they bear as 'responsibility for development' that requires full respect on their part for human rights of all. Participation in 'all spheres' thus forms the cornerstone of development promoting 'full realization of all human rights'. The state in thus devising developmental policy stands summoned to eliminate 'obstacles to development' defined as emanating from violation of human rights, whether endogenously or exogenously caused. Put another way, developmental policy regimes that thrive by offering justifications for the production of human rightlessness constitute an ensemble of 'obstacles' to development.

I have critically reviewed all this in my work entitled *Mabrino's Helmet: Human Rights for a Changing World* (Baxi 1994). Since then various attempts have been made to operationalize this dizzying rhetoric in terms of further United Nations labours concerning the *development of the right to development*, that is, crystallization of the specific range of 'component rights', a task to which Arjun Sengupta, in his role as the United Nations Independent Expert on the right to development, has made a notable contribution. At the very same moment, peoples' movements also map new futures for the human right to development, notably and in so many uncanny modes, summated by the World Social Forum motto: 'Other Worlds Are Possible' (Sen et al. 2004; Sen and Kumar 2003). At stake, then, remains the multitudinous authorship of notions of human rights–based notions of development deflating univocal authority of state/globalizing actors.

This occasion scarcely provides room for any detailed consideration of the contemporary institutional and normative histories of the right to development. It is eminently clear that there exist few enforceable duties corresponding to the core rights to human and social development. Yet the Declaration provides a number of imperfect obligations which still remain important both for policy and struggle. The further concretization of these obligations necessarily remains the work of time and activist judicial actors, including the Supreme Court of India, have often used the Declaration as informing the power of constitutional interpretation in pro-impoverished manner.

The greater challenge to the right to development talk emanates from the amplitude of the notions of *human rights neutral/independent ways* of governance. The developers thus powerfully suggest that governance as an ongoing affair may simply thus become impossible and improbable if even the imperfect duties attaching to the right to development were to be attached to each and every governmental act of choice-making, decision and conduct. A prime example of this stands furnished by international trade and economic diplomacy emplotting comparative economic advantage in a highly competitive globalized trade and commerce. Yet another example stands furnished by the complex Manmohan–Bush 'nuclear deal'. Even granting that all this may have important human rights repercussions, it remains eminently arguable that strategic or economic diplomacy may best proceed by foregrounding the right to development concerns and considerations. Both these are very complex examples but they issue an important reminder: insistence on human rights based governance may ill serve the 'cause' of development. A certain disregard of human rights at the level of economic and security diplomacy remains presented thus as inevitable. The adverse human rights side effects do of course pose some difficulty for 'legitimate', 'good' governance. Politics as governance (both as representational and deliberative) then emerges as the art and craft of 'managing' the perception and reality of the side effects.

The notion of human rights *neutral* governance, and the techniques it spawns, achieves several discernible effects. *First*, it relieves the developers of any major human rights responsibility for developmental failures and disasters, thus further exempting them from any detailed regime of legal accountability and liability. *Second*, and related, it escalates potential for techno-politics, a form of governance which strives to depoliticize developmental decisions by various governance tricks, especially statistical warfare concerning the number of peoples deeply adversely affected by various developmental projects, the magical manipulation of time and budgetary cost overruns in such projects and of the actual measures of compensation, resettlement and rehabilitation.[22] *Third*, it provides for little or no room for popular/participatory monitoring and invigilation of massive corruption and fraud, outside a deeply colonial legal framework provided by the *Prevention of Corruption Act*.[23] *Fourth*, it also weakens overall the role of the Indian Parliament as an 'organization of accountability' (Roy and Mehta 2006); thus, *fifth*, further converting, all over again, Indian *citizens* as *subjects* of governance by the neocolonial expert systems under whose auspices then the developers become enveloped in a culture of high impunity. *Sixth*, all this transfers the burdens of monitoring just development practices to activist judicial actors and popular protest movements, each of which at the end of the day somehow end up by resurrecting and renewing trust in the expert systems.[24] *Seventh*, in the process and end result the 'law' itself becomes a series of

---

[22] See, for example, Ravi Hemadri, Bilaspur Bandh Samnvay Samiti, India, Harsh Mander, Vijay Nagraj, 'Displacement, Resettlement, Rehabilitation, and Development', one of 126 thematic papers submitted to the World Dam Commission; see also, Baxi (2001: 1507–27).

[23] See concerning this, Baxi (1990).

[24] After all, the valiantly recurring Narmada Bachao Andolan endeavours have to invoke conscientious technocrats to achieve a modicum of rehabilitation for the project-affected peoples. Each wave of daring protests demonstrating a lack of faith in the politics of deliberative democracy ends up reproducing forms of trust reinforcing the corrupt sovereign. I do not say this in any spirit of criticism but only by way of designating the *situatedness of all forms of resistance*.

tactics, marking in the immortal phrase of Michel Foucault, not any passages from domination to liberation but only the passages from domination to domination.[25] *Eight*, the presentation of human rights violation as an order of justifiable side effects also short-changes the constituencies of the victims of development. What rights of effective redress may the Bhopal-violated Indian humanity pitted against the Indian state/multinational global combine produced industrial mass disaster actually have under the banner of the right to development? Likewise, what similar rights may accrue to those violated by the Sikh genocide in 1884 or the post-Babri Masjid/Ayodhaya carnage and the Gujarat 2002 violated? How may we further address the devastation signified by mass peasant suicides (recently acknowledged as exceeding 100,000 as of 2003) in terms so roguishly fashioned by the taught and tough 'virtues' of 'good governance'?

I hope that through the foregoing observations I have sufficiently complicated the presentation of human rights' 'neutral' governance: developmentalism diehards may still insist that I insufficiently stress the problematic of 'costs' of development. I may here only say in response that this problematic ought at least to be put in terms of equitable sharing of these 'costs' amidst the dominant 'haves' and the subaltern 'have-nots'. I know that this phrasing needs a lot of refinement[26] provided we in the process do not entirely lose sight of the continued imposition of suffering, deprivation, destitution and disadvantage for the already worst-off peoples most recently, for example, highlighted by Gita Ramaswamy in her study of manual scavengers in Andhra Pradesh (Ramaswamy 2005). Whatever may be its operational shortcomings, the right to development-based conception of

---

[25] At times, these techniques of human rights neutral governance are presented/ promoted even as human rights friendly; for example, in the contemporary Indian political moment the issue of identification of minority benchmarks in the Indian armed forces and the appellate Indian judiciary. I here do not speak to any merits of such policy enclosures save saying that all this highlights the arcs of human rights 'neutral' closure of the deliberative/democratic public commons. But see Khalidi (2003), n. 16.

[26] For one thing, the notion of costs needs careful operationalization, as we all learn from the difficulties of 'cost-benefit' models for analysis; for another, the 'haves' and 'have-nots' may not be either thus essentialized or placed in some dire binary contrasts. Further, it would not be accurate to say that the 'haves' do not bear the costs of development or to say that have-nots never ever benefit from it. Considerations of gender, ethnicity and class complicate the understanding of distributional outcomes even among the worst-off. Nor may be ignored the dimensions of electoral politics and the agency of the have-nots for collective self-articulation.

governance does at least foreground, in my reading, concern with planned injustices, ingrained in callous cultures of developmental governance. This, I believe, ought to suffice for the present purposes.

Development as Political Largesse

The right to development talk still remains insufficiently geared to combat the notion of development as *political largesse*. In some ancient times, largesse was considered in terms of the duties of a pious ruler, which informed constructions of both *rajdharma* and *prajadharma* (that is, ethical obligations of the rulers towards the ruled and of the ruled towards the worst-off peoples). Charity, or *caritas*, remained in some complex ways both a temporal and transcendental notion. Constraints of time, as well of competence, disable me even a momentary luxury of pursuing these pre-secularized conceptions of governance charity.

In the cotemporary forms, political 'largesse' means and signifies a sovereign executive prerogative, the 'rights-free' spaces of executive/ elected official dispensation of developmental aid and assistance as the best possible means of distribution of public goods. This difficult notion stands fraught with questions concerning the notion of public goods, 'distribution' and measurement of impact of public policies. The many traditions of analytical welfare economics as noted earlier, deal rigorously with these and related issues, especially in terms of bringing 'fairness' to the practices of 'welfarism'. It raises, I believe, the necessity of distinction between *principled* and *unprincipled public* distribution, even when what these principles may be remains a matter of erudite contestation.[27] For the moment, allow me to observe that after all welfarism as unprincipled political largesse, almost always, fails to ameliorate and even aggravates the plight of the worst-off.

Perhaps, it remains difficult to improve upon Eduardo Galeano who writes memorably that:

Unlike solidarity, which is horizontal and takes place between equals, charity is top-down, humiliating those who receive it and never

---

[27] See, especially, Sen (1981: 1–39, 1984: 306–24); and more recently see, for a recent analysis, n. 8 and Hockett (2005: 1179–322).

challenging the implicit power relations. In the best of cases, there will be justice someday, in high heaven. Here on earth, charity doesn't worry injustice. It just tries to hide it.[28]

I many not here further pursue the dialectical relationships between 'charity', 'justice' and human 'solidarity', save saying that many developmental international NGOs may still perceive this differently. To take a complex example, the rhetoric and logic of North political largesse emerge in the spheres of international and intergovernmental development assistance and aid policies, which rests on the very phrase—regime of '*donor* countries'. Aid measures are thus couched in languages of developmental political largesse that instantly orphans development aid policy of any normative human rights–based development considerations. Even the NGO-inspired movement for debt reduction for the highly indebted impoverished countries under the now flourishing slogan: 'Making Poverty History' may not fully escape the birthmarks of North 'charity', fully further informed by some surreptitious self-regarding considerations for the North policy actors. Moreover, it remains now incontrovertible that the policies of international and regional financial institutions remain indifferently informed, to say the very least, by human right to development concerns. The reigning paradigm here is that of expedient political largesse, almost altogether divested of any trace of human right to development.

In its myriad staggering forms and within nation contexts political largesse emerges as a domain of peerless executive dispensation, a realm of unquestionable sovereign arbitrariness which presides over the fates of the myriad production of human rightlessness. *To the rightless is owed no more than the grudging and at the very best ethically indifferent 'virtue' of regime charity.* Who may count as victims of developmental violence, what public 'doles' may expediently be offered to them, for how long, at what/whose costs, constitute the ways of expedient governmental succour are questions not always adequately posed. In the Indian context, this means and signifies an endless variety of ad hoc distribution of 'relief' unguided by any normative principle of righting inhuman wrongs.

Thus to take some cruel examples, the expediently invented/recomposed 1984 violated Sikh families suffer as an acknowledgement of their immense suffering in 2006 an upward compensation of about seven lakhs of rupees; the Gujarat 2002 violated remain 'entitled'

---

[28] See n. 4.

to *nothing* and the Bhopal violated are denied forever any further entitlement than belated and meagre individualized compensation amounts secured by the Supreme Court of India induced prejudicial settlement at a pittance of US$470 million as against the claim made by the Government of India as a sovereign plaintiff at US$3 billion! They stand denied all political voice for any pertinent amelioration of their two decades old and continual suffering.

This feudal virtue of state charity, no doubt, episodically though erratically remains invigilated by the pronouncements of the Indian Supreme Court. The Court has variously laboured to produce decisional law that subjects to constitutional discipline of non-arbitrary dispensation of state resources to the NGOs; it has thus held that governmental 'grants' may not be accompanied by unconstitutional conditions.[29] Even so, much of the Court's innovative jurisprudence remains distinctly wayward in the awards of 'compensation' for endless human, and human rights, violation and abuse. Sharply, but not inaccurately put, it remains as constitutionally ad hoc as the distributions from the Prime Minister's National Relief Fund!

The recent vicissitudes of the Members of Parliament Local Area Development Schemes (MPLADS) furnish a riveting example of development as largesse. The Programme itself was conceived as political largesse by, and for, the elected officials; the MPLADS places annually at the sovereign disposal of the members of Parliament as much as ₹5,081 crore. What justified this escalating cost to the public exchequer was a question presumably answered in terms of enlarging the capabilities of the MPs to respond to local needs which somehow the macro/micro level Indian planning 'failed' to achieve. If so, the logic of this failure was never fully explained by the MPLADS.

The issue of accountability in disbursement was thought to be 'well'-addressed by Parliamentary oversight. In some ways, this scheme registers a return to an inaugural form of the constitutional largesse that marked the Privy Purses type dedication of state resources. This early constitutional arrangement was finally eroded by Indira Gandhi withdrawal of this facility to the erstwhile rulers of

---

[29] Such as, the requirement that government representatives may occupy decision-making roles in civil society organization based on the fact of 'doles' being given, unconscionable ways of public audit procedures that cripple autonomous NGO functioning, and even 'arbitrary' ways that constitute the state funding of civil society organizations. I desist from case citation, fully available in treatises on Indian administrative law, especially by Professors M.P./S.N. Jain, S.P. Sathe and I.P. Massey.

Princely States. To be sure, the Privy purses constituted 'conscience money' that facilitated transition to Indian federalism. Likewise, the MPLADS constitutes a like 'fake' constitutional currency, unredeemed by any acts of judicial invigilation, as far as I can discover.

However, on all available public narratives, including the Comptroller and Auditor General's (CAG) Report, disclose that during the period 1993–2000 the MPs utilised only ₹3,221 crore (64 per cent). The balance, ₹1,797 crore, lies either 'unspent' or categorized as 'status not known'. The CAG undertook a review of the scheme covering the periods 1993–97 and 1997–2000 which reported poor utilization, indifferent monitoring by the Ministry and fraud and corruption. In as many as 111 sample constituencies across the country. Indeed, the CAG discovered that expenditure of ₹161 crore under the MPLADS occurred unsupported by any document, testifying to pre–rule-of-law cultures of *oral governance*. In complete plain words, even this flawed narrative suggests that the alleged development work had not been undertaken at all and what took place in its name still manages to survive official acts of scrutiny.

No doubt, the 'cover' was blown by the recent electronic media sting operation named 'Operation Chakravyuh'. Its political aftermath led a deeply embarrassed Indian Parliament to order the expulsion of a few members. I simply lack the requisite time on this occasion to develop this theme any further but still invite you to the labours of detailed reading of the CAG Report, and the March 2006 Report of Parliamentary Committee, word by word, in aid of a fuller understanding of the actual histories of political largesse and their now unfortunately fully entrenched futures.

Yet another recurring instance of political largesse occurs via the ad hoc determination that aims at redistributing constitutional rights across the so-called socially, educationally and other backward classes. Such redistribution remains eminently justified by the original vision of development in the first Indian constitution, despite its so frequently and somewhat extravagantly amended text. The lofty intendment is no longer, one may hope, open to any radical public doubt. However, educational and employment reservations were conceived as an *aspect*, not as the *totality*, of ongoing constitutionally informed redistribution process for the worst-off peoples. In this conception at least stood included—free and compulsory primary education for all, protection of the young from child labour and immunity from some related forms of exploitation, especially forced labour, begging and trafficking in human beings. This is scarcely an occasion to review the vast official and activist literatures fully archiving the constitutional promise and its multifarious betrayals. But it would be no exaggeration to say that the Indian developers have found insufficient time and resources for moving significantly towards this integrated vision of social justice informed/sensitive redistribution of rights and freedoms.

Nowhere does the constitutional conception of just social redistribution authorize peculiar and periodical enactments of redistribution of rights as performances of political patronage and charity, howsoever cross-dressed in some quaint languages of constitutional justice. Abundant empirical evidence suggests that the politics of reservation remains singularly unmindful of the constitutional conceptions of governance, rights, justice and development. No doubt, the deployment of the *politics of ethnic feudalism* marks some sudden bouts of recovery from political amnesia concerning these tasks, thus presenting a poignant moment for any historian of Indian development. Even so, this thrives decisively by the programming of some entirely avoidable violent social contestation/conflagration. The mostly self-styled 'social justice' heroes of contemporary Indian politics who also as well further fully thrive upon some carefully considered scope for civil society violence as and preferred mode of 'doing' competitive politics.

Governance chicanery would have us believe that all this entails a necessary cost of 'development' for 'social justice'. Yet, one may ask with appropriate constitutional sobriety whether this is indeed the case. Surely, any redistribution of constitutional rights invites a serious solicitude according full dignity of voice and representation to the non-dominant and the most backward classes. However, we all know full well the ways in which these borderlines remain craftily constructed.

The 'most backward classes',[30] as is well known, were never accorded the full dignity of public participation shaping such policies.

---

[30] No expression, be it noted, is more constitutionally offensive than this facile phrase—'the most backward classes'. In terms of the sustenance of plebiscitary forms of democracy, these so-called classes have done more than others to sustain Indian democracy. Anthropologists and art historians have archived their contributions to Indian culture and civilization. Indeed, it may be said without even a tinge of romanticization that the values they crystallize through their lived lives—the virtues of contentment with hard and harsh work and labour, everyday integrity, civility and rectitude—which put to shame the political classes and the globalizing yuppie generations. All this fully suggests that this expression, if necessary, may more aptly extend to the actually existing classes of the Indian developers!

They thus remained, overall, *objects* rather than *subjects* of development. The gender dimension (outside the notable exception of restructuration of the *Panchayati Raj* institutions) plays little, indeed no, role whatsoever in such purported redistribution via political largesse. In the main, the forms of Indian political largesse construct the potential *beneficiaries* as *targets* for some vulgar aggrandizing expedient practices of regime power.

The quotidian practices of the politics of reservation further only perpetuate the politics of ethnic feudalism masquerading under the banner of social justice. On all available information, only a minuscule progress has been made to redistribute the real benefits of educational and employment quotas/reservation outside what even the Supreme Court of India was moved to christen as the 'creamy layers'. Surely, the social justice tasks ahead, after 50+ years of constitutional experience, invite some serious attention to the provision of some real-life opportunities for equality for the *atisudras* (the most backward classes) of India, as Babasaheb Ambedkar named the social and economic proletariat. Instead, what occurs under the politics of ethnic feudalism is some extraordinarily vicious political diversion from the pursuit of historically pressing tasks of social redistribution. What occurs constantly is the 'remix' of the *Mandal 1l*, now described as *Mandal 11*! Many further such unconstitutionally fabricated numerals unfortunately also await us in terms of political largesse that continues to constitute some instant, and indifferently enduring, publics and counterpublics, always easy of access for demagogic and democidal practices of manipulation of mass politics.

In saying all this I once again run here a very great narrative risk of being identified as a small time actor allegedly, according to my many critics, singularly uniformed by the rhythms of 'revolutionary' social transformation. I placed myself at such grave risk, as the Vice Chancellor of Delhi University, baptized by, and negotiating nationally, the violence unleashed by the abrupt installation of the regime-favoured reading of the Mandal Commission Report. This, fortunately for me, remains a matter of incontestable public record. I have, in now what remains of my residual life, no desire to re-enact further exposure to such divisive misrecognition. The only point of this autobiographical recall here is to suggest that Indian development discourse scarcely benefits from a planned entrapment into the binary languages of 'for/against' reservations. This unhappily eclipses the fundamental duties of all citizens, in Part IV-A of the Constitution, which require the 'development of the scientific temper', 'spirit of critical enquiry' in social reform measures, respect for the 'composite culture of India', and above all the pursuit of 'excellence ... in all walks of life'. When the practices of politics of reservation border on the constitutionally impermissible mediocre developmentalism, those who suffer the most are surely the worst-off peoples in Indian society.

How may a politics of reservation suffused with the duty of excellence redeem us from the present morass remains a crucial issue. Surely, it needs saying that schemes for reservations may remain possessed of a more secure rights and justice-promising futures when based on the right to development type values and considerations. We need to recast the constantly politically enacted controversies concerning 'reservations' in terms that convert political largesse into some authentic ongoing human rights affairs. The Indian Supreme Court has striven precisely to undertake such historic labours directed to impose a fairness discipline on runaway forms of 'reservation' type political largesse. In this, on all accounts, the Court has benefited by its innovative partnership with the forces and tendencies in civil society. Surely, it needs a degree of redemption from the imposition of the role of a noble scavenger forever clearing the imposed and chequered/caused debris of political dirt and dust; it certainly deserves a better future than being asked to continually engage with some historically unproductive monitoring of the ways of 'fly-now-pay-later' forms of Indian governance.

Towards an Uneasy Conclusion

This has been a very long journey, indeed! Even so, I return, in conclusion, to the principal question: *'Does it make any difference, whether we talk of development as a human right or as political largesse?'* If it makes *any* difference, from *whose perspective* may be the difference be considered significant? And to *what* ends, and at *whose/what costs*? This remains a crucial question.

To be sure, for the wretched of Bharat, these masses of the impoverished developees of constitutionally named Indian developees, what matters is the art and craft of *cheating their ways into everyday survival.* It scarcely matters for them whether their next frugal meal comes from the protean conceptions of human right to development contrasted with those of development as political largesse. This no doubt comes often though in terms of electoral campaign picnics of midday meal schemes and distribution of public foodgrain as objects of political charity, rather than as duties arising from constitutionally, and internationally, enunciated human rights to food and adequate nutrition, immunity from hunger and real-life opportunities/access to dignified livelihood. No doubt, the worst-off developees may also welcome the legal translation of political largesse via laws that provide employment guarantee schemes that at least provide 'secure' income for 100 days a year, even as they must accept as a matter of course the unredeemed patterns of administrative corruption and sex-based violence embedded in any such implementation.

The high-minded 'meta-discourse' of development fails to ameliorate their existential problem of negotiating somehow their decidedly subhuman survival. They know full well in their blood, bones and belongings the enormous cruelty fostered by the United Nations cottage industry of the Millennium Development Goals that contain endlessly revisable datelines for reducing hunger and malnutrition by half (presently the magical year is 2015!).

Fully respecting the dignity of their voice raises a sovereign question all over again: How might the methodologically nuanced and theoretically erudite developmental expertise talk ever advance even the uncertain futures for the amelioration of the Indian, and globally, impoverished masses? How may this discourse be ever moved/haunted by the insistent urgency of the voices of human and social suffering? How may we recover the anguished voice of Mohandas in the current globalizing conjuncture?[31]

The dominant discourse concerning development nurtures only the ways of *sustainable thought*; that is, politically correct forms of articulation of developmentalism. On the other hand, what the developees demand are the ways of *unsustainable and deeply fiduciary*

---

[31] No doubt, John Rawls, Amartya Sen, Martha Nussbaum, Nancy Fraser, Gayatri Spivak, Rajsewari Sunder Rajan among others, provide some future pathways of concerned and fiduciary engagement for rethinking the development discourse, even when these redoubtably represent some post-Monhadasian as well as post-Marxian inheritance.

thought.[32] All this revives to my mind the 1850 observation of Karl Marx, who memorably said, and I quote from bloodied memory, that the classical saint of Christianity mortified his body for the sake of the redemption of the souls of the masses, whereas the modern educated saint mortifies the bodies of the masses for the sake of his/her own redemption.

References

Agamben, Giorgio. 1998. *Homo sacer and bare life.* Trans. Daniel Heller-Roazen. Stanford: Stanford University Press.

Alder, Mathew D., and Chris William Sanchirico. 2006. Inequality and uncertainty: Theory and legal application. Law & Legal Theory Working Paper 8, University of Pennsylvania Politics. http://www.srn.com.

Badiou, Alain. 2001. *Ethic: An essay in understanding of evil.* London: Verso.

Baxi, Upendra. 1982. *Crisis of the Indian legal system.* New Delhi: Vikas.

——. 1990. *Liberty and corruption: The jurisprudence of corruption and corruption of jurisprudence.* Lucknow: The Eastern Book Company.

——. 1994. *Mabrino's helmet: Human rights for a changing world,* 22–32. Delhi: Har-Anand.

——. 1995. Justice as emancipation: 'The legacy of Babasaheb Ambedkar'. In *Crisis and change in contemporary India,* eds. Upendra Baxi and Bhiku Parekh, 122–49. New Delhi: SAGE Publications.

---

[32] This United Nations metaphor has many referents. Sustainability refers *first* to what may be sustained by way of prose and proposal within the discipline of the internal United Nations communicative hierarchy. *Second*, it requires a fair grasp of the canons of global (hegemonic) and within-UN (institutional) political correctness that presides over of smooth regimes of management of finally negotiated developmental texts. *Third*, the 'sustainable' then is always programmatic thought that carefully guards against the 'remembrance of the things past' and promotes a controlled/coordinated articulation of new human, and human rights, futures. *Fourth*, it seeks to contain as far as humanly possible utopic articulations, especially arising from the non-UN global activist traditions of discourse. *Fifth*, a key attribute of the practices and bodies of sustainable thought lies in ways of management of the erasure of past normative and inspirational landmarks. The hermeneutics of retrieval—a notion, which I here refer to only illustratively, contests in particular this selective recall and reiteration of some past instruments, and regards performances of studied silence not so much as a function of chance (harried editorial decision) but rather as acts of necessity (decisions of studied choice serving the production of the regimes of erasure). Concerning this entire constellation, see Baxi (2006d).

Baxi, Upendra. 2001. 'What happens next is up to you': Human rights at risk in dams and development. *American University Law Review* 16: 1507–27.

———. 2005a. The war *on* terror and the 'war *of* terror': Nomadic multitudes, aggressive incumbents, and the 'new international law'. *Osgoode Hall Law Journal* 43: 7–43.

———. 2005b. The Gujarat catastrophe: Notes on reading politics as democidal rape culture. In *The violence of the normal times*, ed. Kalpana Kannabiran, 332–83. New Delhi: Women Unlimited.

———. 2006a. Chapter 5. *The future of human rights*. 2nd revised Ed. Delhi: Oxford University Press.

———. 2006b. What may the Third World expect from international law? *Third World Quarterly* 27: 713–25.

———. 2006c. Justice of rights. In *Political ideas in modern India*, ed. V.R. Mehta and Thomas Pantham, 263–84. New Delhi: SAGE Publications.

———. 2006d. A report for all seasons? Small notes towards reading the larger freedom, 495–514. In *Human rights and development: Law, policy and governance*, eds. C. Raj Kumar and D.K. Srivastava. Hong Kong: Lexis/Nexis.

Braithwaite, John, and Peter Drahos. 2000. *Global business regulation*. Cambridge, Massachusetts: Cambridge University Press.

Dallmayr, Fred. 1998. *Alternative visions: Paths in the global village*. Lanham, Maryland: Rowman and Littlefield.

Dalmia, Vasudha. 2003. *Orienting India: European knowledge formation in the eighteenth and nineteenth centuries*. New Delhi: Three Essays Collective.

Derrida, Jacques. 2003. Autoimmunity: Real and symbolic suicides. In *Philosophy in a time of terror*, ed. Giovanna Borradori, 95–96. Chicago: Chicago University Press.

Devi, Mahasweta. 1990. *Bashai Tudu*. Trans. Samik Bandyopadhyay and Gayatri Chakravorty Spivak. Calcutta: Thema.

———. 2002. *Choti Munda and his arrow*. Trans. with an Introduction, Gayatri Chakravorty Spivak. Calcutta: Seagull.

Dhavan, Rajiv, and Thomas Paul, eds. 1992. *Nehru and the constitution*. New Delhi: Indian Law Institute.

Escobar, Arturo. 1985. *Encountering development: The making and the unmaking of the Third World*. Princeton: Princeton University Press.

Fischlin, Daniel, and Marata Nandorfy. 2002. *Eduardo Galeano: Through the looking glass*. Montreal: Black Rose.

Gell, Alfred. 2001. *The anthropology of time*. Oxford: Berg.

Hein, Jorge. 2006. Which way is Latin America headed? *The Hindu*, Thursday, 20 April, p. 8.

Hockett, Robert. 2005. The deep grammar of distribution: A meta-theory of justice. *Cardozo Law Review* 26: 1179–322.

Ikeda, Daisaku. 1998. *Humanity and the new millennium: From chaos to cosmos*. Tokyo: Soka Gakkai.

Khalidi, Omar. 2003. *Khaki and ethnic violence in India: Army, police, and paramilitary forces during communal riots.* New Delhi: Three Essays Collective.

Koestler Arthur. 1960. *Lotus and the robot.* N.Y.: Harper-Collins.

Leiten, Kristoffel. 2004. *Views on development: The local and global in India and Pakistan,* 1–24. New Delhi: Three Essays Collective.

Lukes, Steven. 1995. *The curious enlightenment of Professor Caritat: A comedy of ideas.* London: Verso.

Mishra, Pankaj. 2004. *An end to suffering: The buddha in the world.* London: Picador.

Pyong-Jik, An. 1979. Han Yougun's liberalism: An analysis of the reformation of Korean Buddhism. *Korea Journal* 19(12): 13–18.

Ramaswamy, Gita. 2005. *India stinking: Manual scavengers in Andhra Pradesh and their work.* Chennai: Navayana.

Randeria, Shalini. 2003. Glocalization of law, environmental justice, World Bank, NGOs, and the cunning state in India. *Current Sociology* 51: 305–28.

Roy, Deepesh, and Mehta, Pratap Bhano. 2006. The Indian parliament as an institution of accountability. The United Nations Institute for Social Development, Democracy, Governance, and Human Rights Program Paper Number 21, January.

Rudolph, Lloyd, and Susanne Rudolph. 2006. *The postmodern Gandhi.* Delhi: Oxford University Press.

Rummel, J.S. 1997. *Death by government.* New York: Transaction Publishers.

Santos, Boaventura de Sousa. 1995. *Toward a new commonsense: Law, science, and politics in the paradigmatic transition.* London: Routledge.

———. 2002. *Toward a new legal commonsense: Law, globalization, and emancipation.* London: Butterworth Lexis-Nexis.

Sen, Amartya. 1981. Rights and agency. *Philosophy & Public Affairs* 11: 1–39.

———. 1984. Rights and capabilities, 306–24. In *Resources, values, and development.* Delhi: Oxford University Press.

———. 1999. *Development as freedom.* Delhi: Oxford University Press.

Sen, Jai, Anita Anand, Arturo Escobar, and Peter Waterman, eds. 2004. *World social forum: Challenging empires.* New Delhi: The Viveka Foundation.

Sen, Jai, and Madhuresh Kumar, eds. 2003. Vol. 1 of *Are other worlds possible: The open space reader.* New Delhi, available with the first author.

Settar, S. 1990. *Pursuing death: Philosophy and practice of voluntary termination of life.* Dharwad: Institute of Indian Art History, Karnatak University.

Shklar, Judith. 1990. *Faces of injustice.* New Haven: Yale University Press.

Tirumallar. 1991. *Tirumantram: A Tamil spiritual classic.* Trans. B. Natarajan. Mylapore, Madras: Sri Ramakrishna Math.

Young, Robert J. 2001. *Postcolonialism: An introduction.* Oxford: Blackwell.

Zizek, Slavoj. 1999. *The ticklish subject: Absent centre of political ontology.* London: Verso.

9

The Power of Uncertainty: Reflections on the Nature of Transformational Initiatives

Mihir Shah

Introduction

I spent the last 20 years of my life living and working with the tribal people of central India, trying with them to forge concrete solutions to some of the most difficult challenges of our time—of water and livelihood security. Over the past 10 months, I have been working as a member of the Planning Commission, handling Rural Development, Water Resources and *Panchayati Raj*. This lecture is an attempt to put together some of my reflections as a participant in the struggle for change, to share with you some of what I have learnt in this process.

My central question before you today is one that has repeatedly arisen over the years and with even greater urgency in the recent past—what is the way to act in a world beset by fundamental uncertainty? If uncertainty (of many kinds, as I will elaborate) is at the heart of the knowledge of the world that is possible for us, what implications does this have for transformational initiatives, whether by government, social activists or citizens? The question gains renewed attention thanks to the grave crisis the world economy has just been going through, and due to the emergence of climate change as a central issue defining our time. This is, therefore, as opportune a moment as any to revisit some of the most fundamental questions regarding economics as a science. I will reflect on the nature of knowledge that economics provides by inter alia drawing upon the work of some of the greatest economists the world has ever seen. I will, therefore, be speaking today as an economist but will also perforce draw upon insights from other disciplines, without which I believe we cannot do full justice to the questions on hand.

Three Kinds of Uncertainty

Uncertainty Related to Time

The natural starting point for an economist dealing with uncertainty is Knight (1921) which introduced the distinction between risk and uncertainty. Briefly understood, risk describes a future outcome whose probability can be reasonably determined, while uncertainty refers to an event whose probability cannot be known in advance. We could even call it a distinction between calculable and incalculable uncertainty.

The most important text that took uncertainty seriously was Keynes' *General Theory*. But Keynes' clearest statement on the matter is to be found in an article in the *Quarterly Journal of Economics* in February 1937, which he wrote in response to critics of the *General Theory*:

> … our knowledge of the future is fluctuating, vague and uncertain … By 'uncertain' knowledge, let me explain, I do not mean merely to distinguish what is known for certain, from what is only probable. The game of roulette is not subject, in this sense, to uncertainty. Or, again, the expectation of life is only slightly uncertain. Even the weather is only moderately uncertain. The sense in which I am using the term is that in which the prospect of a European war is uncertain or the price of copper and the rate of interest twenty years hence. About these matters there is no scientific basis on which to form any calculable probability whatever. We simply do not know. (Keynes 1937)

It is stunning to read perhaps the greatest economist of the twentieth century affirm radical uncertainty in no uncertain terms! Of course, Keynes laid the foundations of the modern welfare state whose interventions he saw as correcting the fallibility of the market mechanism.

Arguing from the opposite end of the ideological spectrum but agreeing with Keynes fundamentally on the nature of knowledge in Economics was Friedrich von Hayek. In his classic 1945 piece, *The*

Use of Knowledge in Society and his 1974 Nobel Lecture, 'The Pretence of Knowledge' Hayek questions the very possibility of rational calculation by central planners. Hayek was highly critical of what he termed scientism: a false understanding of the methods of science, which has been forced upon the social sciences, such as the view that all scientific explanations are simple two-variable linear relationships. Hayek points out that much of science involves the explanation of complex multi-variable and non-linear phenomena. Of course, the irony is that Hayek had a touching faith in the power of unrestrained markets, assigning them near omniscience, quite ignoring his own insights into the nature of knowledge and also ignoring the fundamental revolution in economics inaugurated by the work of Keynes.

Perhaps the economist who captures most beautifully the insights of both Keynes and Hayek is the relatively unsung G.L.S. Shackle. In a much more radical position, he questions both Hayek's naiveté about markets and Keynes' simplistic optimism about state intervention. Shackle introduces the notion of inceptive choice, where the person who chooses cannot:

> foreknow what the sequel of his present choice will be, for if his own choices are inceptive, if his own choices are non-implicit, in some degree, in their antecedents, so are the choices of others and so are all the choices-to-come of himself as well as others. (Shackle 1975: 23)

Since 'the ultimate permissive condition of knowledge is the repetition of recognisable configurations' (Shackle 1972: 6), this limits the possibilities of knowing the courses of action that will be chosen in future. Shackle criticises his teacher Hayek for not fully acknowledging the implications of the decision-maker's 'unknowledge' for the possibilities of self-regulation in a market economy.

Shackle's work potentially takes economics into novel territory such as the role of imagination to assess the plausibility of alternative outcomes while taking economic decisions. But the very freedom that is the basis for imagination makes perfect knowledge an impossibility. Shackle, therefore, posits a fundamental hiatus between freedom and knowledge, as also between time and reason. In an incredibly insightful, less than three-page long, Chapter 2 of his 1972 work *Epistemics and Economics* titled *Time, Novelty, Geometry*, Shackle writes:

> Time is a denial of the omnipotence of reason. Time divides the entirety of things into that part about which we can reason and that part

about which we cannot. Yet the part about which we cannot reason has a bearing on the meaning of the part that is amenable to reason. The analyst is obliged to practice, in effect, a denial of the nature of time. For he can reason only about that which is *in effect* complete; and in a world where there is time, nothing is ever complete. (p. 27)

We must immediately recognize, however, that Shackle's work has remained on the fringes of mainstream economic theory. The standard response to uncertainty in economics can be traced to von Neumann and Morgenstern's (1944) expected utility theory, which led on to Nash's (1951) non-cooperative equilibrium and game theory, Savage's (1954) reformulation of expected utility theory and climaxed in Arrow and Debreu's (1954) derivation of the necessary and sufficient conditions for existence and optimality of general equilibrium under uncertainty. Of course, these formulations were challenged by Allais (1953), and Arrow (1963) himself acknowledged the empirical implausibility of the relevant necessary and sufficient conditions in the face of uncertainty. Indeed, even more recently, Arrow has warned that 'vast ills have followed a belief in certainty, whether historical inevitability, grand diplomatic designs or extreme views on economic policy. When developing policy with wide effects ... caution is needed because we cannot predict the consequences' (Arroe 1962: 46).

Over the last 40 years, but especially following the work of the psychologist and 2002 Economics Nobel Laureate Daniel Kahneman with Amos Tversky on prospect theory, the expected utility hypothesis has been under attack and alternatives proposed. For our purposes, however, it is important to recognize that all of this work is concerned with one project—finding probabilistic solutions aimed at taming uncertainty, attempting to collapse the radical distinction between risk and uncertainty first postulated by Knight and later developed by Keynes and Shackle. For as Keynes has said, 'The calculus of probability was supposed to be capable of reducing uncertainty to the same calculable status as that of certainty itself. Actually, however, we have, as a rule, only the vaguest idea of any but the most direct consequences of our acts' (Keynes 1937).

Before going on to elaborate the other sources of this inescapable uncertainty, I will close this section with a most telling example of the point I am making. Long-Term Capital Management (LTCM) was a US hedge fund founded in 1994, with 1997 Economics Nobel Laureates Myron Scholes and Robert Merton on its Board of Directors. LTCM used complex mathematical models to take advantage of trading strategies such as fixed income arbitrage, statistical arbitrage and pairs trading, combined with high leverage. LTCM was initially highly successful with annualized returns of over 40 per cent. But it lost US$4.6 billion in less than four months in 1998 and collapsed by early 2000. The failure of LTCM is a classic case study of the impossibility of accurately anticipating unforeseen and relatively unforeseeable events such as the 1997 East Asian financial crisis and Russia's 1998 default on its sovereign debt. LTCM collapsed despite having the best economists on its Board because it mistakenly thought it could conjure away an uncertain and unknown future by turning it into a set of calculable risks (Lowenstein 2000). Similar mayhem has occurred across the world in the latest economic crisis.

Uncertainty Related to Context

Apart from the 'time' dimension of uncertainty which has found recognition in economics, we need to also acknowledge the existence of a contextual element in uncertainty, which disciplines like anthropology have best brought to the fore. The question they ask is: how do we understand the 'Other'? Or, what happens when we try to understand the other? One of the most evocative treatments of this question is to be found in the work of the Brazilian anthropologist Eduardo Viveiros de Castro (2003).[1] As de Castro explains:

> The real problem lies in knowing which are the possible relations between our descriptive practices and those employed by other peoples. There are undoubtedly many possible relations; but only one impossible relation: the absence of a relation. We cannot learn these other practices — other cultures — in absolute terms; we can only try to make explicit some of our implicit relations with them, that is, apprehend them in relation to our own descriptive practices. (p. 11)

de Castro cautions us against

> the fantasy of an intellectual intuition of other forms of life 'in their own terms,' for there is no such thing. 'Their terms' are only determined as such in relation to 'our terms,' and vice-versa. Every determination is a

---

[1] I thank Mekhala Krishnamurthy for guiding me to this reference.

relation. Nothing is absolutely universal, not because something is relatively particular, but because 'everything' is relational. (de Castro 2003)

One of the richest descriptions of this relationality is to be found in the work of the German philosopher Hans-Georg Gadamer. In his 1960 magnum opus *Truth and Method*, Gadamer expresses the matter through his notion of the fusion of horizons:

> What do we mean by 'placing ourselves' in a situation? Certainly not just disregarding ourselves. This is necessary, of course, in that we must imagine the other situation. But into this other situation we must also bring ourselves. Only this fulfils the meaning of 'placing ourselves'. This placing of ourselves is not the empathy of one individual for another nor is it the application to another person of our own criteria but it always involves the attainment of a higher universality that overcomes not only our own particularity but also that of the other. To acquire a horizon means that one learns to look beyond what is close at hand, not in order to look away from it, but to see it better within a larger whole and in truer proportion. Understanding is always a fusion of horizons which we imagine to exist by themselves. (pp. 271–73)

Our knowledge thereby loses the certainty of its own voice by acknowledging the need to listen to and understand the knowledge produced by the other whose situation we claim to be trying to transform. Thus, the acknowledgment of the otherness of the other demands recognition of at least five different elements that shape our knowledge:

1. The context where we are trying to intervene is not a blank canvas or as the Roman legal term goes, *terra nullius* ('land belonging to no one' or 'empty land'). These are situations and contexts with a dynamic of their own. The impact of what we do is mediated through the ongoing dynamic of the context where our initiative rolls out. We need to study and understand this dynamic.[2]
2. What is more, there is a great diversity to this dynamic across the contexts where we intervene. So our initiatives need to be sensitive to the variety of dynamics that we encounter.

---

[2] Much of the devastation wrought by colonial settlers in their assignation with the aboriginal/indigenous people across the globe had to do with the presumption of *terra nullius*.

3. These contexts also have knowledges of their own that are often paradigmatically different from ours and from each other. An appreciation of these and an effort to understand them will greatly benefit the course of our own initiative.
4. Whether we like it or not, however unaware we may be of this, our interventions are not unidirectional or omnipotent. They, willy-nilly, transform those who seek to bring about change—beyond their wanting, doing or even knowing. Change will, therefore, never flow univocally from one direction.
5. The presence of the other also compels the question: Who is the calculator? Is there at all a decision-maker acting in pristine isolation and autonomy? What is the meaning of studying the calculation of the individual, atomistic *homo economicus*, in a world characterized by deep interdependencies?
6. Finally, we need to recognize that transformational initiatives are generally located in contexts of deep inequalities and discrimination, some historically inherited, others created anew, whether based on gender, caste, ethnicity, race, community or class. Every intervention inhabits a contested terrain and itself becomes a site for further contention and contestation. This makes outcomes profoundly uncertain and indeterminate. It also demands an understanding of questions of power and justice and the articulation of an appropriate approach towards them.

Uncertainty Related to Nature

Nature has its own dynamic and autonomy that circumscribes and shapes human action. The current crisis of global warming is an example of what happens when we act as if nature does not matter. The roots of the crisis may be traced to the way economics has sought to conceptualize itself and its relationship with nature.

The founders of neoclassical economics, on their own testimony, aspired to create a science patterned exactly on Newtonian mechanics. Newtonian mechanics could visualize change only as locomotion, which is both qualityless and reversible. The economic process is seen here as a circular flow between production and consumption, with no outlets and no inlets. This flow is isolated, self-contained and ahistorical, neither creating nor being affected by qualitative changes in the natural environment within which it occurs. Keynesian macro-dynamics (starting with Harrod) and all its concepts of national income, investment and incremental capital–output ratio also find no place for physical entities. Even the Classical Political Economy of Ricardo expressly saw land as a factor immune to qualitative degradation ('the original and indestructible powers of the soil'), and though Marx was centrally concerned with dynamics, viewing the economic process as essentially historical and qualitative in character, he also did not integrate natural resources into his main analysis. It is true that Marx speaks of labour as a 'process between man and nature' (Marx 1976: 283). But the terms of this interaction are that 'man, through his own actions, mediates, regulates and controls the metabolism between himself and nature' by working on 'objects of labour that are spontaneously provided by nature' (ibid.: 284). This dual conception of 'free gifts of nature' and the imperative to exercise 'control over nature' runs through the entire gamut of thinking in economics. Progress is seen as coterminus with the conquest of nature.[3] Allied to this is the presumption that unlimited quantities of waste can be costlessly dumped into the bottomless sink of the environment. Along with the assumption of free gifts goes also the assumption of free disposal.

Following Debreu (1959), the neoclassicals posited the 'rational expectations hypothesis'[4] which presumes that decision-makers in the market know the probability distribution of future outcomes, the future being visualized as stationary and stochastic (Davidson

---

[3] 'It is the necessity of bringing a natural force under the control of society, of economizing on its energy, of appropriating or subduing it on a large scale by the work of the human hand, that plays the most decisive role in industry' (Marx 1976: 649).

[4] The hypothesis entails 'supposing that the entire sequence of future prices will be "announced" at the initial date in order that the inter-temporal equilibrium is sustained' (Dasgupta and Heal 1979: 337). They deploy the hypothesis despite awareness that:

> we simply do not know how expectations are formed. But we do know that rational expectations yield tidy formulations. These are easy to work with. This forms the motivation for the constructions that follow. But it is worth bearing in mind that as a description the rational expectations hypothesis is likely to be way off the mark here. (ibid.)

Quite clearly, considerations of neatness and ease weigh more heavily than those of accuracy of description.

1982: 182).[5] 'At the initial date there should exist a complete set of forward, contingent commodity markets, on which it is possible to buy or sell goods for delivery in any future time-period and state of the world' (Dasgupta and Heal 1979: 472). Such an approach can provide accurate predictions only if the stochastic process is ergodic—but that is ruled out when we are dealing with irrevocable ecological phenomena which produce a whole range of effects unobservable by the price system.[6] As Shackle has shown, there are a range of phenomena for which no 'pre-image' exists in our minds. We have no previous observations on the basis of which probability distributions can be constructed since the phenomena we are dealing with are unprecedented. This means that we cannot have an 'omni-competent classificatory system' for listing hypothetical scenarios which are endless and beyond human imagination (Shackle 1972: 18).[7]

Another neoclassical device of dealing with the problem of uncertainty is to discount the future. This approach could be said to derive from the contributions of Gray (1914) and Hotelling (1931).[8] The market mechanism supposedly mirrors the preferences of individual economic agents while allocating resources efficiently. When the problem is intergenerational, we run into the ontological difficulty that many of the relevant economic agents are not yet in existence to

---

[5] A stochastic process is stationary if the random variables are well defined for all points in time and if their cumulative probability distributions are independent of time.

[6] After their analysis is complete, Dasgupta and Heal add with complete honesty: 'it is clear that the foregoing construction is of very little use for analysing resource markets in the world we know' (ibid.: 349). At another point they say, 'the rational expectations hypothesis … is so far-fetched. Each individual is required to possess the correct theory of how the economy behaves in order to make the hypothesis credible. Such a requirement is, however, not credible' (ibid.: 436).

[7] Methodologically, this leads Shackle to advocate an exciting diachronic approach for unravelling the 'broad current of self-determining, or organically evolving history' (Shackle 1972: 18).

[8] Right from the start, however, there was a lively recognition of the fact that the whole procedure entailed serious ethical problems, because of which it was not found acceptable by most economists until as late as the 1960s. Ramsey was the first and most trenchant critic: 'we do not discount later enjoyments in comparison with earlier ones, a practice which is ethically indefensible and arises merely from the weakness of the imagination' (Ramsey 1928: 543). Harrod regarded it as 'a polite expression for rapacity and the conquest of reason by passion' (Harrod 1948: 30). See also Pigou (1932) for similar observations.

be able to express their willingness to pay![9] And in discounting the future it is assumed that the future will be brighter than the present. But a high rate of discount will also imply a faster rate of depletion,[10] which could mean that the growth path becomes unsustainable and that the future ends up being bleaker than today. The key problem here is again uncertainty. For 'the discounting of time is at one and the same time the discounting of uncertainty' (Perrings 1987: 116), the latter being an increasing function of time. And the higher the discount rate, the more we will deplete an exhaustible resource while raising the level of economic activity. This will imply higher disposals into the ecosystem, which will in turn bring about environmental changes, raising the level of uncertainty. This will once again raise the discount rate and so on ... Thus, the device meant to tackle the problem of uncertainty only ends up aggravating it![11]

Following the publication in 1971 of Nicholas Georgescu-Roegen's *The Entropy Law and the Economic Process* what is called for is a revolution in economic thinking, nothing short of a Kuhnian paradigm shift, which compels the abandonment of the mechanistic dogma by forcing the realization that qualitative and irrevocable changes necessarily characterize the environment of which economic processes are a part—that both the assumptions of free gifts and free disposal are untenable, there being a dynamic, two-way interrelationship between the economy and the environment. We must see the macroeconomy

---

[9] See Martinez-Alier (1987, Ch. 11) for a brilliant exposition of the consequences of methodological individualism for the intergenerational allocation of resources. Standard discounting procedures do little more than ensuring a 'trickle ahead' for future generations. See Norgaard and Howarth (1991).

[10] In his 1974 Richard T. Ely Lecture, Solow expresses the judgement that 'the market will tend to consume exhaustible resources too fast' (Solow 1974: 12).

[11] In a study of the twin implications for environmental preservation of uncertainty and irreversibility, Arrow and Fisher concede:

[I]f we are uncertain about the pay-off to investment in development, we should err on the side of underinvestment ... Given an ability to learn from experience, underinvestment can be remedied before the second period, whereas mistaken overinvestment cannot, the consequences persisting in effect for all time. (Arrow and Fisher 1974: 317)

The authors cite 'extinction of a form of life, the destruction of a unique geo-morphological phenomenon, the toxicity and the persistence, indeed the increasing concentration, of the hard or non-degradable pesticides' (ibid.: 319) as examples of irreversible changes in the environment produced by economic activity.

as an open subsystem of the finite natural ecosystem and not as an isolated circular flow of abstract exchange value.[12]

Viewed in the light of the Entropy Law, the economic process is, in fact, not circular, but unidirectional, involving a continuous transformation of the flow of low entropy received from the environment into high entropy or irrevocable waste which is returned to the environment. This is a one-way flow, not a circular one. The flow of blood is to the circulation of exchange value as the digestive tract is to the unidirectional entropic flow, beginning with environmental resources and energy, through firms and households, and ending with high-entropy waste into environmental sinks.[13]

What is more, this entropic flow has a continuously degrading impact on the environment from which the economy must incessantly draw its low entropy. Each qualitative transformation of the environment within which the economy operates, demands a readaptation from the economy. Thus, the very sustainability of the economic process depends on its ability to so adapt. No model which seeks to understand the economy can be complete if it ignores the broader ecosystem of which the economy is a part, and the co-evolutionary path of the subsystem and its parent.[14] The changes in the environment are both

---

[12] Alfred Marshall in his magnum opus *Principles of Economics* suggests: 'The Mecca of the economist lies in economic biology' (Marshall 1920: xii, Preface to the 8th edition).

> The forces of which economics has to take account are more numerous, less definite, less well known, and more diverse in character than those of mechanics; while the material they act upon is more uncertain and less homogeneous ... economics, like biology deals with a matter, of which the inner nature and constitution, as well as the outer form, are constantly changing ... economics has no near kinship with any physical science. *It is a branch of biology broadly interpreted.* (ibid.: 637, Appendix C; emphasis added)

However, in Marshall's own body of work, the influence of these insights can be said to be virtually non-existent. This could be because he saw himself as writing only the Foundations, which in his view, 'must give a relatively large place to mechanical analogies' (ibid.: xii, Preface to the 8th edition).

[13] This corresponds to what biologists call the 'metabolic flow' through which a living organism sustains its highly ordered structure by sucking in low entropy from the environment to compensate for the continuous entropic degradation it is subject to (see Schrodinger 1944).

[14] Co-evolution is once again a biological concept which describes the reciprocal relationship between two closely interacting species (see Norgaard 1984).

exogenous and, increasingly in our high-entropy age, caused by the interaction of the global economy with the environment.[15]

One could say that it is the pace at which low entropy is pumped from the environment into the economy that limits the pace of economic development. Constantly, therefore, the economic process calls upon human beings, much like Maxwell's demon,[16] to filter and direct environmental low entropy towards the satisfaction of our economic goals. Based on such a vision, one could describe the challenge of economic development as not merely the multiplication of the filtering mechanism based on existing sieves, but much more as the imaginative task of the innovation of finer sieves (technologies) to filter and thereby reduce the proportion of low entropy ending up as waste.

In such highly complex and highly coupled systems, characterized by both intricate interconnections, as well as novelty, uncertainty has a deep presence. For we still have significant levels of ignorance about upcoming threats, most severely highlighted by the current context of climate change, that are at best poorly understood and at worst completely unknown.

Before going on to the main body of my lecture today, which is concerned with teasing out the implications of uncertainty for the nature of our transformational initiatives, let me try and summarize in yet another way the three kinds of unknowns that we are typically likely to encounter as in Table 9.1.

The most straightforward kind of uncertainty arises from what may be called conscious ignorance or those matters which we know we do not know enough about. But there can be two other kinds of unknowns as well. One which may be called tacit knowledge describes, for instance, the improvisations of a Hindustani classical musician who knows what she sings but may find it hard to describe, explain or exactly pin it down. The same applies to intuitions that arise sometimes about timing and tactics in politics or in the management of

---

[15] 'The virtue of the thermodynamic approach to evolution is its ability to connect life *ecologically* to the rest of nature through shared matter and energy flows' (Wicken 1988: 442).

[16] Maxwell (1871). A fabled minuscule demon posted near a microscopic swinging door separating two gases A and B of equal temperature. The demon would allow only faster molecules to go from A to B and only slower ones to move in the reverse direction, thus raising the temperature of B relative to A, defying the Entropy Law.

Table 9.1: What We Know and What We Do Not Know

		Meta-level	
		Known	*Unknown*
Primary level	**Known**	Known knowns	Unknown knowns (*tacit knowledge*)
	Unknown	Known unknowns (*conscious ignorance*)	Unknown unknowns (*meta-ignorance*)

Source: Bammer et al. (2009).

people in an organizational context. And, of course, there are several issues where we do not know what we do not know. Typically, these arise in the context of our interface with nature, in phenomena which exhibit what Shackle calls 'surprise' or what Georgescu-Roegen has called 'novelty by combination'. The emergence of the HIV virus is one such example. The entire range of phenomena related to global warming is another.

Implications for Action

We have thus established the inescapable presence of what may be termed irreducible uncertainty in our knowledge of the world. We have also understood the many sources and ramifications of this uncertainty. The question for us now is—how is one to act given the nature of the human predicament? Does the recognition of these multiple uncertainties lead to confusion, enfeeblement, non-action? Does it paralyse us? Or does it define a particular course of action, with certain defining characteristics that derive from our recognition of the ineluctable presence of uncertainty? These are large philosophical, existential questions. But to these I propose to give very specific, concrete answers, which are based on what I have learnt from and will illustrate through the work I have done as part of *Samaj Pragati Sahayog*, living in a tribal village over the last 20 years and also by reference to my early work in the Planning Commission over the past 10 months. I summarize the principles that need to guide and features that must characterize transformational initiatives under uncertainty and exemplify these through particular instances. I find it useful to divide the implications for action into four sections:

1. The Approach
2. The Interface with Nature
3. Handling Conflict and Contention
4. Institutional Implications.

The Approach

- *Uncertainty is the best corrective to fundamentalism:* The biggest contribution of a recognition of uncertainty as an essential feature of human knowledge about society is that it leads to a rejection of the notion of a *single* truth or *the* correct path. What saves science from degenerating into a dogma is the acknowledgment of the limits of knowing. This liberates us from the tyranny of certainty, whose claim is a part of the arrogance of power and the aspiration for which leads to a suppression of dissent, enquiry and the sense of wonder and mystery that has to be the beginning of all science. Uncertainty demands humility, the non-presumption of the arrogance of complete knowledge or certainty. It calls for a non-assertion of the definitive correctness of one's own viewpoint—an acknowledgment that truth resides in a matrix, not in any one location. That it flows from multiple directions and is embodied in relationships.
- *Uncertainty demands nimble-footedness:* Uncertainty requires an openness to mid-course correction as new knowledge is acquired over time. This means an abandonment of the heavy-handed inflexibility which characterizes so many of our development interventions.
- *Uncertainty calls for dialogue:* The loss of certainty opens up the possibility that we must also look elsewhere, to other sources for help and support in our quest for knowledge. Uncertainty, therefore, necessitates deep listening and the building of common ground across differences, respecting a diversity of approaches and standpoints regarding the same problem. It calls for an attempt to learn from the context where change is being attempted—an open and rich dialogue, a true engagement, which is both transparent and participatory. For it is transparent and participatory processes that are also more accountable and open to mid-course correction. They also facilitate the building of social trust, which is a powerful and often indispensable resource in situations of uncertainty (Luhmann 1979).

- *This dialogue neither romanticizes nor devalues so-called people's knowledge:* It would be a mistake to valorize any one form of knowledge over another. We need a corrective to the stridency of both the bottom-up activist and the top-down planner. Neither is appropriate or adequate by itself. What matters, what enlightens, is deep dialogue, an engagement from which something quite unanticipatable, something novel emerges and guides action.

- *Uncertainty demands a fusion of horizons à la Gadamer in at least three senses:* historical, embracing different stakeholders and across multiple disciplines. Since we attempt change in a specific context and this context has a unique history, is characterized by a range of stakeholders and requires an understanding of issues that reside in a multiplicity of disciplines, effectiveness of action demands that we make the requisite effort to bring together diverse perspectives in each of these three dimensions.

The Interface with Nature

- *We must weave our interventions into the contours of nature:* Once we recognize the contours defined by the balances in nature, our entire approach needs to shift from an attempt to control nature towards a creative weaving of our interventions into the flows and dynamics of natural processes. This requires a new imagination, to use Shackle's term, to visualizing the future. The best positive examples of this are the watershed approach and the move towards organic farming. The most significant negative illustration is the interlinking of rivers project. In a country like India which gets seasonal rainfall from monsoons, the periods when rivers have 'surplus' water are generally synchronous across the subcontinent. Further, given the topography of India and the way links are envisaged, it might totally bypass the core dryland areas of Central and Western India, which are located on elevations of 300+ metres above the mean sea level (MSL). It is also feared that linking rivers could affect the natural supply of nutrients through curtailing flooding of the downstream areas. Along the east coast of India, all major peninsular rivers have extensive deltas. Damming the rivers for linking will cut down the sediment supply and cause coastal and delta erosion, destroying the fragile coastal ecosystems. Most significantly, the plan could threaten the very integrity of the monsoon system. The presence of a low salinity layer of water with low density is a reason for maintenance of high sea-surface temperatures (greater than 28°C) in the Bay of Bengal, creating low pressure areas and intensification of monsoon activity. Rainfall over much of the subcontinent is controlled by this layer of low saline water. A disruption in this layer consequent upon massive interlinking of rivers, which would curtail the flow of fresh river water into the sea, could have serious long-term consequences for climate and rainfall in the subcontinent, endangering the livelihoods of a vast population.

- *The unity and integrity of natural cycles must compel giving up our silo-based approach to transformation:* We cannot expect to find a solution to India's water crisis unless we come out of the silos into which we have divided water and take a holistic view of the hydrologic cycle. We face a situation where the left hand of drinking water (under the Department of Drinking Water Supply located within the Ministry of Rural Development) acts as if it does not know what the right hand of irrigation (within the Ministry of Water Resources) is doing. Today groundwater is both the single largest source of rural drinking water (over 80 per cent) and irrigation (over 60 per cent). Both tap the same aquifer without any coordination whatsoever. Indeed, we are close to entering a vicious infinite regress scenario where our proposed solution (deep drilling by tube wells) only ends up aggravating the problem it seeks to solve. If one continues along the same lines, the initial problem will recur infinitely and will never be resolved. This regress appears a natural corollary of what has been termed 'hydroschizophrenia' (Llamas and Martinez-Santos 2005), which entails taking a schizophrenic view of an indivisible resource like water, failing to recognize the unity and integrity of the hydrologic cycle. I am happy inform you that this is the central message emerging from the Mid-Term Appraisal (MTA) of the 11th Plan we have just completed.

- *Our interventions need to be location-specific* reflecting every element of diversity—social, cultural and physical. Since we intervene in very diverse contexts, we need to give up the bureaucratic one-size-fits-all, monocultural approach. Across India we are faced with multifarious variations—in rainfall received, in soil and rock type, in slope and contour, in animal forms, in kinds of vegetation, crop or forest—and each of these and each combination of these, has different implications for the possibilities of striking, harvesting and storing water as also the possible forms of livelihood (agriculture or pastoralism, nature of crops that can be sustained, kind of livestock to be raised, etc.). Many of these variations occur even within a small micro-watershed. And this natural diversity has a complex interplay with the sociocultural tapestry of these regions. That includes values regarding life-goals, priorities (for example, security in view of pervasive, inherent uncertainty), understanding of and relationship with natural forces and resources, which have evolved over centuries, if not millennia. This canvas of *differentia specifica* poses a unique challenge to the development planner, the scientist, the social worker. Those who seek to intervene in any context, but especially in one with such diversity and potential fragility, cannot do so on the basis of a notion of mastery over nature and society. With mastery and control, comes the resort to simple tech fixes—monocultural, unilinear, indiscriminate. Irrespective of the specific challenges of each situation, an unthinking, insensitive bureaucracy seeks to impose its own pet solution—tube wells, eucalyptus, soya bean, Holstein Friesian. Appropriateness does not matter. Sustainability is of no concern. Dialogue is not attempted. History is given a go by, with disastrous consequences.

In our development programmes, unfortunately, we have sought to impose simplistic answers, top-down, without making the effort to understand the context, in all its diversity and complexity. We have been narrowly preoccupied with single variables like aggregate income, neglecting completely the entire range of issues involved in ecosystem resilience and stability. Disciplines, narrowly defined through specialization, have not spoken to each other. Nor have they spoken to the people in whose name solutions are sought to be developed. They have not been mindful of the balance that must be retained if our interventions are to be sustainable. Nature and society are not to be mastered or subdued. They are, rather, to be deeply understood so that we can weave our interventions in a creative manner into their delicate fabric. Consistently learning each step of the way—light, nimble and innovative in our tread.

·I am again glad to inform you that the MTA of the 11th Plan attempts a corrective in this direction. There are many examples of this. I will limit myself to only a few. One of the limitations of the Total Sanitation Campaign (TSC) that we have identified is the narrow range of technology options offered in a country with such immensely diverse geographic, hydrologic, climatic and socio-economic conditions (high water table, flood prone, rocky ground, desert/water scarce areas and extreme low temperatures). This has led to many problems, including non-acceptance by local communities, water pollution in shallow water table regions and waste of public funds. We highlight the need to broaden the range of models permissible under TSC and offer an initial menu of alternatives derived from detailed consultations with experts and practitioners.

Similarly, the MTA highlights the fact that problems surrounding groundwater overuse are not just a matter of the share of extraction in annual replenishment. The relationship between extraction and replenishment is complex and depends upon the aquifers from which groundwater is extracted.[17] The foundation of good groundwater management is a clear understanding of aquifers, which requires knowledge of geology—of rock types and rock structure. For groundwater, availability is dependent on the water storage and transmission characteristics of these underlying geological strata. The geological diversity in India makes aquifer understanding challenging, but all the more important because the local situation dictates the approach to managing groundwater. Moreover, these local situations also determine how groundwater overuse, droughts, floods, etc., impact drinking water security. The vulnerability of different hydrogeological settings to the level of groundwater development is different.

---

[17] An aquifer is described as a rock or rock material that has the capacity of storing and transmitting water such that it becomes available in sufficient quantities through mechanisms like wells and springs.

About 54 per cent of India (comprising mainly the continental shield) is underlain by formations usually referred to as 'hard rocks'.[18] Groundwater resource in hard rocks is characterized by limited productivity of individual wells, unpredictable variations in productivity of wells over relatively short distances and poor water quality in some areas. The initial thrust of irrigation by tube wells following the Green Revolution was restricted to India's 30 per cent alluvial areas, which are generally characterized by relatively more pervious geological strata. But from the late 1980s, tube well drilling was indiscriminately extended to hard rock regions where the groundwater flow regimes are extremely complex. Deeper-seated aquifers often have good initial yields, but a tube well drilled here may be tapping groundwater accumulated over hundreds of years. Once groundwater has been extracted from a deeper aquifer, its replenishment depends upon the inflow from the shallow system or from the surface several hundred metres above it. The path this water has to traverse is characterized by relatively unfavourable media, which greatly slows down the rate of groundwater recharge. This poses a severe limit to expansion of tube well technology in areas underlain by these strata. Similarly, in the mountain systems, which comprise 16 per cent of India's land area, effects of groundwater overuse do not take very long to appear. As the processes of groundwater accumulation and movement are vastly different in different geological types, the implications of any stage of groundwater development will vary significantly across types of geological settings. Clearly, therefore, a much lower level of groundwater development across 70 per cent of India's land area (hard rock and mountain) could be as 'unsafe' as a comparatively higher level in alluvial settings.

* *Factoring in uncertainty demands creation of more resilient systems:* Location-specific interventions, deeply cognizant of diversity necessarily give rise to polycentric, diverse and deeply interconnected systems, which are more resilient in the face of external perturbation. The best example of this is provided by the recent moves towards biofarming as shown in Figure 9.1.

---

[18] Hard rock is a generic term applied to igneous and metamorphic rocks with aquifers of low primary inter-granular porosity (for example, granites, basalts, gneisses and schists).

Figure 9.1: Flow of Resources in a Biofarm

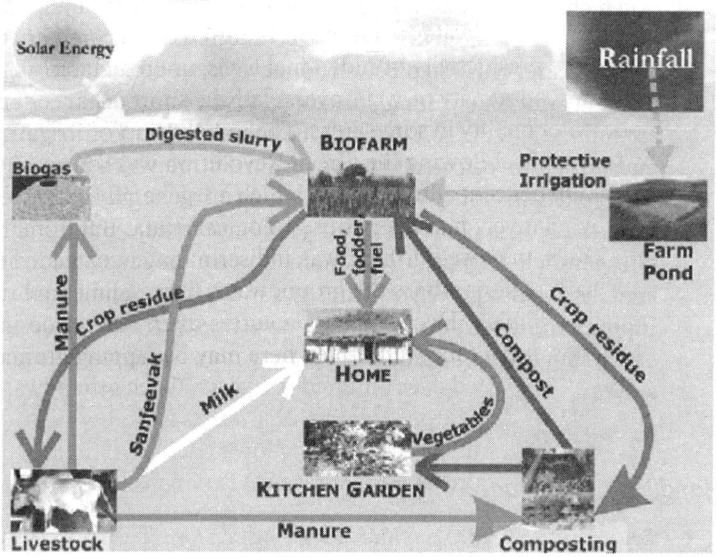

Source: Author.

The internal stability of an agro-ecological system could be defined as its elasticity towards any sort of external perturbation (Tiezzi et al. 1991). This stability is a function of the network of links that can be forged between various components of the system. Such links typically break down when monocultural production practices are adopted as in the Green Revolution or due to processes of environmental destruction such as deforestation and infringement on the domain of common property. These interventions weaken the internal linkages of the system, making it increasingly dependent on external.energy subsidies (such as fossil fuels–based chemical fertilizers, pesticides, etc.). This makes the system vulnerable to external shocks and market fluctuations which cause a further decline in stability. On the other hand, an integrated agro-ecological system, such as a biofarm, characterized by energy conservation and material recycling, is considerably more stable. In this system, several new links are forged within the elements of the natural resource base (climate, rain-fed agriculture, wastelands, forests, crop residues, animal and human wastes and

decentralized energy sources). With soil and water conservation technologies, surface runoff is minimized which improves
the level of soil moisture. Loss of essential soil nutrients is also
reduced, and harvested runoff is recycled to agricultural land
through water harvesting structures. Part of the crop residues
are returned to the soil through microbial decomposition. Animal wastes are directed to biogas plants, from which bioenergy
is supplied to households for cooking. The organic residues
from the biogas plant (digested slurry) go to enrich the soil as
nitrogen-rich fertilizer. The biomass surplus generated from
land, as a consequence of water and nutrient recycling, in turn,
supplies more residues, supports more livestock and creates an
expanding decentralized energy base within the agro-ecological
system.

Handling Conflict and Contention

• *Uncertainty related to conflict—Power, justice, love:* The fruits of India's development have been shared very unequally, especially
in certain geographies (*Adivasi* enclaves, drylands, hills) and
with specific social groups (Dalits, Muslims). In recent years,
India has witnessed the fastest growth of high net-worth individuals worldwide. In the same period in the 'other India',
across 200 districts, lakhs of people have committed suicide
or taken to the gun. Martin Luther King suggests a different
response to injustice—the path of love. But the love he spoke of
was no ordinary love. King (1958) elaborates the very different
meanings of three words for love in the Greek New Testament.
Eros, in Platonic philosophy, means the yearning of the soul
for the realm of the divine. It has come now to mean a sort
of aesthetic or romantic love. *Philia* signifies the intimate love
between friends, a reciprocal love, where we love because we
are loved. But the love King advocates is best expressed in the
Greek word *agape*. *Agape* implies understanding. It intimates a
creative, redeeming goodwill for all, an overflowing love which
seeks nothing in return. *Agape* is not a weak, passive love. It is
love in action (King 1957).
     Through a profound inversion of Nietzsche's critique of Chris-
tianity, King provides a reconceptualization of the relationship

between power and love. Nietzsche sought to determine the conditions of a new affirmation of life by overcoming what he regarded as the nihilistic despair produced by Christian values. King interrogates the very terms of this *problématique* by providing a radical restatement of his own spiritual tradition. He questions the legacy of viewing love and power as polar opposites, where love appears as a rescinding of power, and power as a rejection of love. King (1967) argues that 'power without love is reckless and abusive, and love without power is sentimental and anaemic' (p. 247). And this new understanding of power helps King positively formulate the unbreakable bond between love and justice: '[P]ower at its best is love implementing the demands of justice, and justice at its best is power correcting everything that stands against love' (ibid.).

Love must necessarily take on the larger structures of injustice that stand in its way. This love includes but goes well beyond isolated acts of kindness. At the same time, because love is our weapon, we do not seek to defeat anyone and must try not to end up humiliating those positioned against us. For the struggle is not against persons, it is for transformation of the opponent's view and the system of oppression. And even more for the self-renewal of those who work for change. As King (1958) says:

> [T]o retaliate with hate and bitterness would do nothing but intensify the hate in the world. Along the way of life, someone must have sense enough and morality enough to cut off the chain of hate. This can be done only by projecting the ethics of love to the centre of our lives. (p. 19)

Such an organic link between inner transformation of the individual and larger social change is invariably missing in our politics. But there is more. In our pursuit of structural change we cannot overlook the immediacy and enormity of suffering. Sadly, this has been the record of many movements for justice. The millennial quest, based on various teleological certainties of the dynamic of History (with a capital H), has often led to people being treated as cannon fodder. The finiteness of their lifetimes appears to have little import for leaders, who invariably belong to classes quite distinct from those who suffer injustice.

As a result, the desperation for finding tangible solutions appears much less evident in leaders than for the masses they lead.

We are confronted with a paradox. Narrow preoccupation with daily issues results, for example, in the sterile 'economism' of the working class. But the quest for millennial goals of a distant Shangri-La means a striking lack of concern for real-time solutions and an unyielding 'protest for the sake of protest'. The former reflects a complete absence of broader vision, the latter a cruel neglect of immediate anguish. The challenge of creative politics is to strike an imaginative balance between the two, without disadvantaging either.

We must stop viewing conflict as an arena of our victory over the 'other'. It is better regarded as a problem in search of a solution. A conflict needs not so much a victory, as a resolution. Indeed, a 'defeat' that moves society forward on the moral landscape, that empowers the disadvantaged and sensitizes those in power, deepening democracy in the process, could even be preferred to a 'victory' that fails to achieve any of these.

A key to moving forward in this direction is to give up the antediluvian unitary and insurrectionist conception of Revolution (with a capital R). The unique appeal of 'scientific socialism' was its claim to have discovered the 'laws of motion of society' that definitively predicted the inexorable coming of a new dawn. This teleology has ended up becoming the chief weakness of Marxism. If change is visualized in these terms, means-ends questions will be run roughshod over and horrors of the Stalinist kind will continue to be perpetrated.

The standpoint of *agape* love finds strong support in recent advances in Neuroscience and Economics, both of which have traditionally been bastions of selfishness as the central motive of human behaviour. Neurobiologists like Donald Pfaff (2007) marshal a new understanding of genes, neuronal activity and brain circuitry to explain our concern for the other. The path-breaking work of economists like Samuel Bowles questions standard textbook assumptions of the selfish *homo economicus* and emphasizes the role of altruism in the very survival of humankind in the difficult years ahead.

A one-track, single-event notion of revolution must also be discarded because it leads to complete neglect of crucial nitty-gritty detail that forms the heart of the transformation we dream of. It is this dry spadework that also contains solutions to immediate distress. Running midday meals in schools under active supervision of mothers, local people managing sanitation and drinking water systems, social audits in vibrant *gram sabha*s, participatory planning for watershed works, women leading federations of self-help thrift groups and workers running industrially safe, non-polluting factories as participant shareholders—all these and many more are the immediate, unfinished, feasible tasks of an ongoing struggle for change. Unfortunately, activists typically push these questions into a hazy future, to be all answered after the revolution, so to speak. These are difficult questions that necessitate intricate answers, and we need to begin looking for these here and now, in the living laboratories of learning of our farms and factories, villages and slums. Not in some imaginary distant future after a fictitious insurrection.

- *Social mobilization of the weak and voiceless essential part of any intervention:* If uncertainty related to a context of contention and conflict is to be adequately recognized we need to dedicate specific time, human and financial resources to the social mobilization of the disadvantaged in each of our development interventions. In the MTA of the 11th Plan, I have tried to provide a road map for this in the specific context of various development initiatives such as the *Mahatma Gandhi National Rural Employment Guarantee Act* (MGNREGA), sanitation and drinking water supply. The Parthasarathy Committee had already outlined this approach for the watershed programme and this has been incorporated into the Common Guidelines issued during the 11th Plan. One has to resist the rush to universalize without adequate preparation so that quality outcomes with genuine inclusiveness can be attained.

- *Uncertainty flowing from contention also demands inclusive approaches to the land question:* Land acquisition initiatives such as the *SEZ Act* and the proposed *Land Acquisition (Amendment) Bill* (LAAB) portend a serious conflict in India's countryside. The fact that the Supreme Court has held that the state is the 'trustee of all natural resources' must be regarded as posing a challenge to the doctrine of eminent domain, for it qualifies the assertion of absolute sovereign power by the state over natural resources. The inclusion of labourers, SC/ST families, vulnerable persons (disabled, destitute, orphans, widows, unmarried girls, abandoned women or persons above 50 years of age, without alternative livelihoods) and the landless is a very significant provision in the Rehabilitation and Resettlement (R&R) Policy which must become part of the LAAB. The LAAB and the *SEZ Act* also appear inconsistent with land ceiling laws and do not incorporate the special protection for Scheduled Tribes in the Indian Constitution, whether those under Schedules V and VI, the *Panchayats (Extension to the Scheduled Areas) Act*, 1996 or the *Scheduled Tribes and Other Traditional Forest Dwellers (Recognition of Forest Rights) Act*, 2006.

It needs to be clearly understood that the process of industrialization or infrastructure development in rural India cannot be sustained in the long run if opposition by Project Affected Families (PAFs) continues unabated or and they are not made the very first beneficiaries of its outcomes. It has been estimated that 70 per cent of 190 infrastructure projects in the pipeline have been delayed due to land acquisition problems. Enlightened state policy aimed at ensuring long-term sustainability of the process must gain decisive ground over a short-sighted recourse to available legal loopholes. There are many possibilities here, which need to be regarded as very small investments that ensure the long-term sustainability of the development process. One is to provide land in the command area of irrigation projects, as mentioned in the R&R policy. The other is to utilize the long period that separates project initiation and land acquisition as also the gap between first notification, displacement and project construction to train PAFs in skills that could be used on the project. Facilities and products created by the project could be made available to PAFs. Compensation could also be tied more closely to future valuations, which is an inflation-adjusted monthly pension combined with a savings bond. The pension could be partially tied to the profits of the project. The best route could be to make PAFs shareholders in the proposed project given their contribution to a key element of share capital. The safest way to disincentivize land acquisition from degenerating into a real estate proposition (as it has, reportedly in quite a few cases) is to resort to leasing or temporary alienation, which will not sever the relationship of the landowner with her land. This would mean that if the project does not take off or shuts down or comes to a close, the land would be returned to the original landholder.

Each of these initiatives can help restore the faith of people in the democratic process, which is under strain in the remote hinterlands of India. The way forward is to move away from the vision of 'subjects' inherent in the eminent domain doctrine towards that of citizens, whose rights are guaranteed under the Constitution. Ultimately, we have to go beyond narrow legality to seek broader legitimacy. This demands giving a cutting edge to many provisions of the R&R Policy, making each of them mandatory and not reducing them to what they are in effect—conditionalities without consequences (Ramanathan 2008). But it also requires an unequivocal commitment to imaginatively exploring ways of rebuilding the livelihoods of those adversely affected by development projects.

Institutional Implications

- *Uncertainty demands forging of partnerships:* Certainty is the requirement and characteristic of top-down, unilinear visions of change. Rejecting the illusory certainty of a single voice is a liberating, enriching, inclusive experience. It potentially provides the benefits of multiple perspectives and standpoints, each of which has a unique value. We need to recognize that a multidimensional, multi-stakeholder, multidirectional and multidisciplinary matrix of relationships governs the dynamics of change in a deeply interconnected way. While we may never fully fathom the depths and intensities of these interconnections (which is the residual uncertainty that ineluctably characterises our interventions), the more we are cognizant of these and the more we forge partnerships that bring all of them together, harnessing their respective strengths and insights, the more sustainable will our interventions become (in social, ecological and financial terms). Emerging from iterative, consultative, inclusive processes, they will also, therefore, be both more richly informed and more acceptable. What we need, therefore, are consortia or partnerships of players and agencies, each of which are poles of change. Both civil society and the state need to be open to and prepared for such partnerships. By prepared

I mean not only willingness but a degree of prior preparation for what would in most cases be a novel and certainly demanding experience. As so many examples already illustrate, no real change is possible without that.[19] But above all what I have learnt of living and working in the tribal areas of central India for 20 years is that the people of this country will need to be prepared to activate themselves. Democracy ultimately is a lot of hard work that demands that we move way beyond the victim mode. Neither waiting passively for the state to deliver nor activating ourselves only to fight for our rights can bring about real change. Transformational initiatives will succeed only if they are energized by the active participation of the people themselves. The space for this needs to be created by the state, which has to also facilitate this participation by building people's capacities and supporting their initiatives in this direction. I illustrate this point in a minute through the example of MGNREGA.

- *Recognition of uncertainty calls for and enables the growth of new kinds of organizations:* An acknowledgment of uncertainty in all the dimensions we have explicated creates the conditions for the creation of lean, learning organizations based on partnerships. This kind of nimble-footed organization is engaged in a process of continuous self-transformation even as it facilitates learning by its members (Pedler et al. 1997). It pledges itself to building partnerships with other organizations, which show a similar commitment to remaining lean and open to learning from others. Rather than unilinear 'command and control' strategies, it follows 'adaptive management' practices where surprises are expected and learning through experience and evolving knowledge is built into the organizational DNA (Kasperson 2009) as shown in Figure 9.2.

Following Shapiro (1988) and Thompson (2008), we could even describe these as 'clumsy institutions', in which 'contestation is harnessed to constructive, if noisy argumentation' (Thompson 2008: 172). Clumsiness is preferable to its alternative elegance, which would seek optimization around just one of the definitions of the problem and a unique solution,

---

[19] One of the most striking of these is the partnership between the Government of Andhra Pradesh and the Mazdoor Kisan Shakti Sangathan for NREGA social audits.

Figure 9.2: Adaptive Management in the Face of Uncertainty

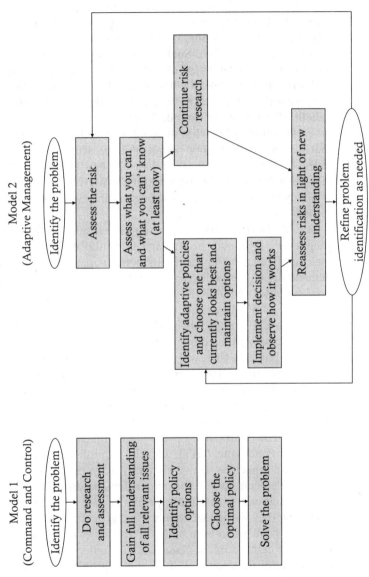

Model 1
(Command and Control)

Identify the problem

Do research and assessment

Gain full understanding of all relevant issues

Identify policy options

Choose the optimal policy

Solve the problem

Model 2
(Adaptive Management)

Identify the problem

Assess the risk

Assess what you can and what you can't know (at least now)

Continue risk research

Identify adaptive policies and choose one that currently looks best and maintain options

Implement decision and observe how it works

Reassess risks in light of new understanding

Refine problem identification as needed

Source: Author.

thereby silencing other voices. Clumsy institutions are agile and flexible enough to facilitate adaptability to turbulent environments. They can absorb plural perspectives and frames of reference found in inter-organizational partnerships.

- *A new definition of reform:* Such an institutional design hints at a completely new definition of 'reform' for the neglected parts of India. Over the last 20 years, reform has been restricted to the corporate sector. But the large mass of this country will not benefit till reforms are extended to the public sector in rural development. It is here that we need new institutional designs that will make the poorest people of India active participants in the development process. Perhaps the best example is provided by what is being attempted through MGNREGA, which is clearly the most radically new programme ever conceived in the history of independent India.

The MGNREGA has given rise to the largest employment programme in human history and is, unlike any other in its scale, architecture and thrust. Its bottom-up, people-centred, demand-driven, self-selecting, rights-based design is new and unprecedented. MGNREGA enjoins the state to provide a guarantee of employment to each rural household that demands work. But it also demands of the people that they participate actively in the design and implementation of the programme. For only then will it realise its true potential. Thus far, the programme has suffered because it continues to rely on the same ossified structure of implementation that has failed rural development for six decades. The programme demands a new imagination to be brought to bear on its institutional design. We need to empower the main implementing agency, the Gram Panchayats (GPs), with the requisite personnel and build their capacities so that they can make people aware of their entitlements, as also the unique demand-driven character of the programme. And move people beyond their long-held belief that they will get work only when government decides to 'open' work. We also need build GP capacities to enable them to develop detailed micro-plans that truly reflect the needs and aspirations of the people. Without this effort what is truly new about MGNREGA will not come into play. This empowerment initiative is what will strengthen the roots of democracy in India and place rural governance on a completely new and

stronger foundation. This demands lively partnerships with civil society, organizations and research institutions who can provide critical inputs in each of these vitally important aspects.

MGNREGA is also exciting because it has a self-limiting
character which has not yet been adequately recognized. The
ultimate potential of MGNREGA lies in a renewed focus on
improving the productivity of agriculture and convergence to
engender allied sustainable livelihoods. Millions of small and
marginal farmers are forced to work under MGNREGA because the productivity of their own farms is no longer enough
to make ends meet. Among agricultural labour households
in India, the percentage of those who own land is around 50
in Rajasthan and Madhya Pradesh, 60 in Orissa and Uttar
Pradesh and over 70 in Chhattisgarh and Jharkhand. And if
we focus on tribals, the proportion shoots up to as high as
76–87 per cent in Chhattisgarh, Jharkhand and Rajasthan.
MGNREGA will become really powerful when it helps re-
build this decimated productivity of small farms and allows
these people to return to full-time farming, thereby also reducing the load on MGNREGA. There are many such examples
to be found under MGNREGA, although they still remain
small in number. For example, the First Annual Report of
the National Consortium of Civil Society Organisations on
MGNREGA (2009) reports that earthen dams on common
land have recharged wells of thousands of poor farmers who
earlier worked as labourers to build these dams. These farmers are now busy making a series of investments to improve
their own farms. Rising incomes also improve capacity utilization and happier expectations act as incentives for more
investment. Under MGNREGA, farmers have come back to
land they long abandoned, as increased output, in an atmo-
sphere of renewed hope, spurs further investment. Converg-
ing MGNREGA with other programmes for rural livelihoods
would carry this momentum forward in a positive upward spi-
ral, which will broad-base the growth process via downstream
multiplier-accelerator effects (Shah 2009).

Our endeavour has to be to not merely help MGNREGA
realise its full potential but to carry that positive momentum
forward in a redesign on similar (though necessarily different
and specific) lines of all our other development initiatives.

Conclusion

The totalitarian state, the invisible hand of the market and science and technology—these were the three main bastions of certainty in the twentieth century. As the century ran its course, each one of them, at different points of time, palpably and demonstrably reached their limits. It is in the space created by their dethronement that the power of uncertainty has the potential to flower. It is only this fracturing of fundamentalisms that has forced each of these fulcrums of power to seek answers to unresolvable challenges in other domains. It is now for us to seize the moment by showing the requisite imagination and creativity in very concrete terms to harness the possibilities created by this unleashing of the insuperable recognition of uncertainty.

This needs to be very carefully understood. For, there is a very real possibility in precisely the opposite direction. So overwhelmed by the collapse of these certainties, we could allow ourselves to be gripped by the worst cynicism and despair, an alarmist fear of cataclysmic consequences. Leading either to an extremist stance of counter-violence or a giving up, translating in its most desperate form, into large-scale suicide. Both of these responses are in evidence in contemporary India. Both can, in one sense, in a large swathe of compassion, even be understood. But neither serves any useful purpose whatsoever. Violence, as is already evident, only incites the draconian character of the state. And surely we can find a better option for our farmers, than their swallowing the poisonous fluid.

Our challenge is not to allow ourselves to be overwhelmed by the undeniable darknesses of the time but to seize the light that still shines within so many endeavours, small, unsung but powerful, many outside the government but also several within it and envision the forging of strong alliances among them. I speak to you today of a hope in this direction. Where we exercise our imagination to creatively utilise the spaces that democracy is perforce obliged to provide its citizens, exemplified in recent years, after the watershed General Elections of 2004, by the *Right to Information Act*, the MGNREGA, the *Forest Rights Act*, the *Right to Education Act* and the upcoming *National Food Security Act*. These have resulted from an acknowledgment of the need to forge new instruments once the certainties of old had all run their course.

But let us hasten to remind ourselves that these are spaces that have as yet only been just created. To realise their full potential will require all the resourcefulness at our command. That will give reform a completely new, intricate and powerful meaning. That will demand forging of new kinds of institutions and partnerships. Building these will not mean a denial of the state, markets or science and technology. Rather, it will mean a harnessing of their respective strengths in a completely new alignment of forces.

The Prime Minister has described the Planning Commission as 'an essay in persuasion'. The word essay has an incredible range of meanings that includes trial, test, effort, attempt, especially an initial tentative effort and the result or product of an attempt. My aim as Member, Planning Commission is an *aagraha* (an attempt to persuade) with key players in the central and state governments, as also in civil society and academia across disciplines, to forge partnerships with each other that would help roll out a wide range of best practices that are already in place in isolation but need to be mainstreamed at scale without the customary loss of quality that such scaling normally entails. I invite all of you to join in this endeavour, where we work together, deeply cognizant of our own individual, discrete limitations but fully aware of the enormously powerful potential of our coming together.

References

Allais, M. 1953. 'The Behaviour of the Rational Man Faced with Uncertainty', *Econometrica* 21 (4): 503–46.

Arroe, K. 1962. 'The Economic Implications of Learning by Doing', *Review of Economic Studies*, 29 (3): 155–73.

———. 1963. 'Uncertainty and the Welfare Economics of Medical Care', *The American Economic Review* 53 (5): 941–73.

Arrow, K.J., and A.C. Fisher. 1974. 'Environmental Preservation, Uncertainty and Irreversibility', *Quarterly Journal of Economics* 87: 313–19.

Arrow, K.J., and G. Debreu. 1954. 'Existence of an Equilibrium for a Competitive Economy', *Econometrica* 22: 265–90.

Bammer, G., M. and Smithson, eds. 2009. *Uncertainty and Risk: Multidisciplinary Perspectives*. London: Earthscan.

Bammer G., M. Smithson and The Goolabri Group. 2009. 'The Nature of Uncertainty', in G. Bammer and M. Smithson eds, *Uncertainty and risk: Multidisciplinary perspectives*. London: Earthscan.

Carvalho, F. 1983. 'On the Concept of Time in Shacklean and Sraffian Economics', *Journal of Post-Keynesian Economics* 6 (2): 265–80.

Cernea, M., and H.M. Mathur, eds. 2008. *Can compensation prevent impoverishment?* New Delhi: Oxford University Press.

Costanza, R., ed. 1991, *Ecological Economics: The Science and Management of Sustainability.* New York: Columbia University Press.

Dasgupta, P.S., and G.M. Heal. 1979. *Economic Theory and Exhaustible Resources.* Cambridge: Cambridge University Press.

Davidson, P. 1982. 'Rational Expectations: A Fallacious Foundation for Studying Crucial Decision-making Processes', *Journal of Post Keynesian Economics* 5 (2): 182–98.

de Castro, E. Viveiros. 2003. '"AND", After-dinner Speech at "Anthropology and Science"', the 5th Decennial Conference of the Association of Social Anthropologists of Great Britain and Commonwealth, 14 July. Published in Manchester Papers in Social Anthropology 7.

Debreu, G. 1959. *Theory of Value: An Axiomatic Analysis of Economic Equilibrium.* New Haven: Yale University Press.

Gadamer, Hans-Georg. 1960. *Truth and Method.* New York: Continuum.

Georgescu-Roegen, N. 1971. *The Entropy Law and the Economic Process.* Cambridge: Harvard University Press.

Gray, L.C. 1914. 'Rent under the Assumption of Exhaustibility', *Quarterly Journal of Economics* 28: 466–89.

Harrod, R.F. 1948. *Towards a Dynamic Economy.* London: Macmillan.

Hotelling, H. 1931. 'The Economics of Exhaustible Resources', *Journal of Political Economy* 39: 137–75.

Kahneman, D., and A. Tversky. 1979. 'Prospect Theory: An Analysis of Decision Under Risk', *Econometrica* 47 (2): 263–91.

Kasperson, R.E. 2009. 'Coping with Deep Uncertainty', in *Uncertainty and Risk: Multidsciplinary Perspectives*, eds G. Bammer and M. Smithson. London: Earthscan.

Keynes, J.M. 1936. *The General Theory of Employment, Interest and Money.* London: Macmillan.

———. 1937. 'The General Theory of Employment', *Quarterly Journal of Economics*, February, 14 (1): 109–23.

King, M.L. 1957. 'Non-violence and Racial Justice', in *A Testament of Hope: The Essential Writings and Speeches of Martin Luther King Jr*, ed. J.M. Washington (1986). New York: HarperCollins.

———. 1958. 'An Experiment in Love', in *A Testament of Hope: The Essential Writings and Speeches of Martin Luther King Jr*, ed. J.M. Washington (1986). New York: HarperCollins.

———. 1967. 'Where Do We Go from Here?' in *A Testament of Hope: The Essential Writings and Speeches of Martin Luther King Jr*, ed. J.M. Washington (1986). New York: HarperCollins.

Knight, F.H. 1921. *Risk, Uncertainty and Profit.* Boston: Houghton-Mifflin.

Llamas, R., and P. Martinez-Santos. 2005. 'Intensive Groundwater Use: Silent Revolution and Potential Source of Water Conflicts', *American*

Society of Civil Engineers Journal of Water Resources Planning and Management 131 (4): 337–41.

Lowenstein, Roger. 2000. *When Genius Failed: The Rise and Fall of Long-term Capital Management.* New York: Random House.

Luhmann, N. 1979. *Trust and Power.* United Kingdom: John Wiley.

Marshall, A. 1920. *Principles of Economics,* 8th edn. London: Macmillan (1st edn. [1890]).

Martinez-Alier, J. 1987. *Ecological Economics.* Oxford: Blackwell.

————. 1991. 'Ecological Perception, Environmental Policy and Distributional Conflicts: Some Lessons from History', in *Ecological Economics: The Science and Management of Sustainability,* ed. R. Costanza, 118–36. New York: Columbia University Press.

Marx, K. 1976. *Capital,* Vol. 1. Harmondsworth: Penguin.

Maxwell, J.C. 1871. *Theory of Heat.* New York: Longmans, Green, and Co.

Nash, J. 1951. 'Non-cooperative Games', *Annals of Mathematics* 54: 286–95.

Norgaard, R.B. 1984. 'Coevolutionary Development Potential', *Land Economics* 60: 160–73.

Norgaard, R.B., and R.B. Howarth. 1991. 'Sustainability and Discounting the Future', in *Ecological Economics: The Science and Management of Sustainability* ed. R. Costanza, 88–101. New York: Columbia University Press.

Pedler, M., J. Burgogyne and T. Boydell. 1997. *The Learning Company: A Strategy for Sustainable Development,* 2nd edn. London: McGraw-Hill.

Perrings, C. 1987. *Economy and Environment: A Theoretical Essay on the Interdependence of Economic and Environmental Systems.* New York: Cambridge University Press.

Pfaff, D.W. 2007. *The Neuroscience of Fair Play.* New York: Dana Press.

Pigou, A.C. 1932. *The Economics of Welfare,* 4th edn. London: Macmillan.

Ramanathan, U. 2008. 'Eminent Domain, Protest and the Discourse on Rehabilitation', in *Can Compensation Prevent Impoverishment?* ed. M. Cernea and H.M. Mathur, New Delhi: Oxford University Press.

Ramsey, F.P. 1928. 'A Mathematical Theory of Saving', *Economic Journal* 38: 543–59.

Savage, L.J. 1954. *Foundations of Statistics.* New York: Wiley.

Schrodinger, E. 1944. *What is Life?* Cambridge: Cambridge University Press.

Shackle, G.L.S. 1972. *Epistemics and Economics.* Cambridge: Cambridge University Press.

————. 1975. *Time and Choice.* Oxford: Oxford University Press.

Shah, M. 2009. 'Multiplier Accelerator Synergy in NREGA', *The Hindu,* 30 April.

Shapiro, M. 1988. 'Judicial Selection and the Design of Clumsy Institutions', *Southern California Law Review* 61 (3): 1555–69.

Slovic, P. 1993. 'Perceived Risk, Trust and Democracy', *Risk Analysis* 13: 75–82.

Solow, R.M. 1974. 'The Economics of Resources or the Resources of Economics', *American Economic Review* (Richard T. Ely Lecture) 64: 1–21.

Thompson, M. 2008. 'Cultural Theory, Climate Change and Clumsiness', in *Contested Grounds*, ed. A. Baviskar. New Delhi: Oxford University Press.

Tiezzi, E., N. Marchettini and S. Ulgiati. 1991. 'Integrated Agro-industrial Ecosystems: An Assessment of the Sustainability of a Cogenerative Approach to Food, Energy and Chemicals Production by Photosynthesis', in *Ecological Economics: The Science and Management of Sustainability*, ed. R. Costanza. New York: Columbia University Press.

von Neumann, J., and O. Morgenstern. 1944. *Theory of Games and Economic Behaviour*. Princeton: Princeton University Press.

Washington, J.M. 1986. *A Testament of Hope: The Essential Writings and Speeches of Martin Luther King Jr*. New York: HarperCollins.

Weber, Bruce H., David J. Depew and James D. Smith (eds.). 1988. *Entropy, Information, and Evolution: New Perspectives on Physical and Biological Revolution*. Cambridge, MA: MIT Press.

Wicken, J.S. 1988. Thermodynamics, Evolution and Emergence: Ingredients for a New Synthesis', in, eds Bruce H. Weber, David J. Depew and James D. Smith, 139–69.

10

Lineages of Political Society

Partha Chatterjee

The Mythical Space of Normative Theory

It is sometimes said that modern political theory of the normative kind takes place in an ahistorical timeless space where perennial questions about the right and the good are debated. In fact, that is not quite the case. Rather, it would be more correct to say that these normative debates take place in a time-space of epic proportions, which emerged fully formed only after the victorious conclusion of an epochal struggle against an old order of absolutist, despotic or tyrannical power. There is, thus, a definite historical past that is posited by modern political theory as an era that has been overcome and left behind, even if it appears only as an abstract and negative description of all that is normatively unacceptable today. Sometimes, this abandoned past is given a location in real historical time, as, for instance, the absolutist order of the ancien régime overthrown by the French Revolution, or the restricted rules of suffrage extended by the reform acts in Britain in the nineteenth century, or the regime of racial discriminations undone by the civil rights legislation in the United States. But it is also clear that in its abstract and negative character, this historical past is limitlessly elastic in its capacity to include virtually any geographical space and any historical period and designate them as the past that must be overcome for modern politics to become possible.

The curious fact is that this negatively designated historical past could even be found to coexist with the normatively constituted order of modern political life in a synchronous, if anomalous, time of the present. Thus, when the demand became vociferous in many Western countries in the early twentieth century for unrestricted voting rights for women, the existing restrictions were described as unacceptable remnants of a past order. If there is, in some not too distant future, a serious campaign for the abolition of the House of Lords, the existing upper house of the British Parliament will, I am sure, be similarly consigned to a premodern past. Thus, even in its apparent indifference to the historical mode of argument, modern political theory of the normative kind uses a definite strategy of historicization in order to demarcate and serially redefine its own discursive space.

If I am permitted to adopt, somewhat insincerely (but only partially so), a position of externality in relation to the space-time of Western political theory and take a panoramic view of its progress since the beginning of the modern age, I would end up with the impression that there is an elemental sameness in all of modern political theory in the last three hundred years. It is as if all the major political developments of the modern world were anticipated, indeed foretold, at the birth of modern political theory in the late seventeenth-century England. Thus, whether we speak of the abolition of feudal privileges, or independence from an imperial power that refused to grant representative government to its colonial subjects, or the abolition of slavery, or universal adult suffrage without discrimination on grounds of religion, race, class or gender—the basic structure of arguments appears to be contained within modern political theory from the moment of its formation. Consequently, it doesn't really matter if John Locke could not even imagine women as autonomous and rational members of the Commonwealth, or if Immanuel Kant could do little more than hope that the Prussian Monarch would be enlightened enough to rule according to the dictates of reason. Those views of individual political philosophers were remnants of a premodern political order that had managed, in a purely empirical sense, to coexist in the same contemporaneous time-space as modern political life. They could, by an appropriate historicizing strategy, be explained away from the normative space of modern political theory, which would then be left free to traverse the entire discursive field opened up by its epic victory over absolutism. Needless to say, this discursive field can only be abstractly constituted.

As someone from the postcolonial world introduced from a very young age to the normative verities of Western political theory, I must confess that I have found all this quite baffling. How was it possible, I have asked myself, that all of the bitter and bloody struggles over colonial exploitation, racial discrimination, class conflict, the suppression of women, the marginalization of minority cultures, etc., that have dominated the real history of the modern world in the last hundred years or so have managed not to displace in even the slightest way the stable location of modern political theory within the abstract discursive space of normative reasoning? How is it that normative political theory was never pushed into constructing a theory of the nation, or of gender, or of race, or indeed of class? How could those contentious topics have been relegated to the empirical domains of sociology or history? How could it be that all of the conceptual history of modern politics was foretold at the birth of modern political theory? I have often heard it said, to the accompaniment of derisive sniggers, that Hegel's confident pronouncement in the early nineteenth century that 'what the spirit is now, it has always been implicitly ... the spirit of the present world is the concept which the spirit forms of its own nature' (Hegel 1975: 150) was only a piece of idealist mystification, or worse, German delusion. I am not sure that Hegel's detractors among contemporary political philosophers are necessarily free of that defect, even if they do not share the same national cultural traditions.

Having searched for several years both within and outside the domains of normative political theory, I think I now have the outlines of a possible answer to the question: How has normative political theory as practised in the West managed to fortify itself against the turmoil of the real world of politics and assert the continued validity of its norms as pronounced at its moment of creation? The answer will take us well outside the philosophically well-tempered zones of the Western world.

Two Senses of the Norm

Although the epic time of modern political theory appears to begin in seventeenth-century England, the conceptual innovations that enabled that abstract time-space to be constructed and secured against the incursions of the real world of politics appeared, I think, only around the turn of the nineteenth century. By then, European countries, of course, had the experience of conquering and ruling over vast territories in the Americas. But the European empires in the western hemisphere never seriously posed the problem of having to incorporate within a European political order the forms of law, property and government of the indigenous American peoples. The latter were not regarded as having a credible political society at all that needed to be integrated into the new imperial formation. Only the colonial settlements of Europeans and mestizos mattered—and these came to be organized on the most modern European normative principles of the time. But the European conquests in Asia that began in the second half of the eighteenth century posed entirely different problems. The existing political institutions of those defeated Oriental kingdoms could not be entirely set aside, for utterly 'real' political reasons. They had to be given a place within the new imperial order of European rule over its Eastern colonies. Thus began a new journey of normative Western political theory.

A key moment in the British history of the emergence of its modern empire was the debate in Parliament from 1781 to 1792 over the conduct of Warren Hastings as Governor General of India. Charged with corruption and high crimes, Hastings, in his defence, argued that India could not be ruled by British principles. If he had, in his own conduct, deviated from British norms, it was because Indian conditions demanded it. 'The whole history of Asia is nothing more than precedents to prove the invariable exercise of arbitrary power ... Sovereignty in India implies nothing else [than despotism].'[1] Edmund Burke, in his reply, was merciless:

> ... these Gentlemen have formed a plan of Geographic morality, by which the duties of men in public and in private situations are not to be governed by their relations to the Great Governor of the Universe, or by their relations to men, but by climates, degrees of longitude and latitude.... (Burke 1991: 346)

This was a license for corruption and abuse of power. 'My Lords', Burke thundered in Parliament:

> we contend that Mr. Hastings, as a British Governor, ought to govern upon British principles...We call for that spirit of equity, that spirit of justice, that spirit of safety, that spirit of protection, which ought to

---

[1] Speech by Warren Hastings in his defence in the House of Commons on 1 May 1786, cited in P.J. Marshall, ed., 1991, *Writings and Speeches of Edmund Burke* (Vol. 6), 348–49. It is speculated that these passages in Hastings's defence were actually composed by Nathaniel Brassey Halhed. See Rocher (1983).

characterise every British subject in power; and upon these and these principles only, he will be tried. (Burke 1991: 345–56)

Burke's claim was that Indians had their own ancient constitution, their own laws, their own legitimate dynasties. A British governor, ruling by true British principles, ought to have respected those institutions and customs and not, like Hastings, arrogantly cast them aside in order to introduce British forms with the substance of despotism.

The impasse created by debates such as this in the domain of normative theory was resolved, in the tumultuous age of revolutions, by a set of conceptual innovations that had little to do with the great political conflicts of the time. Writing his *Principles of Morals and Legislation* in 1789, Jeremy Bentham declared that the methods and standards of legislation he was proposing were 'alike applicable to the laws of all nations' (Bentham 1789: 2). More interestingly for us, in an early essay on 'The Influence of Time and Place in Matters of Legislation', Bentham proposed the following method:

I take England, then, for a standard; and referring every thing to this standard, I inquire, what are the deviations which it would be requisite to make from this standard, in giving to another country such a tincture as any other country may receive without prejudice, from English laws? ... The problem, as it stands at present, is: the best possible laws for England being established in England; required, the variations which it would be necessary to make in those of any other given country, in order to render them the best laws possible with reference to that country.[2]

In providing an instructive example of this method, Bentham chose a country that presented 'as strong a contrast with England as possible'.

Such a contrast we seem to have in the province of Bengal: diversity of climate, mixture of inhabitants, natural productions, force of the country, present laws, manners, customs, religion of the inhabitants; every circumstance, on which a difference in the point in question can be grounded, as different as can be ... To a lawgiver, who having been bred up with English notions, shall have learnt how to accommodate

---

[2] Bentham (1843: 171). I have been unable to determine the exact date when this essay was written. It appears to be sometime in the early 1780s.

his laws to the circumstances of Bengal, no other part of the globe can present any difficulty. (Bentham 1843: 172)

But Bentham also insisted that 'human nature was everywhere the same' and that different countries did not have 'different catalogues of pleasures and pains'. Then why should not the same laws hold good for all countries? Because the things that caused pleasure or pain were not the same everywhere. 'The same event ... which would produce pain or pleasure in one country, would not produce an effect of the same sort, or if of the same sort, not in equal degree, in another' (ibid.). But these grounds of variation were not all of the same kind either. Some were physical, such as the climate or the nature of the soil, and these were invariant and insurmountable. Others, no matter how difficult or inexpedient, were subject to intervention and change, such as 'the circumstances of government, religion, and manners' (ibid.: 177). Different sets of laws would be appropriate for different circumstances. Further, by the application of appropriate laws, the mutable circumstances could be subjected to the forces of change.

Bentham thought of these variations as amenable to more or less precise and detailed qualitative and quantitative comparison—that is to say, they were all subject to some common measure. He suggested that the legislator should be provided with two sets of tables relating to the country for which he was legislating. One set would consist of the civil code, the constitutional code, a table of offences and punishments, etc., and the other set would comprise tables of the moral and religious biases of the people, a set of maps, a table of the productions of the country, tables of the population and the like (ibid.: 173). Armed with these, he would be able to devise the best possible laws for any country.

Reading Bentham today, one can almost imagine an anticipation of the statistical handbooks of social indicators with which any undergraduate of the twenty-first century is now able to rank the countries of the world according to standards of living, mortality rates, quality of governance, human development and dozens of other evaluative criteria. Unlike in the writings of eighteenth-century historians and travellers brought up on Montesquieu, cultural difference here is no longer incommensurable. Rather, it can now be seen in terms of its consequences, plotted as deviations from a standard and hence normalized. Governments everywhere have been brought within the same conceptual field. All deviations between states were now comparable according to the same measure. States could be divided into ranks and grades.

Moreover, once normalized, deviations could be tracked over time: the deviation of a state from the norm could close or widen. Thus, in time, a country could conceivably enter the grade of 'advanced societies' or drop out of it. The important innovation here was the handle that was afforded for the intervention of 'policy' to affect the distance of an empirical state from the desired norm. Indeed, as the philosopher Ian Hacking has shown, the statistical elaboration of the idea of normality in the nineteenth century would establish two senses of the norm: one, the normal as the right and the good—the normative, as political philosophy, for instance, would have it; and the other, the normal as the empirically existent average or mean, capable of improvement (Hacking 1990: 160–69).

Norms and Exceptions

The significance of this conceptual innovation for the emergence of the new practices of government in the nineteenth century has not been adequately stressed. We see the concepts elaborated for the first time by Jeremy Bentham and his 'utilitarian' theories of legislation. But these formal properties of the comparative method would become part of the background assumptions of virtually all schools of thought on the subject of modern government, including many that had no truck with the baggage of utilitarianism as a political philosophy. Notwithstanding Bentham's exaggerated confidence in the ability of his method to provide exact and unimpeachable solutions to every policy problem, what it did mark out was a conceptual field that could in principle integrate into a single theoretical domain all questions of governance in every society that exists in the world. Its comparative method of normalization would establish an enduring modality of relating the domain of the normative to that of the empirical, something that would long outlast the limited appeal of utilitarian political philosophy.

Bentham's comparative method would also establish another global paradigm. If constitutionally established representative government was now to be recognized as the universally valid normative standard, then the universally valid and legitimate exception to that norm could only be some form of enlightened despotism. Despotism is unlimited and arbitrary power, unconstrained by constitutional rules. In this sense, it was often distinguished in the classical literature of the seventeenth and eighteenth centuries from absolutism, which was unlimited power but legitimately constituted within certain fundamental laws. The form of government recommended by the new normative theory for European colonies in the East was absolutist in the sense that while it did not recognize any limits to its sovereign powers within the occupied territory, it did claim to be constituted by, and to function within, certain fundamental laws. But it was despotic in its foundational assumptions since the authority that was to lay down those fundamental laws was arbitrarily constituted and was not in any way responsible to those whom it governed. But when despotism claims to be enlightened, it places a limit on itself and promises to itself to be responsible—it becomes limited by and responsible to enlightened reason. When that happens, there is effectively no difference between despotism and absolutism. Despotism has to justify its actions to itself by their results (Krieger 1975: 39). Since the empirically prevailing average social conditions in the 'backward' colonies were different from those in the advanced countries, the normative standard of the latter would have to be altered to suit the former. The universally valid norm would have to be withheld in favour of a colonial exception.

This structure of norm and exception can be seen in virtually every justification of colonial empires in the nineteenth and twentieth centuries. The puzzle posed by postcolonial political theory—by Uday Singh Mehta, for example—of liberal democratic governments of Europe holding overseas territories under their despotic rule, thus apparently contradicting their cherished normative principles, dissolves when one realizes the power of the norm–exception construct (Mehta 1999). Thus, John Stuart Mill, one of the greatest liberal political theorists of all time, while making an extended case for the universal superiority of representative government, specifically argued that it could not apply, at least not yet, to dependencies such as India or Ireland (Mill 1861, Ch. xviii). The latter were exceptions; hence, there was really no contradiction in Mill's normative liberal theory. He recommended a paternal British despotism for those countries, until such time as their peoples became mature enough to govern themselves. Of course, neither Mill nor any other liberal could suggest an impartial way of deciding when and if such a stage had been reached.

Apparently, there was no alternative but to rely on the good sense of the paternal guardians to grant self-government to their wards.

The method of normalization as a key aspect of modern disciplinary practices is, as Michel Foucault has shown, ubiquitous in the operations of the modern regime of power.[3] The norm-exception formula too is used widely to deal with the exigencies of heterogeneity and uncertainty in a policy field that has been presumably normalized. What I am also suggesting through my thumbnail sketch of the conceptual history of political institutions in the modern West is that, contrary to the long enshrined received narrative, those institutions and their normative principles were not the products of an exclusively endogenous development but the result of Europe's encounters with its colonial territories, first in the Americas and then in Asia and Africa. Let me now move to our contemporary times and look at the formerly colonized parts of the world to see how the universal verities of Western political theory have fared in those places.

The Civil and the Political in Alien Spaces

I will have to be somewhat schematic in laying out the background conditions that made postcolonial political theory possible. The period of decolonization following the end of the Second World War made the nation state the universally normal form of the modern state. Popular sovereignty became the universal norm of legitimacy—even military dictators and one-party regimes began to claim to rule on behalf of the people. But decolonization was achieved not necessarily because the paternal guardians decided that their immature wards had at last achieved adulthood. On the contrary, in most colonial countries, the people declared their determination to rule themselves by rebelling against their masters. This meant that the pedagogical role of those who were the guardians of the norm and the declarers of the exception came to be questioned. As we shall soon see, this would have important implications for the relation between the norm and the exception.

The normative principles of modern politics as established in the West held enormous sway over the new ruling elites in postcolonial

---

[3] Especially Foucault (1977).

countries, not least because of the influence of colonial education. But decades of colonial rule did not necessarily close the deviation of the empirical social indicators from the universally desirable norm. The sociologically grounded theories that now came into vogue re-phrased the old arguments of colonial difference in a new language of modernization, calling the deviation a historical lag that had to be made up. Underlying these theories was, as Sudipta Kaviraj has recently pointed out, an assumption of symmetrical development, that is to say, an expectation that all of the functionally interrelated processes within modernity should emerge simultaneously (Kaviraj 2005: 497–526). If they did not, then it was a case of imperfect or failed modernity. A little reflection will show that this expectation of symmetrical development is not unrelated to the abstract homogene-ous discursive space cleared out and occupied by normative political theory.

But soon there began to emerge arguments about alternative or multiple modernities. These, Kaviraj has shown, are better under-stood as implying a sequential theory of development. This theory suggests that the particular sequence in which the different processes of modernity occurred in Western history need not be repeated else-where. In that case, the resultant forms of the modern in those places might look quite different. Thus, to take an example, if the particular sequence 'commercial society – civic associations – rational bureauc-racy – industrialization – universal suffrage – welfare state', which may be taken as a schematic representation of the trajectory of the modern state in the West, is replaced by a sequence in which rational bureaucracy and universal suffrage precede the others, then it is likely that the form of the state that would result would not be a replica of the state in the West. It is from a consideration of these alternative sequences of modernity rather than from that of multiple or postmo-dernity that postcolonial political theory was born.

But this raised entirely new theoretical problems regarding the re-lation between the two senses of the norm, viz. the empirical average and the normatively desirable. Let me illustrate this with reference to two sets of issues—the first, of legality, and the second, of violence.

Leaving out the white settler colonies, the domain of civil social institutions and modern representative politics was, in most parts of the colonial world, restricted to only a small section of the colonized population. Mahmood Mamdani has described how in anglophone, francophone and lusophone Africa, there emerged a modern civic space that was racially divided but regulated by a modern code of civil law, while a huge domain of traditional society was organized under customary law. Following independence, the conservative regimes de-racialized civil society while leaving the traditional sphere of customary law largely intact, while the radical regimes tried to impose uniform citizenship on all by means of authoritarian power structures, leading to resistance and conflict (Mamdani 1996). In India, the new republic was founded on a liberal democratic constitution, universal suffrage and competitive electoral representation. But the space of politics became effectively split between a narrow domain of civil society where citizens related to the state through the mutual recognition of legally enforceable rights and a wider domain of political society where governmental agencies dealt not with citizens but with populations to deliver specific benefits or services through a process of political negotiation. In some of my recent work, I have described the anomalies that result in the application of the norm of equality of all citizens before the law and how those anomalies are sought to be resolved through the intervention of politics (Chatterjee 2004).

Take the familiar example of squatter settlements of the poor in numerous cities of the postcolonial world. These urban populations occupy land that does not belong to them and often use water, electricity, public transport and other services without paying for them. But governmental authorities do not necessarily try to punish or put a stop to such illegalities, because of the political recognition that these populations serve certain necessary functions in the urban economy and that to forcibly remove them would involve huge political costs. On the other hand, they cannot also be treated as legitimate members of civil society who abide by the law. As a result, municipal authorities or the police deal with these people not as rights-bearing citizens but as urban populations who have specific characteristics and needs and who must be appropriately governed. On their side, these groups of urban poor negotiate with the authorities through political mobilization and alliances with other groups.

On the plane of governmentality, populations do not carry the ethical significance of citizenship. They are heterogeneous groups, each of which is defined and classified by its empirically observed characteristics and constituted as a rationally manipulable target population for governmental policies. Consequently, if, despite their illegal occupation of land, they are given electricity connections or allowed to use municipal services, it is not because they have a right to them but because the authorities make a political calculation of costs and benefits and agree, for the time being, to give them those benefits. However, this can only be done in a way that does not jeopardize the legal order of property and the rights of proper citizens. The usual method is to construct a case such that the particular illegality associated with a specific population group may be treated as an exception that does not disturb the fundamental rule of law. Governmental decisions aimed at regulating the vast populations of the urban poor usually add up to a huge pile of exceptions to the normal application of the law.

Populations respond to the regime of governmentality by seeking to constitute themselves as groups that deserve the attention of government. If as squatters they have violated the law, they do not necessarily deny that fact, nor do they claim that their illegal occupation of land is right. But they insist that they have a right to housing and livelihood in the city, and if they are required to move elsewhere they must be provided with rehabilitation. They form associations to negotiate with governmental authorities and seek public support for their cause. Their political mobilization involves an effort to turn an empirically formed population group into a moral community. The force of this moral appeal usually hinges on the generally recognized obligation of government to provide for the poor and the underprivileged. This obligation may be seen as part of the general democratic temper of our age. But I believe it is also specifically a consequence of the anti-colonial movement that overturned the paternal despotism of imperial rule and established the sovereignty of the people.

If we consider the example of elections in India, for instance, we will find that the overwhelming bulk of the political rhetoric expended in election campaigns concerns what governments have or have not done for which population groups. The function of rhetoric here is to turn the heterogeneous demands of populations into the morally coherent and emotionally persuasive form of popular demands. In this sense, as Ernesto Laclau has argued, populism is the only morally legitimate form of democratic politics under these conditions (Laclau 2005). It is important to emphasize that unlike the symmetrical theory of modernity which would regard such populism as a perversion of modern democratic politics, the sequential theory would consider it with utter seriousness as a new and potentially richer development of democracy.

However, the negotiations that take place in political society frequently involve an invitation to the authorities to declare an exception. Thus, when squatters claim that they be allowed to occupy their settlements or hawkers that they be allowed to set up stalls on the streets, they do not demand that the laws of property be abolished or that all trade licenses and regulations be set aside. Rather, they demand that the authorities make a political judgement to use the sovereign power of the state to declare their case as an exception to the norm laid down by the law.

It is true, of course, that the law is also frequently broken by the propertied and the wealthy, that is, by those who claim to be proper citizens inhabiting civil society. Thus, municipal building regulations, trade regulations and tax laws are widely believed to be broken by the urban rich, many of whom, being influential and well connected, even flaunt their impunity. But these violations are unable to mobilize the moral justification that the illegalities of the poor manage to do. Hence, they are dealt with through corruption, evasion or the blatant use of power. They fail to become issues of negotiation in political society.

We should also remember that vast sections of the poor in postcolonial cities find a living in the so-called informal sector of employment which is largely unregulated and in which production or service units frequently violate labour, tax and environmental laws. Quite often, these enterprises have owners who are themselves workers and it is not unusual for them to value the survival of their units and the livelihood of their employees above the objective of making profits for further accumulation. They frequently use collective political mobilization and seek the help of political parties and leaders to ensure the conditions of their survival, often by demanding that the usual tax, labour or environmental regulations not be applied in their case. Here again, politics intervenes to suspend the norm and create an exception, supposedly in a justified cause.

This raises another interesting problem for contemporary political theory. Is justice better served by the non-arbitrary procedures of the equal application of the law or by the contextual and possibly arbitrary judgement that addresses the peculiarities of a particular case? It is useful to recall here an observation of Alexis de Tocqueville from the time when the modern democratic state was in its youth. Distinguishing between tyranny and arbitrary power, he says, 'Tyranny may be exercised by means of the law itself, and in that case it is not arbitrary; arbitrary power may be exercised for the public good, in which case it is not tyrannical' (Tocqueville 1990: 262). We could say that political society, operating under conditions of electoral democracy in India, affords the possibility of inviting the arbitrary power of government to mitigate the potentially tyrannical power of the law. As a matter of fact, it could even be said that the activities of political society in postcolonial countries represent a continuing critique of the paradoxical reality in all capitalist democracies of equal citizenship and majority rule, on the one hand, and the dominance of property and privilege, on the other.

It is relevant to point out, for instance, that this critique has a genealogy going all the way back to the origins in the eighteenth century of British colonial attempts to impose a regime of the non-arbitrary rule of law in the newly conquered territories of India. Ghulam Husain Tabatabai, the most perceptive Indian historian of the eighteenth century, and Mirza Abu Taleb who travelled to Britain at the turn of the nineteenth, both wrote extensively and critically on what they thought was an expensive, slow, distant and unconscionably inflexible judicial system introduced by the British in Bengal. Both thought that direct access to an impartial judge who was knowledgeable about and sensitive to the specific circumstances of a case was far more likely to serve the cause of justice.[4] The critique has continued to inform popular beliefs and practices about the judicial system of modern India. Thus, for example, one of the most sought-after services of elected local bodies in rural West Bengal is arbitration in property, family and community disputes. Even though this is not one of their statutory functions, elected local representatives are preferred by rural people for resolving conflicts than the slow, non-transparent and frequently corrupt institutions of the police and the courts (Bhattacharya et al. 2006). The latter are seen as instruments that only the wealthy can manipulate to their advantage; the poor avoid them to the best of their ability.

If one thinks of this widely shared popular critique of the modern normative idea of the non-arbitrary and equal application of the law

---

[4] Khan (1972: 196). There is a four-volume edition of the 1788 translation of Ghulam Husain's work *Sair ul-mutakkherin* published in 1902 (Seid-Gholam-Hossein-Khan 1902). A facsimile edition of the 1926 edition is now available from New Delhi, Inter-India Publications, 1986.

within a sequential rather than symmetrical framework, one could be led in some unexpected directions. Thinking symmetrically, one might conclude, like many conservative colonial officials of British India, that the impersonal procedures of rational law and bureaucracy were unsuited to backward societies used to customary rather than contractual obligations and that the exercise of personal but impartial authority was more appropriate. This would be the familiar declaration of a colonial exception. But if we take the sequential logic more seriously, we might be moved to suggest not the irrelevance of the norm of the impersonal and non-arbitrary application of the law but its critical re-evaluation in the light of emergent practices in many postcolonial countries that seek to punctuate or supplement it by appealing to the personal and contextual circumstances.

It is important to stress that the normative principles of Western political theory continue to enjoy enormous influence all round the world as models that are worthy of emulation. But the actual practices of modern political life have resulted not in the abandonment of those norms but in the piling up of exceptions in course of the administration of the law as mediated by the processes of political society. The relation between norms and practices has resulted in a series of improvisations. It is the theorization of these improvisations that has become the task of postcolonial political theory.

One other area where such improvisations have led to a distinct reformulation of the received norm is that of the secular state. The French republican ideal of *laïcité*, having travelled to Turkey as *laïque*, has in recent years provoked much controversy and conflict over state recognition of religious practices without as yet producing any redefined norm (Gole and Ammann 2006). In India, while the secular state is a central feature of the constitutional structure, its practice has come to mean neither the mutual separation of state and religion nor the strict neutrality of the state. Rather, an altogether new norm of the modern secular state seems to have emerged, which Rajeev Bhargava has theorized as that of principled distance, which implies disestablishment but not the strict non-intervention of the state in religion (Bhargava 1998). In this context, one must also mention the massive but as yet untheorized process of the establishment of modern secular states all over East Asia apparently without any serious debate over the question of secularism. What is it about the sequence of modernity in that part of the world that made this possible?

The Political Management of Violence

A study of squatter settlements in the city of Calcutta (now Kolkata) carried out by Ananya Roy brings out an interesting gender dimension of political society (Roy 2003). The livelihood of families living in these illegal settlements greatly depends on the employment of women as domestic help in neighbouring middle-class houses. This is, of course, an informal sector of employment lacking any form of labour organization. The men of the settlements often do not have regular jobs. But they form associations to seek the support of political parties in order to protect their settlements. The associations are entirely male. The reason is not merely that political work is traditionally seen as a male pursuit, but also because politics in the slum neighbourhoods is thought to be dangerous, involving frequent incidents of violence. Political society, consequently, tends to be a masculine space.

The point is illustrated graphically in Thomas Blom Hansen's study of the Shiv Sena in the towns and cities of Maharashtra, especially Mumbai (Hansen 2001). The political effectiveness of the Shiv Sena as a right-wing populist party claiming to defend Marathi interests and Hindu dominance has crucially depended on its control over the urban slum population and the informal sector of labour. Hansen shows that a key figure here is the local *dada*, the strongman who builds a personal network of loyalty and protection and projects the image of masculine, assertive and often violent power. The modality of this power is performative; it is effective precisely to the extent that it works as a demonstrated threat that brings about the desired result. The issues on which the Shiv Sena intervenes are everyday matters of political society among the urban poor—jobs, housing, living conditions in the slums, prices of essential items of consumption, dealing with the police and the authorities. The methods are direct and often theatrical—the image of local strongmen projecting raw power to secure instant justice is what is expected to attract their followers. For the most part, the actual violence is kept within carefully controlled limits. Only rarely is there widespread organized violence and that too only after a decision of the central leadership of the party, as in the 1992 killings of Muslims in Mumbai.

The subject of violence brings into view the dark underside of political society. It is clear that the real world of politics is quite far removed from the Weberian ideal of the state having a monopoly of the means of legitimate violence. Since many of the practices of political society involve the transgression of the law, it follows that agents other than the state authorities must also acquire the means of using force to defend those practices when necessary. Once again, political parties and leaders try to mobilize such means, with or without the acquiescence of the authorities. This is undoubtedly the principal reason why there has emerged the phenomenon of what is often called the 'criminalization' of politics, that is, the increasing presence of persons with criminal records among elected representatives at local, state and even national levels. That violators of the law can become legitimate representatives of the people is not necessarily a symptom of popular foolhardiness or of the perversion of electoral democracy. Rather it is a sign of the inability of the normative regime of law to fully bring under its order the real heterogeneity of power relations in society. It is also significant that in most local formations of political society, a certain 'normal' level of violence tends to be established which represents some sort of empirical equilibrium among prevailing power relations and that there are recognized thresholds beyond which the limits of normality are crossed. On the other hand, when a situation has to be demonstrated as intolerable or outrageous, there is frequently a spectacular show of violence, usually involving the destruction of public property or attacks on governmental institutions and personnel. Violence here is not mindless or blind, but even in its most passionate expressions, calculated to elicit the desired response from the government and the public.

Redefining the Norms

A consideration of postcolonial politics against the background of Western normative theory might suggest the abandonment of moral norms in favour of realist politics. This would be to trivialize the challenge posed for postcolonial political theory. Even though the demand for realism has much merit, it cannot mean, as Raymond Geuss has pointed out, the claim that morality has no place in politics (Geuss 2008). Rather, as we cannot fail to see in numerous accounts, postcolonial politics frequently presents a moral critique of the normative standards upheld by Western political theory and improvises practices that run parallel or counter to the approved forms. The theoretical challenge that is thereby posed is twofold: The first is the challenge to break the abstract homogeneity of the mythical time-space of Western normative theory by emphasizing the real history of its formation through violent conflict and the imposition of hegemonic power. The second is the even greater challenge to redefine the normative standards of modern politics in the light of the considerable accumulation of new practices that may at present be described only in the language of exceptions but in fact contain the core of a richer, more diverse and inclusive, set of norms.

References

Bentham, Jeremy. 1789. *Principles of Morals and Legislation*, Chap. xvii, Section 2.

———. 1843. 'Essay on the Influence of Time and Place in Matters of Legislation', in *The Works of Jeremy Bentham*, vol. 1, ed. John Bowring, 171. Edinburgh: William Tait.

Bhargava, Rajeev, ed. 1998. *Secularism and Its Critics*. Delhi: Oxford University Press.

Bhattacharya, Dwaipayan, Partha Chatterjee, Pranab Kumar Das, Dhrubajyoti Ghosh, Manabi Majumdar and Surajit Mukhopadhyay. 2006. *Strengthening Rural Decentralization*. Calcutta: Centre for Studies in Social Sciences.

Burke, Edmund. 1991. Opening of Impeachment, February 16, 1788. In *Writings and Speeches of Burke*, vol. 6, ed. Marshall, 345–56.

Chatterjee, Partha. 2004. *The Politics of the Governed: Reflections on Popular Politics in Most of the World*. New York: Columbia University Press.

Foucault, Michel. 1977. *Discipline and Punish: The Birth of the Prison*, trans. Alan Sheridan. Harmondsworth: Penguin.

Geuss, Raymond. 2008. *Philosophy and Real Politics*. Princeton: Princeton University Press.

Gole, Nilufer, and Ludwig Ammann, eds. 2006. *Islam in Public: Turkey, Iran and Europe*. Istanbul: Istanbul Bilgi University.

Hacking, Ian. 1990. *The Taming of Chance*. Cambridge: Cambridge University Press.

Hansen, Thomas Blom. 2001. *Wages of Violence: Naming and Identity in Postcolonial Bombay*. Princeton: Princeton University Press.

Hegel, G.W.F. 1975. *Lectures on the Philosophy of World History*, trans. H.B. Nisbet. Cambridge: Cambridge University Press.

Kaviraj, Sudipta. 2005. 'An Outline of a Revisionist Theory of Modernity', *Archives européennes de sociologie* 46 (3): 497–526.

Khan, Abu Taleb. 1972 [1814]. *Travels of Mirza Abu Taleb Khan in Asia, Africa, and Europe during the Years 1799 to 1803*, trans. Charles Stewart, Ch. xxii. New Delhi: Sona Publications.

Krieger, Leonard. 1975. *An Essay on the Theory of Enlightened Despotism.* Chicago: University of Chicago Press.

Laclau, Ernesto. 2005. *On Popular Reason.* London: Verso.

Mamdani, Mahmood. 1996. *Citizen and Subject: Contemporary Africa and the Legacy of Late Colonialism.* Princeton: Princeton University Press.

Mehta, Uday Singh. 1999. *Liberalism and Empire: A Study in Nineteenth-century British Liberal Thought.* Chicago: University of Chicago Press.

Mill, John Stuart. 1861. *Considerations of Representative Government*, Ch. xviii.

Rocher, Rosane. 1983. *Orientalism, Poetry and the Millennium.* New Delhi: Motilal Banarasidass Publishers Pvt Ltd.

Roy, Ananya. 2003. *City Requiem, Calcutta: Gender and the Politics of Poverty.* Minneapolis: University of Minnesota Press.

Seid-Gholam-Hossein-Khan. 1902. *A Translation of the Sëir Mutaqherin; or View of Modern Times, Being an History of India, from the Year 1118 to the Year 1194 (this Year answers to the Christian Year 1781–82) of the Hedjrah;* vols. 1–4. Calcutta: R. Cambray.

Tocqueville, Alexis de. *Democracy in America*, vol. 1, trans. Henry Reeve, revised by Francis Bowen, ed. Phillips Bradley. New York: Vintage.

11

The Politics of Social Justice

Pratap Bhanu Mehta

Introduction

India is going through enormous changes. There is, rightly, a great sense of optimism. For the first time in our history real social and economic change seems like a possibility, and the sheer unleashing of aspiration and energy across different sections of Indian society is staggering. But there are some concerns about the form the politics of justice will take, even in this newly buoyant and optimistic era. This is the theme of this chapter. The chapter is divided into two parts. The first reflects on the limited set of instruments we have that can do full justice to the aspiration of social equality. The second part reflects, somewhat more briefly, on why caste still remains such an entrenched category around which the politics of social justice is constructed, and what the consequences of this entrenchment might mean. The aim of this lecture is, to borrow Judith Shklar's phrase, to be more tour of perplexities than a guide for the perplexed.

The Challenges for Social Justice

The present challenge of the politics of social justice must be seen against the backdrop of a general, perhaps more global and historical pessimism about the relationship between democracy and equality. Democracies, in principle, derive their legitimacy from a certain form of political radicalism, promising new beginnings, a constantly challenged and renewed social order and an affirmation of equality. But in practice, democracies have turned out to be remarkably conservative institutions. Perhaps a little historical perspective is in order. In the eighteenth and nineteenth centuries, many perceptive observers of 'democracy' saw its conservative potential. Adam Smith had very presciently predicted that a republic, the United States, would be the last to abolish slavery, much after many monarchies had done so. Alexis de Tocqueville, the most insightful observer of democracy had commended it in part because democracies make revolutions rare. While democracies relentlessly abolish formal distinctions of social status, they are quite compatible with high levels of economic inequality. Contrary to those who feared democracy, Tocqueville argued, that democracies promote stability in property relations. This is so for various reasons. But one reason was quite subtle. In countries where formally inequality has been abolished, and a *myth* of formal equality becomes part of the self-understanding of a society; it becomes, paradoxically, harder to critique real inequality.

There is a wider debate to be held about why democracies have turned out to be so compatible with high levels of inequality. And this is, in some senses, a truly global debate. In the United States, political scientists are puzzled by the fact that the democratic system has allowed inequality to grow immeasurably over the last two decades, with most of the gains of growth going to the top 10 per cent of the population and a decline in real wages for much of the middle class. There are several reasons advanced for this—from the role ideological mystification plays in democratic politics to the susceptibility of democracies to special interests. But in very different contexts, from the debate over democracy in China to the health of democracy in the United States, one question is being asked. Is the inability to mitigate inequality a contingent feature of democracy? Or are there deeper, far more structural reasons as to why democracies are unable to mitigate inequality?

On the contingent view, the inability of democracy to mitigate inequality can be explained by contingent features of the way in which democracy is organized. The structure of election finance, forms of party organization, the susceptibility of media control, voter apathy, lack of information, all contribute to making democracies less self-aware than they should be. Others, like Adam Pzeworski argue that there may be deeper structural reasons why addressing inequality is difficult (Pzeworski 2010). One major reason has to do with what I call 'small liberty effects'. In a society, which allows some basic freedoms, even small differences can over time accumulate and transform into great ones. The most powerful illustration of small liberty effects is illustrated in a classic paper by Debraj Ray and Dilip Mookherjee. Their reasoning goes something like this. Suppose productive assets were equalized. But there were very very small differences in rates of return due to a variety of reasons. Some get a return on 0.02 per cent and others suffer a small loss of minus 0.02 per cent. After 50 years such minute differences of return will translate into one group having almost eight times the wealth of others. And this is with minor differences (Mookherjee and Ray 2003: 369–93).

Instruments of Redistribution

There may be other reasons as well. Is it the case that the instruments of redistribution that democracies can use have severe limitations? And it might be worth considering briefly, the set of instruments democracies have used for this purpose and the politics around them in a country like India. The most obvious instrument is redistribution through taxation. But there is no serious politics structured around using this instrument for several reasons.

First of all, countries like India have recent and vivid memories of the distorting effects of high taxes in the context of low enforcement capacity. There is a generalized scepticism about the efficacy of high direct taxes. How far this scepticism is justified can be debated in economic terms. But in the matter of taxes, there is an interesting ideological phenomenon also at work. The rich benefit from the fact that most people, at any level of society, do not like being taxed more; high taxes, even for the very rich are often seen as a slippery slope for legitimizing high taxes for all. So, while most democracies have some forms of progressive taxation, there are limits to how much they can tax.

Second, in the context of globalization and mobility of capital there is scepticism about the efficacy of very high tax rates. Third, and this is a point I will return to later, taxes provide redistribution, through the instrumentality of the state. Often there is scepticism about a state's capacity to use taxes wisely. Indeed the case for lower taxes and an ideological delegitimization of the 'public sector' as it were, go hand in hand. And certainly the historical performance of states gives grist to the mill of those who are sceptical that more resources must be poured into the state. But even when the state works, the welfare effects of the state are likely to be higher than its equality effects. So broadly speaking, there appear to be political limits to taxation as an instrument of redistribution.

The second major instrument of redistribution was collectivizing productive assets, particularly industrial capital. This instrument has simply turned out to be an unviable historical option. The third instrument of redistribution is the focus of one particular asset, land. Certainly after independence it was thought that land redistribution would be the major instrument of producing equality. But, and this is a global phenomenon, democracies have not been very successful at radical land reform. Most of the cases of successful land reform have been either through revolution or colonial powers destroying a landed aristocracy as the Japanese did in Korea. Land reform in democracies has been, at best ameliorative rather than radical. But at the present conjuncture, in the context of our uneven development, the politics of land is playing out very differently. At one level the issue of land is absolutely central to conflicts in our society. Many major fault lines in our society involve land, whether it is tribals desperately trying to secure use rights to their traditional lands, to farmers contesting land acquisition, to conflicts over shaping urban zoning.

State regulation of land has also become central to the political economy of Indian democracy. There is a joke that after liberalization the state controls only three things: land, liquor and learning. And these are three areas where the visible hand of rent seeking is tremendously powerful. Historically, of course, land reform has been associated with better economic outcomes—states with relatively more egalitarian distribution of land produced a more egalitarian politics. But in a way this fact only highlights one of the paradoxes of land politics—you already need a certain degree of asset equality to shape politics in a more egalitarian direction. The politics of land itself has turned out to be greatly path dependent. Politics itself seems a rather weak instrument for producing asset equality. But while land remains an issue of great social contention, it is, with some exceptions, not the locus of an egalitarian politics for several reasons.

As Partha Chatterjee and many others have pointed out, in much of rural India, the quest is now to get off the land. The fragmentation of landholdings (combined with large-scale shifts in lifestyle aspirations) are making working on land less desirable. While regularizing the rights of tenants and share croppers can have empowering effects, particularly in states like Bihar, the blunt truth is that access to small landholdings is not seen as considerably empowering. In rural India the greatest fault lines are often between the interest of small farmers and landless labour; in some states the greatest complaint about NREGA raising wage rates has come from small and marginal farmers. In short, often the conflicts between 'adjacent' classes are more consequential and immediately severe than those between the top and the bottom, making politics less a matter of attacking privilege than holding onto small distinctions. Land politics in India is very complicated. But here I simply want to make one point. It is the axis of conflict. But it is no longer the main fulcrum of distributive politics. Parenthetically, one can make a stronger argument is that land assets are the means by which inequality is being reproduced and exacerbated rather than reduced.

Land acquisition has also become a mechanism for exacerbating inequality in India in three ways. First, property rights were weakened in India to facilitate land reform. Ironically, weakened property rights, which were meant to help the poor, ended up dispossessing them even more. Second, what farmers think of land acquisition depends, amongst other things, upon two factors—location and their existing assets. Again, ironically, farmers in an area with a real estate boom or high circle rates like Haryana are more likely to be willing to part with their land than farmers in poorer states. It is not an accident that land acquisition is harder in backward states like Orissa, West Bengal and parts of UP. The poor get a poorer deal in a poor state. High growth states like Gujarat have less of a challenge. As the recent conflict in UP has shown, large farmers also have a greater capacity to bargain, compared to small farmers, and are likely to get better deals. So dispossession is also unequal in its effects. Finally, there is one aspect to inequality in land discourse that is deeply insidious. There is some focus on monetary compensation and promise of jobs. But let us face two ugly truths. In most areas we have not invested enough in the skills of dispossessed people for them to get meaningful jobs. Studies are showing that, particularly in backward areas, companies do not employ local labour—partly because of skills deficit, partly because of fear that local labour will unionize easily. But there is also an aspirational dimension.

Even in Singur, it was startling to see the government promise jobs as janitors to those dispossessed. Contrast this with what the mayor of a Chinese city is supposed to have told those displaced. He admitted that the adults will have to sacrifice, but the promise was that the children of those displaced would have the same opportunities as those of the most privileged. And the state would ensure that. Whether or not this is entirely implemented is not the point. The point is whether any Indian politician looks at the children of the dispossessed in the eye and promises them something genuinely aspirational—a first rate, instead of a third rate school; a dream of a great job, instead of jobs low in the hierarchy. Land acquisition is often an occasion for reproducing social distance rather than closing the gap. It is important to be reminded of this backdrop because land conflicts are not just over compensation. The compensation issue has become a distillation of a complex set of issues: low trust in the state, resentment at inequalities that your encounter with the land lottery can only exacerbate and a politics that rests on the conviction that power is arbitrary and access to it simply a means of making money. But cumulatively land politics is exacerbating inequality.

The fourth instrument for producing some kind of distributive justice is the state itself. On this view the primary mechanism through which redistribution happens is not transfer or collectivization of assets, but through the state provision of public goods, particularly health and education. At one level there is something powerful in this narrative. Welfare states have been the instrumentality through which the lives of the poor have been improved. But the welfare state has a very complicated relationship to the politics of equality along several dimensions. First and most obviously, the effectiveness of welfare states depends upon a number of factors, including state capacity. In India that state capacity is very unevenly developed across time and space. State capacity is often a function of structural features like ability to generate revenue but it is also a product of contingent political formations. But the unevenness and distrust of state capacity has meant, at the very least, that support for public provisioning is still very limited in India.

One striking illustration of this is the fact that fact our discourse on universal entitlements is so under ambitious. There is a powerful narrative that UPA wanted to project of universalising a set of basic entitlements from the right to education to employment. But you often get the feeling that these rights are so tepidly defined, and even more haphazardly implemented that they are fighting yesterdays battles, not tomorrows challenges. The *Right to Education Act*, for example, has been enacted just at the moment where formal enrolment in a school is no longer a major challenge. What *is* a major challenge is ensuring quality education for all. Yet the focus of the legislation is largely on the infrastructural inputs. While many of the bye laws of this legislation have to be drafted, there is a real danger that this Act could hinder rather that support the pursuit of quality education. Similarly in Food Security, what is being proposed lags behind the practice of many states, including Tamil Nadu and Chattisgarh. Tamil Nadu has universalised food security much more effectively than the Centre is proposing to do. So while welfare schemes are amelioratively, helping people their relationship to the politics of equality is much more tangential than should be the case.

The Politics of Welfare

There is another issue in the politics of welfare that needs some attention. Historically, the Indian state has been relatively bad at targeting. To take just one example, unde-inclusion and over-inclusion in BPL lists is often as high as 50 per cent. Just the history of targeting failures in India suggests that there is an administrative case to be made for universalization.

For policy purposes the BPL is a disingenuous construct. Normatively speaking, this line is an exercise in bad faith because it arbitrarily separates those who can avail benefits from those who cannot. The difference between those immediately above and below the poverty line is miniscule, almost irrelevant from a practical point of view. Yet that cut-off arbitrarily determines access to benefits. A BPL line, rather than being an expression of a commitment to equality, is a subtle exemplar of discrimination. The cut-off also bears no relationship to the particular objectives of public policy. It also does little justice to the fact that the poor are unevenly deprived along different attributes. A list has to be made with reference to objectives, but here the existence of the list defines the limits of the programme. The BPL is a classic case of state inversion that confuses ends and means. Second, the process of creating BPL lists produces a strange intellectual contortion. First there is a survey that supposedly caps how many poor people there are. Then criteria are evolved to identify which particular households fall within the set. This exercise is a bit of sleight of hand—the identifying criteria selected should be such that they do not yield a figure higher than the cap that has been predetermined.

If you go by criteria, caps make no sense. If you are committed to the caps, the criteria look arbitrary. Another instance of the state engaging in circular reasoning unhinged to any objectives. Third, there is the practical difficulty of implementing any criteria for selection. Again distinguished economists and planners have performed a heroic task of identifying easily implementable criteria that do not rely on complicated and dubious surveys. But objectively verifiable criteria that do not over-include or under-include are hard to design. Then the state resorts to including whole groups, or sometimes districts, in a blunt way that again makes the list discriminatory. It is small wonder that the states are deeply dissatisfied with the Centre setting the parameters of the criteria; the Centre in turn is suspicious that allowing the states to do their thing is a recipe for anarchy. But the most unconscionable practical consequence is the horrendous rate of under-inclusion and over-inclusion that has characterized these lists, often in excess of 50 per cent. The lists marginalise the poor rather than empower them.

So why does the state continue to persist with so flimsy a construction, one that is normatively dubious and practically difficult? In some schemes the state has made a departure, by making goods universal or by allowing self-targeting. But the mystique of the BPL remains strong. In part its hold may be attributed to state inertia; the state often continues along inherited ways of structuring the world even when circumstances have rendered those strategies futile. Part of it is ideological: to show that something is being done for the poor, you first have to set the poor apart as a category, and make them a special object. How can we be seen for standing up for the poor, if we are treating them as equal citizens rather than as special wards of the state? It is also a way of ensuring that schemes for the poor by being exclusively for them, receive little attention from others. Ironically, all subsidies which the privileged enjoy, like petrol, are mostly couched in universalistic terms. Part of it is a false fiscal scare. On this view, if you don't target, and universalize schemes, the costs may turn out to be prohibitive. But this assumption is mostly false. As states that have universalized PDS, like Tamil Nadu, have demonstrated, there is self-targeting that limits the fiscal burden.

Finally, there is also political expediency. The Ministry of Agriculture and Food and state governments would rather let a catfight break out over who gets included or excluded, than focus attention on the real issue at hand: how do you design delivery systems with minimal leakage? The messiness of the BPL lists shifts the blame to civil society. If food is not reaching the poor, it can be blamed on the fact that people are gaming BPL lists, whereas the real culprits are delivery mechanisms that include everything from FCI to the ownership of food shops. Again, states that have done well with PDS focus less on futile controversies over lists, and more on structures and technologies of delivery. What lists are needed depends upon the objective of the programme. But at this historical juncture it is clear that the BPL lists are serving very little purpose. For most schemes that matter to the poor they are unnecessary; these schemes can either be universalized or criteria can be evolved that bear some relation to the purpose of the scheme rather than rely on an antecedently given list like BPL that we have not got right in over five decades. It will also remove this great scramble in the states to make poverty their sole revenue generation industry. Government needs to make a distinction between two kinds of waste. There is a form where the state incurs slightly higher costs, but the objective is fulfilled; universalization of PDS will probably take this form. Then, there is the form of waste where neither does the state save money, nor is the objective of the scheme fulfilled. But the BPL abets this more insidious kind of waste, as our unconscionable nutrition outcomes show.

UID and the Welfare State

There is great hope being placed in the fact that Unique Identification (UID) will help overcome some of these problems. The UID is certainly a necessary instrument for an effective state; the state needs to identify its citizens, and poor citizens in turn need an identity. But it is more likely that UID is more useful for universal schemes than targeted ones. UID will certainly help solve one problem in a universal scheme—identification of citizens. What is less obvious is whether it will be able to solve the challenge of targeting. As a matter of intellectual history, universal identification have gone hand in hand with the creation of universal rather than targeted welfare states. But this is a technical discussion. For our purposes what is important is this. BPL lists have two consequences for the politics of justice. First, it is usually the case, as the saying goes, that schemes for poor people are poor schemes. As a matter of simple political economy, schemes in which the privileged do not have a stake are not subject to great accountability. But second, instead of producing widespread support for strengthening welfare schemes, it has produced more a politics of getting access to state resources by manipulating the categories of access, which again paradoxically ends up pitting the poor against the slightly less poor.

There is a final point to be made about welfare states in relation to the politics of equality. Where welfare states function well, they can certainly contribute to the *improvement* in the lives of the poor. In that sense they are necessary aspects for the politics of equality. But welfare in this sense does not *constitute* the politics of equality for a couple of interesting reasons. In principle access to health and education and other public goods that form part of the welfare basket should enhance the capabilities of citizens to take advantage of opportunities. But these goods also enhance what one might call *individuation*. They allow the pool of citizens who are capable of being upwardly mobile. But they do not address the challenge of structural inequality.

One way of seeing this point is to see how ideologies of education play out in relation to equality. As a normative point it cannot be debated that all citizens must have access to high quality education. But the comparative history of the relationship between education and equality is a little sobering in the following respects. First, access to equal opportunity in education is quite compatible with high levels of inequality. All the equal opportunity does is widen the pool from which successful candidates are drawn; it does not, by itself erase inequalities between different classes. Or rather, to be more precise, equality is more a function of compensation patterns for different jobs than it is of education itself. In an openly competitive system, where the job market does not have the right kind of distribution across incomes classes, equality of educational opportunity is quite compatible with inequality. For equality depends upon the penalties associated with not coming out on top. The more egalitarian an occupation structure, the less severe are the perceived penalties for not coming out on top. Europe has in part escaped the neurosis, a meritocratic competition can induce because there is greater background equality. In short, education alone may not produce a politics of equality. The real debate we need is on the kind of occupational structure we see emerging. What is the relationship between education and that occupational structure?

Consequences of Meritocracy

Meritocracy also has two peculiar psychic consequences. One of its unintended consequences is that it inculcates the idea that those who are left behind are somehow less worthy; and it creates a new form of inequality in turn. There is also an argument to be made that over the last 20 years or so, it is precisely meritocracy that has ideologically underpinned an ideology of great inequality. As some social observers have noted, people who rise through the system based on an idea of merit also have a greater sense of entitlement to all the fruits of their effort. What is interesting about income inequality in places ranging from the USA to China is not the fact that it exists. It is that people at the top in particular and society more generally also came to the view that those at the top deserved what they have. They deserved it in part because they rose by the dint of their own talent. There is an odd sense in which privilege has to justify itself, but merit does not. Since the idea of equality of opportunity in education is so aligned with the idea of meritocracy (or rather the two legitimize each other), education is often not seen as the locus of equality.

This little excursus on meritocracy is interesting in relation to the politics of justice for another reason. In upper classes which have a sense that they have risen on the dint of merit, there is the possibility that there is less support for an egalitarian politics. This is because a society where achievement is linked to education attainment also gives those who achieve a sense of *entitlement*. It is perhaps easier to shame an aristocracy by claiming their wealth is undeserved; it is harder to induce guilt in those whose self-perception is that they have attained wealth by legitimate means. The expansion of a professional middle class may be conducive for supporting expansion of education. But this class may at the same time have less patience with any politics of redistribution because it is the very ideology of education that supports their sense of entitlement.

There is therefore something of a crisis in articulating an egalitarian politics of social justice. Traditional Marxists believed that there is a subject or bearer of egalitarian politics, namely the proletariat. But there is no such natural subject, in part because all classes are now placed in very complex and contradictory relationships. There 'instruments' of equality have very limited reach. And even when they are successful in delivering certain goods, they often enhance the ethic of individuation, mobility and competition rather than a politics of equality. It is, therefore, possible to articulate a discourse of improvement, but there is no locus of social justice.

Challenges of Indian Democracy

If this is the case, then a profound challenge opens up for Indian democracy. At the moment when our republic was founded, Ambedkar very famously articulated the life of contradictions India was about to enter. On the one hand, our constitution promised political equality. On the other hand, actual social life was going to be marked by deep social and economic inequality. In some respects, this contradiction was not unique to Indian constitutionalism; it has been a feature of most democracies. In fact, the kind of political equality that modern constitutions introduce is often seen as Janus faced. On the one hand, these constitutions instantiate a normatively attractive conception of political equality. One central feature of this conception is that who one is should not matter to what political or even legal rights one has. The modern conception of citizenship is, in many ways, founded on this ideal. But this very attractive normative feature is also seen as, in some respects threatening. For this doctrine of equality is, as many have pointed out, as much a doctrine of anonymity. To repeat, who one is, is irrelevant to what rights one has.

Why is this conception of equality a threat? The worry is that this anonymity, while it opens up certain formal avenues of access, can actually also throw a veil over inequality. Indeed, Tocqueville had argued that in societies governed by formal equality (or anonymity), it is harder to mobilize an egalitarian politics. So, as Ambedkar had rightly worried, constitutional anonymity can leave real structures of inequality intact. This is a general challenge faced by democracies. But in a society marked by the particular form of inequality India had, this fear of constitutional anonymity was real and powerful. The challenge was to address this fear, while at the same time retaining the attractive normative features of constitutional anonymity. It was in this context that the recognition of caste as an axis of equality became central to Indian politics. The idea was that whatever constitutional anonymity might do, it must not render this particular form of inequality invisible, particularly in the case of Dalits.

But I want to draw attention to two features of this politics and the impact it has had on the politics of social justice. The first, I have discussed at some length in *The Burden of Democracy*, but the gist of the argument bears repeating here, because it explains some difficulties of egalitarian politics in India. But later in this section I will draw out some new implications of this argument to address one interesting analytical question about the salience of caste over class politics in India. Although I must make full disclosure and state emphatically that I worry about the new forms in which caste is being entrenched in Indian political discourse. But here I try and analyze why caste defines the contours of what we think of as equality so insistently.

Democratic aspirations are in some senses tied to the idea of equality. The idea of equality is complex and immediately invites the question, 'Equality of What?' Income? Wealth? Political Equality? Opportunity? But understanding the political trajectory of Indian democracy does not require beginning with an answer to this question. In any society, especially democratic ones, the meaning and scope of equality will be fiercely contested and will be the basis for ideological divisions. Rather, it is the psychological impulses that lie behind the demand for equality; the existential burdens that any demand for equality seeks to address that leave their imprint on politics. The variety of structures, caste, class, patriarchy, that maintain and reproduce inequality are all too familiar, and Indian society exemplifies many of these to an unconscionable degree. But inequality is not simply a structural condition in which people find themselves; a condition measured by such objective indicators as Gini coefficients or development indices. Inequality is resented, and becomes salient for politics, because it is experienced existential burden that inflicts complex psychic costs by diminishing a sense of self. Not all forms of inequality are unjust. And the ways in which the experience of inequality shapes the self is a complex subject. But fundamentally inequality imposes the profoundest existential burdens when it seen as denying individuals the minimum regard due to them, or when it constantly puts them is situations that are experienced as humiliating.

It is now a commonplace observation, thanks largely due to Rousseau who most vividly wrote about the psychic burdens of inequality, that most human beings, unless they have been dehumanized to an unimaginable degree, place some value upon themselves. This does not mean that they are selfish; it is rather that they place some *value* upon themselves and wish that this value be somewhere affirmed. The institutions and practices of most inegalitarian societies deny individuals this basic form of recognition, the recognition that they are valuable in some sense, that they have some moral standing. In most societies this quest for having one's worth affirmed will take debased forms. The only way in which you can secure others' acknowledgement is either by seeking to dominate them, or by putting a convincing show of attributes and accomplishments that are capable of winning the acknowledgement of others. This is because the only way you can get acknowledged is by having power over them, by being able to say, 'I know I am worth something, because I have power over you.' Those who are not in a position of being able to dominate secure acknowledgement in other more self-debasing ways. They say something like, 'Pay attention to me, because I can make your comparative sense of self worth even more pronounced by debasing my self for you, by flattering you.' Inegalitarian societies where there is no public acknowledgement of individual self worth will be characterized by both a fierce competition to dominate, and paradoxically, an exaggerated sense of servility. These are the two strategies of securing acknowledgement. Both desire to dominate and a kind of self-abasement, Rousseau suggested, would lead us to lead inauthentic lives—lives that were not governed by values or concerns that were properly our own. Such societies would also frequently give individuals reasons to consider their self-respect injured—inegalitarian societies will routinely humiliate their members.

The aspiration to democracy is in part an aspiration to have one's moral worth acknowledged. The charge that an arrangement or a set of procedures is 'undemocratic' carries moral resonance, not simply because it describes a faulty procedure, but because it is accompanied by the sentiment that in being undemocratic someone's moral standing has been slighted. Acknowledgement by others of your moral worth is at least partly constitutive of an individual's sense of self-respect. A sense of self-respect is necessary to have a firm sense of one's own value, to have the conviction not only that life is worth living but worth living well. The absence of self-respect can be corrosive; it can make most pursuits meaningless.

In some senses, equal voting rights are a dramatic expression of individual's moral worth. But unless the collective arrangements of society give individuals the minimum bases for social self-respect, of which the equal right to vote is just one aspect, society is likely to be characterized by an odd combination of a fierce competition for domination on the one hand, and abject servility on the other, and when neither succeeds, violence as a way of announcing ones moral standing. What institutions and objectives can satisfy the minimal requirements of acknowledging people's moral worth is a debatable one. But at the very least, freedom from abject necessity, removal of invidious and humiliating forms of discrimination, some equality of opportunity and access to set a of goods that are minimal requirements for being a capable agent in the modern world. The great liberal hope, embodied in the Indian constitution, was that ameliorating serious material deprivation, and an effective equal standing in the eyes of the law would go some way towards mitigating the desire to have one's worth affirmed, either by dominating others, or by having one's own sense of self fashioned by what we think might get others attention. Indeed, arguably, if the basis for social self-respect is adequately protected, the existence of other inequalities might matter less, because they could not be used as a base from which to dominate, despise or negate others.

Conceptually speaking, there are many different ways in which equality of moral worth can be affirmed. One might say, for instance, that we are equal in the eyes of God. Within Indian history, religious traditions, and traditions of dissent, these modes have always been available; but they did issue in effective and enduring demands for ordering the texture of social relationships. It is not indeed an impossibility to assert both that we are equal in the eyes of God and that a hierarchical social organization such as caste is defensible; indeed the theoretical radicalism of so many claims to equality in the past was compromised by their practical conservatism. It can be granted that Indian history provides at least some conceptual resources for affirming equality. But the introduction of democracy is radical. Democracy is a way of affirming human dignity by granting individuals civic standing. In a democracy, the desire for having one's moral worth affirmed for emptying social space of humiliation is given open social legitimation and expression.

But, paradoxically, the struggles to affirm one's moral worth do not necessarily take the form of a demand for justice. Indeed, if Rousseau's diagnosis is plausible, the desire for having one's worth acknowledged can express itself in all kinds of debased forms, ones that require debasing others. Indeed, the paradox is that while individuals and groups can be acutely conscious of society's indifference towards them, they can, in turn be acutely indifferent towards others. Indeed, you would almost experience this to the case in highly inegalitarian societies. The only meaning empowerment has in such a society is power *over* others, some claim of power or privilege or access that sets *you* apart, rather than a generally shared sense of empowerment as such. *The paradox is that the more unequal the background institutions and practices of society, the more likely it is that politics will be a struggle to displace the holders of power rather than an ambition to bring about social transformation.* The struggle to move ahead will not be a common struggle for justice—for little commonality exists—but a competitive quest for power. A society that is adept at humiliating its members is, as Rousseau convincingly argued, more likely to make them adept at humiliating others than it is to teach them about justice. This perhaps explains one of the paradoxes at the heart of Indian politics. There are few other democracies where the universalist language of injustice, rights, even constitutionalism is so profusely used and has become part of so many political mobilizations. But it is a stratagem for particular individuals or groups to gain access to power, not an acknowledgement of the due claims of all.

Discourses of law, constitutionalism, rights, justice, obligations, do not signify that a particular set of values are being taken as authoritative and these set genuine moral constraints for individuals. Rather, they are the languages in which particular grievances are expressed or interests advanced without the least acknowledgement of reciprocal or parallel interests and grievances of others. A sense of justice towards someone presupposes a sense of reciprocity; it presupposes that you acknowledge others. The more the social distance, the less likely that such reciprocity obtains. It is quite possible for a democracy to experience great clamour for recognition by particular individuals and groups without these resulting in diffusion of norms of justice. This follows the general pattern of the ways in which Indian society has been democratized. *Democracy in India has advanced through the competitive negotiations between groups, each competing for their interests rather than the diffusion of democratic norms. It is, in some senses, a contingent outcome of social conflicts, not necessarily a deep-seated norm. The purpose of political mobilization has not been to make the state more accountable but to get access to or share in its power.*

The Conception of Politics

This conception of politics was most dramatically manifest in the way in which citizens often thought of the state. Given the commanding presence of the state, underwritten by an ideology of state-led development, access to state power became, for good or for ill, the principal means of improving the life chances of individuals. In an economy with slow and sluggish growth, averaging under 3 per cent, the state became a disproportionate provider of opportunity. Even access to opportunities and resources outside the state were mediated through state influence. Indeed, in one sense, politics, through access to state power has become the swiftest route towards social mobility. In a strange kind of way, compared to the market, or educational institutions, politics of all kinds, from the most ambitious aspiration for power, to the interest in gaining smallest benefits, came to be seen as a surer route to social mobility.

Access to the state gave jobs and a likely class status that was better than anything available outside the state; the discretionary power the state conferred on all its officials was experienced by many as empowerment, or at least an escape from the subordination that resulted from being at the receiving end of that power. Access to state power was about the only way of ensuring that one counted for somebody. Big scams do not tell the real story of the connection between corruption and social mobility. It is the thousands of petty fortunes that are made through the state that seemed to most citizens a surer bet of improving their class status than the uncertainties of a market. One of the peculiar features of Indian society has been that political power became almost the sole means of social mobility. Is there any other sphere of activity that is less stratified and more representative of Indian society than politics?

But the consequence of the growth of the state and its undoubted success in producing a kind of social mobility is attended by a paradox. This paradox is, namely, that once the state is seen as a means for social mobility, it is not, for the most part seen as the provider of public goods. The state is adjudged to be successful, the more opportunities for large numbers of private individuals it can create through its own spending—if the number of government jobs expands for instance, even when not required, this is adjudged to be a political success, regardless of the opportunity costs this form of job creation imposes on others. The state exists primarily to satisfy the private interests of collusive interest groups. Although it is undoubtedly true that the dominant proprietary classes will have a disproportionate share of the state's resources, there is enormous fluidity in the nature of social groups that have at different times gained access to the state. But the net result was that almost never has that state been governed by a public philosophy; it is rather a high stakes competitive game in which individuals or groups seek advantages on particularistic lines.

The raison d'être of politics, the aims of public representation are no longer to respond to fundamental issues impinging upon common life but to organize the state's power in such a manner that its resources can be channelled in the direction of particular groups or individuals to protect their exclusive interests. The cumulative impact has been a view of the state and constitutional fabric that see them as institutions to be manipulated according to particularistic interests. One can appropriate Hegel's melodramatic phrase, 'the state exists no longer'. What Hegel meant in his context is that the state and constitution were being manipulated to serve particular interests, and that the decisions that emanated from it did not carry the necessity of principle, but only the arbitrariness of expedience. To be sure, there are restraints internal to expedience, but how effective these restraints are will be a matter of some concern. It is extraordinary that the association of the state with the 'public' or the state with the 'common', the two sustaining associations of the state, are wearing so thin.

But this politics continues because it has also acquired great normative depth. And it is this normative depth that I want to focus on, in the remainder of this talk. What I mean be normative depth is this. This de facto competition of groups to gain access to state power is now being given constitutional depth in different ways. First, as Sudipta Kaviraj pointed out several years ago (Kaviraj 2005), India had a discourse of equality in which equality was not about transcending caste. *It was rather about claiming equality on the basis of caste.* The measure of equality becomes the share of caste power in institutions like the state. The most extreme version of equality on the basis of caste is the legitimacy of what you might call the mirror theory of representation. On this view institutions are legitimate only in so far as the distribution of power within them mirrors, broadly speaking the relevant social cleavages in society. To a certain extent, the attraction of this ideal is understandable. If groups are systematically excluded from structures of power, there is prima facie a case that a society is operating on mechanisms of exclusion. There was consensus that these mechanisms very visibly and oppressively operated in the case of Dalits. But slowly this narrative was expanded to include other 'Backward Castes'. And one of the strange ironies of modern India is that the historical narrative of subjugation and marginalization that was specific to Dalits has now been appropriated by other groups.

A society like India requires some form of affirmative action. What form that should take, who the state should target, why we should target them and how we should target them is an important subject that is best left for another occasion. Here I simply want to focus on some of the political and normative underpinnings of the kind of emphasis on reservation that we have institutionalized, and the implications of these assumptions for the politics of social justice. One way of bringing out the peculiarity of these assumptions is to ask the question how the demand for equality will be expressed. How will society ensure that constitutional anonymity does not throw a veil over inequality? One other possible criterion for ensuring this that has often been debated in the public sphere is the use of economic criteria. There was an understanding at the time of independence that this criterion would not cater to the specific form of injustice and discrimination Dalits faced. But using this criterion could help address other forms of Backwardness.

Institutionalization of Caste

We have come to believe that using economic criteria or class as a basis for reservation or affirmative action does not express a politics of social justice. Part of the reason often cited for this administrative—caste is thought of as a more easily identifiable characteristic than income. Part of the reason is that the caste/class overlap was very strong particularly in the case of Dalits. But this overlap is becoming much more complicated, particularly amongst non-Dalits, as the caste and occupation linkage is becoming weaker. But there is also a deeper reason at work. Reservations based on anything other than ascriptive criteria like caste are not seen as expressing a politics of equality for the following reasons. The first reason can be best highlighted by a little semantic experiment. Think of what the phrase 'equality of classes' might mean. As applied to distributive justice it can mean only the abolition of classes; otherwise, the phrase equality of classes is a little bit of an oxymoron. But for reasons mentioned earlier, we do not have any instruments for the abolition of class. But the phrase 'equality of caste' is not, in this sense, an oxymoron. It does not require neither the abolition of caste. And the degree to which we have achieved equality of caste can be crudely measured by the share of different caste groups in structures of power.

Just continue this line of thinking for a second. What are the differences between how we represent caste mobility and class mobility? If a poor person becomes middle class, this may reflect a salutary fact that society has opened up avenues for opportunity. But precisely by virtue of this mobility the person is able to *change* his class. And a society with great class mobility is a desirable one; at the very least is a potent expression of the thought that where one is born does not determine the opportunities one might have. But class mobility is compatible with two things. First, class mobility presupposes the continued existence of classes and inequality—all it suggests is that individuals can change their position. And the individuals who are so able to change their position *no longer represent the class they came from.*[1] A poor person becoming middle class is an instance of a poor person becoming middle class. In class mobility, your position on the axis of deprivation being measured changes. Such a movement provides a measure of *mobility*; it is not seen as providing a measure of *equality*.

But caste operates somewhat differently. A Mala or Maddiga becoming rich may change their class status. But they remain a Mala or a Maddiga. *They can still represent the caste* from which they came in the calculus of power sharing. They may have become rich or powerful, but their position on the axis of deprivation being measured (in this instance, caste) does not change. In fact, one of the ethical dilemmas posed by reservation is the way in which it perpetuates a compulsory identity on citizens through officially sanctioned categories—once a member of a particular caste, always a member of a particular caste. But this normatively disturbing feature of the way in which we want to perpetuate caste as a compulsory identity also makes it attractive as a locus of social justice. This is because caste now comes to be a measure of equality in virtue of an immutable characteristic. In a way 'caste' answers the question 'equality with respect to what' in a way no other characteristic does, precisely because of its constructed immutability. Equality with respect to 'class' would require the abolition of class. Equality with respect to caste does not

---

[1] I do not mean that they cannot have views that are sympathetic to the poor, or that they cannot identify with the poor or act on their behalf. The reference to representation here is not a reference to substantive views in this sense. It is simply that on the dimension of class they have become someone else.

require this abolition. This immutability can also be combined with a simple measure—simple count the 'representatives' of each caste in the share of power. Again, with class this is impossible to do, because the mere act of access to power transforms the individual's structural relation to class.

This institutionalization of caste as the basis of equality has some interesting consequences. First, it is a form of legitimizing class difference. Since we have limited instruments to achieve deep equality, class is now seen almost as a legitimate form of inequality. Caste has become the form in which the politics of social justice has come to be sublimated.

Second, in India there is no serious discourse on the relationship between justice and discrimination. This is in part due to the fact that the category of discrimination was specific to the Dalit experience. But the appropriation of the Dalit narrative by other communities has meant that power sharing rather than discrimination has become the central normative category in our thinking on justice. And in a way for 'upper castes' as well there is a tacit assumption that since a share to power has been reserved, discrimination is no longer a category one needs to think about.

Third, because equality can now be claimed only on the basis of an immutable identity, there is a growing clamour for the state to institutionalize these. Almost everyone knows that the politics of social equality depends on particular categories of identity being recognized and codified. The latest demand for a caste census is an inevitable outcome of this recognition. Social classifications recreate and solidify the realities rather than merely representing them. But the focus of politics of justice has shifted to what are the appropriate identity categories that need to be so codified. This will, in coming years take new forms. For instance, there will be greater political pressure to create new subdivisions within broad categories like Dalit or Other Backward Classes. The demand for these subdivisions is inherent in the logic of equality on the basis of caste.

Fourth, identity politics and other forms of politics centred around welfare and justice are often posed as alternatives. Recent Indian history has shown that identity politics is the form in which the politics of social justice is expressed. And there is no reason to believe that the force of identity politics is going to diminish in the near future. Its forms may change, the categories deployed will be contested, and there will be a demand to expand this politics to new domains, including the private sector. But its central axis is going to remain demanding equality on the basis of an immutable characteristic.

Conclusion

The politics of social justice is at a deep impasse. The fear that constitutional anonymity must not draw a veil over inequality has led to the constitutionalization of caste, as it were. It has provided a ready locus and measure of equality. But its price has been a move away from the ideals of Indian constitutionalism and the essence of democracy in two respects. It has reinforced the tyranny of compulsory identities and has reduced justice to crude and limited measures of power sharing. But caste becomes the locus of a politics of equality in part because there is deep structural pessimism about addressing other forms of inequality. India is going through a profound change, and the gains in both growth and poverty reduction are very real and widespread. But these changes do not, by themselves, address the politics of social justice.

India's growth has opened up new possibilities. It has certainly given the state more resources and potential for institutionalizing welfare schemes. It is also producing new forms of improvement and mobility. But it has also increased the potential for rent seeking. Perhaps the best that we can hope for at the current conjuncture is 'small equality' effects that growth and welfare can produce. But how we will resolve the contradictions that Ambedkar talked about, still remains an open question. Where will be the locus of a politics of justice? Will the historical logic that made caste the dominant paradigm in which we think of justice continue? And will it crowd out the essential challenge we face. This challenge is best summed up in the words of the Chinese thinker Qin Hui. He put it in a striking formulation, 'What is excessive now is not liberalism or social democracy, but oligarchy and populism. It is therefore essential to critique both oligarchy from a liberal standpoint and populism from a social democratic standpoint.' When I read these words, I wonder whether there can be any better formulation of the challenges for Indian democracy. And I wonder how far we are from meeting these challenges.

References

Kaviraj, Sudipta. 2005. 'Democracy and Inequality in India', in *Transforming India*, ed. Zoya Hasan and Francince Frankel. Oxford: Oxford University Press.

Mookherjee, Dilip and Debraj Ray. 2003. 'Persistent Inequalities', *Review of Economic Studies*, 70 (2): 369–93.

Pzeworski, Adam. 2010. *Democracy and the Limits of Self Government*. Cambridge: Cambridge University Press.

About the Editor and Contributors

Editor

R. Maria Saleth is Director, Madras Institute of Development Studies, Chennai, India. He has earlier worked at the International Water Management Institute, Colombo, Institute of Economic Growth, Delhi and Institute for Social and Economic Change, Bangaluru, India. He has three books, four edited volumes, and several papers in journals and edited volumes. He has won several awards for some of his papers, books, and works from organizations such as the Indian Society of Agricultural Economics, American Water Resources Association, and International Water Association. He is the editor of the journal *Review of Development and Change*.

Contributors

Bina Agarwal is Professor and Director, Institute of Economic Growth, Delhi, India. She is a prize-winning feminist economist who studies gender, development and agriculture in India and throughout South Asia. She focuses on the importance of land and control of land for women. Her book *A Field of One's Own: Gender and Land Rights in South Asia* won the Coomaraswamy Book Prize in 1996. She is the winner of several awards, including the Leontief Award and Malcolm Adiseshiah Award. She was awarded the Padma Shri by the President of India in 2008.

U.R. Ananthamurthy is a writer of eminence in both Kannada and English languages. He is well known for his much acclaimed novels, short stories and poetry. He has won the Jnanpith Award for his lifetime contributions to literature. He has held several distinguished positions such as Professor of English, University of Mysore; Vice-Chancellor, Mahatma Gandhi University, Kottayam; Chairman, National Book Trust of India; President, Sahitya Akademi and Chairman, Film and Television Institute of India, Pune.

Amita Baviskar is Associate Professor, Institute of Economic Growth, Delhi, India. Earlier, she was with the Department of Sociology, University of Delhi. She is widely recognized as the premier sociologist of social movements involving environment and development in contemporary India. She has held visiting positions at US universities such as Yale, Stanford, Berkeley and Cornell and also at the London School of Economics, UK. She has received numerous prizes and awards, including the V.K.R.V. Rao Prize, Malcolm Adiseshiah Award, and Infosys Prize. She is currently the co-editor of the journal *Contributions to Indian Sociology*.

Upendra Baxi is currently Professor of Law in Development, University of Warwick, UK. Earlier, he served as Professor of Law, University of Delhi (1973–96) and as its Vice-Chancellor (1990–94). He has also served as Vice-Chancellor of University of South Gujarat, Surat (1982–85), India. He was the President of the Indian Society of International Law (1992–95). As a widely published author, Professor Baxi has contributed substantially to social action (public interest) litigation in the Supreme Court of India and, thereby, enhanced democratization of access to judicial process and power by the disadvantaged groups in Indian society.

Amit Bhaduri is Professor Emeritus at Jawaharlal Nehru University, Delhi, India. Currently, he is also a visiting professor at the Council for Social Development, Delhi. Previously, he was associated with the Delhi School of Economics and the Indian Institute of Management, Calcutta, India. He was Visiting Professor at various academic institutions (Colegio de Mexico and Universities at Stanford, Vienna, Linz, Bologna, Bremen and Trondheim). He has also served as Research Officer at the United Nations Industrial Development Organisation, Vienna, Austria and as Visiting Fellow at the Centre for Development Studies, Trivandrum, India.

Partha Chatterjee is Honorary Professor of Political Science and was the Director of the Centre for Studies in Social Sciences, Calcutta,

India. He is currently a Professor of Anthropology and South Asian Studies at Columbia University, New York, USA. He has held many visiting professorships across Europe, Asia and North America. He was a Founder-Member of the Subaltern Studies Collective. He is a multidisciplinary scholar, with special emphasis on political science, anthropology and history. He has published several books and scholarly articles in these areas. He is Joint-editor of *Baromash*, a bi-annual Bengali literary journal published from Kolkata. He has received the Fukuoka Asian Culture Prize in 2009 for his academic contributions.

Dipankar Gupta is Professor, Centre for the Study of Social Systems, Jawaharlal Nehru University, New Delhi, India. For a brief period, he was with the Department of Sociology, University of Delhi. He held many visiting positions in universities in North America and Europe. He has made significant contributions to the research and teaching in several major aspects of Indian society and polity. He has authored or co-authored 15 books and written over 70 research articles. He is a member of the National Security Advisory Board, the National Broadcasting Authority, and the Government of Punjab.

Pratap Bhanu Mehta is President, Centre for Policy Research, New Delhi, India. He was previously Visiting Professor of Government and Associate Professor of Government and of Social Studies at Harvard University, USA. He was also Professor of Philosophy and of Law and Governance at Jawaharlal Nehru University, New Delhi, India. He has also been a Visiting Professor at New York University Law School, USA. His areas of research include political theory, constitutional law, society and politics in India, governance and political economy and international affairs. He was Member-Convenor of the Prime Minister of India's National Knowledge Commission and is currently a member of the National Security Advisory Board.

Mihir Shah is currently a Member, Planning Commission, Government of India. After his early career at the Centre for Development Studies, Thiruvanandapuram, India, he traveled extensively in rural and tribal India. These travels culminated in 1990 in the formation of Samaj Pragati Sahayog, one of India's largest grassroots initiatives for water and livelihood security, working with 122 partners across 72 districts in 12 states of India. Dr Shah was Adviser to the Commissioner appointed by the Supreme Court of India in the *Right to*

Food case and an Honorary Adviser to the Technical Committee on Watershed Programmes set up by the Government of India.

Jandhyala B.G. Tilak is Professor, National University of Educational Planning and Administration, New Delhi, India. He is an established scholar in the field of economics of education. He has been a consultant economist to the World Bank. He held visiting positions at the University of Virginia, USA; Hiroshima University, Japan and University of Rochester, USA. He has authored eight books and numerous journal articles. He is a winner of the UGC Swami Pranavananda National Award and Malcolm Adiseshiah Award. He is currently the President of the Comparative Education Society of India and editor of the *Journal of Educational Planning and Administration*.

L. Venkatachalam is Associate Professor, Madras Institute of Development Studies, Chennai, India. He is also a visiting faculty at Indian Institute of Technology Madras, Madras School of Economics and Indian Maritime University, Chennai. He works on environmental economics with a focus on non-market valuation, environmental policy, and climate change and has published papers in reputed journals and edited volumes. He held Fulbright–Nehru Senior Research Fellowship, Indo-France Scholars' Exchange Fellowship and Indo-Canadian Faculty Research Fellowship, and won the Japanese Award for outstanding Research on Development.

Index

politics
  conception of, 241–44
  practice in India, 7
  role in democratic systems, xii
  of welfare. *See* Welfare, politics of
poor, dispossession of, 40–41
post-reform period, impact of, xi
pre-liberalization era, 7
private institutions, 125
Private Universities Bill (1995),
  126–27
Project Affected Families (PAFs),
  196
property, gender gap in command
  over
  effects of welfare, 69–71
  empowerment of women, 71–72
  gaining of efficiency, 71
  importance of land, 67–69
  nature of, 65–67
  women unequal access to land,
    implications of, 69
property rights, gender inequality
  in, 11
Prospect theory, 175
Public Distribution System (PDS), 3
universalization of, 233
public investment, on social science
  research, 1
public spending, on education and
  school attendance, 112
Pzeworski, Adam, 227

Radhakrishna, R., xvi
Ramaswamy, Gita, 160
redistribution, instruments of,
  228–32
reference public, 97. *See also* Lipsky,
  Michael
reform, definition of, 200
Registration of Shops Act, 130
Rehabilitation and Resettlement
  (R&R) Policy, 196–97. *See also*

Land Acquisition (Amendment)
  Bill (LAAB)
resource-intensive production,
  36–38
Right to Development Talk, 157–61
Right to Education Act, 231
risk, distinction between
  uncertainty, 173
Roy, Ananya, 222
Rural Land Contracting Law
  (RLCL), 68
Rural Non-Farm Employment
  (RNFE), 10, 56–59

Sainath, P., 88
Sardar Sarovar project, 91
Sastra Sahitya Parishad campaign,
  91
Scheduled caste politics, rise of, 49
Scheduled Tribes and Other
  Traditional Forest Dwellers
  (Recognition of Forest Rights)
  Act, 2006, 196
Scholes, Myron, 175
Schultz, Theodore, 104
Secondary education, share in Five-
  Year plans, 110
Sen, Amartya, 80, 103, 140
Sengupta, Arjun, 158
Sengupta, Nirmal, 90
service sectors, xi
SEZ Act, 195–96
Shackle, G.L.S., 174–75, 180, 186
Shah, Mihir, 16–18, 172–203
Shetty, H.B.N., xvi
Shiv Sena. *See also* Violence,
  political management of
  Hansen study on, 222
  political effectiveness of, 222
Singur incident, 230
small liberty effects, 227
Smith, Adam, 227
social inequality, 5